Black
Men
Can't
Shoot

Black Men Can't Shoot

SCOTT N. BROOKS

THE UNIVERSITY OF CHICAGO PRESS • *Chicago and London*

Scott N. Brooks is assistant professor of sociology at
the University of California, Riverside.

The University of Chicago Press, Chicago 60637
The University of Chicago Press, Ltd., London
© 2009 by The University of Chicago
All rights reserved. Published 2009
Printed in the United States of America

18 17 16 15 14 13 12 11 10 09   1 2 3 4 5

ISBN-13: 978-0-226-07603-4 (cloth)
ISBN-10: 0-226-07603-2 (cloth)

Library of Congress Cataloging-in-Publication Data

Brooks, Scott.
    Black men can't shoot / Scott N. Brooks.
        p.   cm.
    Includes bibliographical references and index.
    ISBN-13: 978-0-226-07603-4 (cloth: alk. paper)
    ISBN-10: 0-226-07603-2 (cloth: alk. paper)
1. Basketball—Social aspects—Pennsylvania—
Philadelphia. 2. African American basketball
players—Pennsylvania—Philadelphia—Social
conditions. I. Title.
    GV885.73.P55B76   2009
    796.32309748'11—dc22   2008045158

To Maya, Clay, Kenan, and Kara and Sallie Man

CONTENTS

PREFACE: WHAT'S IN A TITLE

The Origins of This Research

In the 1992 movie *White Men Can't Jump*, two basketball players, one black and the other white, establish a partnership and travel around Los Angeles conning black basketball players, who assume the white partner cannot play well. The partners bet money that they will win, and they usually do. The con works by playing on the stereotype that white men do not play basketball as well as black men because they are athletically inferior—white men can't jump, but black men can. If white men can't jump, meaning their athletic achievements and skills do not come naturally, then the implication is that they become good athletes as a result of hard work, discipline, and a level of intelligence. They practice and learn, while black men, the natural athletes, simply play. The idea of "natural" athleticism is often invoked to explain why blacks make up such a large, disproportionate percentage of the NBA (approximately 80 percent). I find this idea problematic because black athletes do work at becoming elite players. They learn and work hard to develop the skills necessary for playing collegiate and professional basketball. They do not and cannot simply show up and dominate. The movie title and discussion of natural athleticism inspired the title of this book, *Black Men Can't Shoot*.

Notions of "natural" ability or superior genes have not been validated scientifically. Race has not been systematically tested to find the "race" gene, which would be necessary to support the myth of black genetic superiority. There is more variability within a "race" than between races. How much blackness is enough? Black covers a large, geographically and phenotypically diverse population: Africans, Afro-Caribbeans, Afro-Europeans, Afro-Latinos, African Americans, and other people of mixed ancestry. Race is a social construct and social fact. It is a human invention used to establish hierarchy/stratification and to justify differential and unequal treatment of people. Still, there are deep consequences to this social fact shown by the gross inequality between races in numerous areas (employment, wages, and education, just to name a few).

Blacks are just as complicit in racializing athletic ability as people from other racial/ethnic groups.[1] It is a part of our racial socialization that we believe people belong to groups and that groups do things and behave in certain ways because of their race. Further, social position is tied to these racial behaviors and values. The real problem with racializing athletic ability is that it reflects our society's stereotypes about blacks and encourages wrong and sometimes malicious thinking and theorizing. Blacks continue to be pathologized and blamed for the wage, education, and wealth gaps between blacks and whites. The hypersexualizing of black people—blacks are awesome natural specimens as a product of breeding—renders athletic success and achievement automatic and not an example of their hard work, thinking, and strategizing toward becoming an athlete (Smith 2007). But success and achievement are not merely "natural"; they require both nature and nurture.

Sociologist Charles Horton Cooley explains that achievement, even in physical skills, is connected to learning, influences, and environment:

> When we say that a child is a born musician we mean, not that he can play or compose by nature alone, but that if he has the right kind of teaching he can rapidly develop power in this direction. In this sense, and in no other, can a man be a born lawyer, teacher, poet, or a born counterfeiter or burglar. I knew a family in which the boys had a remarkable aptitude for football. Several of them became distinguished players, but certainly unless they had all been sent to college, and to one in which football ability was prized and encouraged, this aptitude would never have been discovered. (1902, 7–8)

Aptitude must be activated by discovery. How does a person know that they are good at something if they don't have the opportunity to participate in that activity? Resources are significant, in the form of right teaching and opportunity, as well as setting—where the activity is prized and encouraged.

Another sociologist, Daniel Chambliss, claims that excellence in Olympic swimmers is mundane and a qualitative distinction. Olympic-caliber athletes swim differently (in terms of technique) as opposed to simply practicing more. It is how they swim and not how much they swim. Therefore, it is important to understand that the "actions, ordinary in themselves, performed consistently and carefully, habitualized, compounded together, added up over time" (1989, 85), make a significant difference in performance.

This book traces the career of known basketball players in Philadelphia—and looks at how basketball skill and status develop in Philadelphia, the mundanity of basketball excellence, and the decisions and strategies by some that lead to predictable outcomes. This book is *not* about hoop dreams or whether or not sports improve black men's mobility at the macro level.[2] It is concerned with what young black men in Philly do to go from being good players to great players (and college prospects) and the impact of this work on their local status and social position.

My Approach

Black Men Can't Shoot is an ethnography, a systematic study of culture made through in-depth and consistent participant observation. It is an insider's point of view that will reveal the process some black athletes engage in to become a *known* player.[3] The process of becoming known is social: being known is a recognition given by others that entails learning how to play and perform, gain exposure, increase opportunities for buzz and pub(licity), and utilize networks and contacts. Elite players are known beyond their neighborhoods and cities. Players develop strategies and construct plans for success and management of their careers.

I did not just observe players; I also coached and followed play-ers who were in the midst of their ascent, and I immersed myself in their careers.[4] I spent four years as a coach and staff person in one of Philadelphia's most prominent basketball leagues. My responsibilities included attending and running practices four or five days a week in a South Philadelphia recreational center and going to league games during the week and on weekends, whether my teams were playing or not. I assumed additional roles and became close friends with people in this social world of basketball.

I captured numerous encounters in my field notes[5] after I "got with folks": sitting in homes with players, grandmothers, moth-ers, aunts, fathers, uncles, and siblings; playing basketball on different playgrounds throughout the city; tutoring players in al-gebra, geometry, physics, and Spanish; giving personal support; going to family court and clothing stores with players; driving or "riding" players to games in other leagues where I also stayed and watched; and having telephone conversations with players and their families about prospective school transfers, unemploy-ment problems, and their hopes and aspirations.[6] Therefore, this book is as much about the everyday lives of the kids I coached and their personal support systems as it is about the process of becoming known.[7]

ACKNOWLEDGMENTS

I have been blessed by this research and benefited greatly from personal, financial, and academic support from a number of folks. I can't acknowledge or remember everyone but would like to recognize the following people who have contributed in some significant way to this project and my development as a human being and sociologist (professors, colleagues, and students in no particular order): Elijah Anderson, Benjamin Bowser, Harry Edwards, Kenneth Shropshire, Camille Zubrinsky-Charles, Tukufu Zuberi, Doug Massey, Howie Becker, Nikki Jones, Raymond Gunn, Aiden & Joe, Gary Alan Fine, Bob Emerson, Jack Katz, Michael Katz, Mitch Duneier, David Grazian, Furqan Khaldun, Susan & Mel Clampett-Lundquist, and the undergraduate and graduate students at UCR who have had to put up with basketball stories, talk, and movies.

This work is not a singular effort. It has taken a village or villages to produce this book. Thanks to Doug Mitchell, my editor guru Erin DeWitt, Tim McGovern, Robert Hunt, Mike Brehm, Christina Samuell, and the whole gang at the University of Chicago Press. Thank you to the reviewers along the way who have provided invaluable feedback. I hope that you all feel recognized by this work.

Special thanks to Jermaine and Ray (you know who you are—I told you I'd put you in the book!), the Blade Rodgers League, T.D., Blade, and everyone involved; Marc Brooks and family, Todd Brooks and family, Marvin Davis and family, and the whole Martin, Brooks, Davis, Cephas, and Smedley clans; Arabelle and Tom Brown, Mike Mitchell, Jay Franklin & Ramona Boys Basketball;

and to my Philly family, Super Kathy and Chuck, Rev, Sis, Mida and Uncle Rachel, Ms. Selena, and Gingi and Jason Wingard.

I also owe an unforgivable debt to Kara, my partner, and our kids, Kenan, Clay Ali, and Maya; my Moms and Pops, who have been editors, friends, and parents; and Mamay and Papa C, who have been unwavering and supportive throughout this process. Of course, there's also *my man*, the real Chuck Green—a best friend who has taught me much about life.

This book is in memory of Peanut, Sweets, Johnny Sample, Michael Blackshear and Philadelphia's Big Dipper and all of C.G.'s guys—past, present, and future.

INTRODUCTION

This book began in 2000 when my family of three (with one on the way) moved from Oakland, California, to Philadelphia, Pennsylvania. I had been accepted into the University of Pennsylvania's sociology graduate program and felt strongly that Philly was the place for me to study urban sociology. In my first semester, I enrolled in Dr. Elijah Anderson's urban ethnography course and was given the ideal assignment: pick a street corner, hang out, write field notes, and report back. I didn't follow his directions exactly—instead I took on more than a corner. I wanted to figure out something about the entire city. Why is Philly known as a basketball city?

I took a recreational basketball player approach. I played at different parks and playgrounds throughout the city and in Penn's gym. Between games, I asked people about Philly basketball and where to play. I also read a book on the nation's best places for pickup basketball games. I received a lot of information, but one league name came up over and over again, the Blade Rodgers League.[1] I called the league and they referred me to *their* historian. Yes, the league had a historian, Henry Ryan, who was a former sports journalist. I contacted him and arranged a meeting. We met in the living room of his North Philly row house. It was cluttered with stacks and stacks of newspapers lying around on chairs, sofas, and his dining-room table. It appeared as though things had not been moved for some time. In his defense, he wore a cast on one leg and did not move around well. He was extremely generous with his time—we spoke on four separate occasions for a total of eight to nine hours. At the end of our last talk, he referred me to several basketball guys.

I made a number of calls, but only one person called me back, Chuck Green. This was fortuitous because Chuck is a coach and a teacher and enjoys showing his basketball acumen. He was excited about teaching an outsider. Chuck is a cofounder of the Blade Rodgers League and has coached at all levels for forty years. He is also a Philadelphia basketball legend. Most importantly, Chuck is what local folks consider an "old head": an older man, wise from experience, who shares his knowledge with others, especially younger people. He called one afternoon, and we talked for about an hour. He offered a lot about the history of basketball, Philadelphia's place in that history, and much more. We agreed to meet in person.

Coach Chuck Green was in his late sixties, about six feet six inches tall, with a scruffy salt-and-pepper beard. It was hard to make out his face, hidden under an Afro topped with a bucket hat and framed in square, medium-size gold eyeglasses. His long arms, broad shoulders, thin frame, size-fifteen shoes, and unusually large hands were a dead giveaway that he was a basketball player. He had won championships at the high school and semipro levels, including a national Junior Olympic championship that is honored in the Basketball Hall of Fame.[2]

Chuck drove me around Philadelphia for hours showing me particular black communities and giving me an insider's view of the city. We ate Philly food—hoagies, cheesesteaks, and water ice. Chuck is a South Philly guy and naturally claimed that the city's best food could only be found in South Philly. I met countless people that he was connected to via basketball. They were black, white, shop owners, homeless persons, retirees, drug addicts, convicts, former professional players, college coaches, and white-collar workers. He knew them as former players, friends, foes, and parents.

Chuck gave details about his basketball career and asked me about my background. I told him about my short hoop career that ended in my senior year of high school. I was an average player who had one great summer. A California scouting and report journal mentioned me as a "player to watch" after I had worked really hard to change my attitude and improve my skills. This was very short-lived. I clashed with my coach, reverted to old habits and poor performance, and quit midway through the season. In retrospect, I blame myself and my coach. I was not assertive enough and didn't know how to become a star player. I questioned my coach's management of players and felt he was weak in motivational and interpersonal skills. He was an overachiever but couldn't get the most out of a smart and athletic player. I was recruited to a Division 2 college basketball program but decided not to attend. My family persuaded me to go to Cal (University of California, Berkeley), a much bigger and more prestigious school. I considered "walking on," trying out for the team, but questioned how being a practice dummy (even if I made the team) and getting sneakers and sweat suits would help pay for books and the rent. So I gave up on becoming a college player.

Chuck asked me to visit the Blade Rodgers Neighborhood Development League to see "the best league in the world for young people." Our relationship developed quickly, though it had its ups and downs (see the methodological appendix). After several visits to the league and becoming a volunteer, Chuck asked me if I would like to help him coach and get an even closer look at Philadelphia basketball. This was a chance to become one of Chuck's guys. It would also be a great laboratory for doing research. I accepted and worked as an assistant coach under him for four years. I learned more about basketball and working with kids while under Chuck than I had learned in all of my other years combined. Chuck and I also became lifelong friends.

The position of assistant coach inserted me into this basketball world. I entered the lives and homes of our players and their families, coaches, and supporting cast. I was a part of my research, having influence and power in the lives of our players. They impacted me too. From this close vantage point, many things were revealed, and I developed many more questions to research. I tracked several players closely and learned the amazing complexities of what it takes for young men to *get known*—to become recognized publicly as good basketball players—and how they earn college scholarships.

1

JERMAINE AND RAY

Chuck and I coached three teams per year—a sixth-, seventh-, and eighth-grade team, a ninth- and tenth-grade team, and an eleventh- and twelfth-grade team. We won more games than we lost, including some undefeated seasons. Jermaine and Ray, two young black South Philly ballers, played four years for us. They were fifteen (ninth grade) and sixteen (tenth grade) when they joined our team. Their lives embodied the inner-city story, so becoming successful at anything was a challenge. Yet they were watchful and paid close attention to what others said and did, and to the stories of poor black boys who made it. They tried to learn from others' mistakes and their own. This was necessary, if they were to become known basketball players.

Jermaine

Jermaine is dark skinned, six feet four inches tall (he's often listed taller in published reports), lanky, and broad shouldered. His first goal was to become a professional athlete. Later he also considered television/movie production, after meeting a television editor on an eighth-grade field trip. He dreamed of attending the University of Southern California, known for its film school. Jermaine got a late start at playing basketball. He had been a football player for years but began to play basketball when many of his friends were playing seriously and some were beginning to be praised by others, as he explained:

I started playing at the end of my eighth-grade year, going into my ninth-grade year. I grew up playing football, and the reason I stopped was 'cause, like, in middle school my grades, they was okay, but I could only choose two high schools [after placement tests], and the schools I chose they only had basketball; they didn't have football. And I wanted to play sports, so I switched over. I had played a little [basketball] my eighth-grade year, though, in Brown [Middle School], but it wasn't serious; I just did it for recreation and to get out of school early.

Yeah, and I played a little at the park sometimes, Espy [Park], but I sucked. Everybody was destroying me, 'cause I didn't know what I was doing. Like I didn't know how to shoot, how to dribble. 'Cause they just put me there because I was tall and I could rebound the ball, 'cause I was taller than everybody else. But I really wasn't good. I didn't never get laughed at 'cause people was scared of me. But, you know, they had their inside jokes and all that.

Hanif Martin, Todd Darling, and Sharif Johnson [were the best players around], 'cause they was the most talked-about players in the city at the time. Everybody in the city, from North Philly to South Philly, was talking about them three players. How good they were, what they gonna do in high school when they get there, and all that. I used to hang with them after school, and a lot of times at school they had games, and sometimes I'd go to the games and I'd hear them [people] talking [about them]. And I saw them play and they scored a lot of points, so I assumed they was good.

Jermaine witnessed the kind of public recognition and status good players received. Hanif, Todd, and Sharif earned citywide reputations in the eighth grade. Fortunately, Jermaine had time to catch up.

Jermaine knew where he needed to go to get better, but not what he needed to do. He headed to Espy, a local playground. He became one of several young men wanting to get known. He worked at his skills and watched and listened to older men who played. He hoped to make the high school team and earn a lot of playing time. The playground had informal resources—a group of kids who could challenge one another, and old heads with extensive knowledge and local reputations who could support and encourage him.

Jermaine, his mother, Monica, and his older brother, Khalid, lived in a two-bedroom, low-income housing project on Bank Street in South Philly. The housing project was two blocks (spanning three streets) of three-story row houses, of a "top" and a "bottom," built in the 1980s. Tops had two or three bedrooms, and bottoms had one or two. Jermaine's family lived in a "top" for most of his life. Most families in this community are longtime residents with long-term "visitors," extended family or friends who moved in temporarily but have stayed on or extended family who live in the same housing project or nearby. Jermaine's aunt and grandparents lived within walking distance.

Monica, Jermaine's mother, had Khalid and Jermaine in her mid-twenties. She attended a technical college and completed a medical assistant certificate program. She worked steadily until most of the jobs in her field moved to the suburbs. Monica then moved into medical administration and human resources. However, this work soon migrated as well, and there were limited opportunities matching her skill set in the city. Her employment was spotty during Jermaine's and Khalid's high school years and included an eighteen-month stint of unemployment. One job lead closed and left an awful taste in Monica's mouth.

> "They called me on Tuesday and told me to come in on Wednesday. The guy whose place I was supposed to take, he had come in there with a union rep. And he said that he wasn't leaving."
>
> "That's too bad," I said.
>
> "So, I go up there and they take me to administration and they lay this on me. So, you know I was ready to pull a .45 [caliber gun] or something, but I can't act that way. So, if you hear anything [about a job], please keep me in thought because they put a wrench in my whole program."

Monica's unemployment had an impact on the family. Khalid, as the oldest son, had to help. Initially, he just gave Jermaine city-subsidized tokens for the train and bus so that Jermaine could get to school and play basketball. Khalid missed a lot of school and fell behind, even failed some classes. This was a sacrifice. Khalid had been admitted to one of the top academic public schools in the city and was a high-achieving student. High achievement in his freshman and sophomore years earned him a spot in a local university's summer BRIDGE program for aspiring math and science majors. Khalid's delinquency had a steep cost—he lost the opportunity to go directly into a selective four-year college or university.

Jermaine was affected by Monica's struggles with employment in a different way. When he was eight or nine years old, he was hit by a driver running a red light; his doctor advised that he would not be able to play competitive sports. However, Jermaine continued to play sports, and at fifteen he was scheduled to undergo arthroscopic surgery to relieve the pain in his right knee. But Monica's unemployment meant the family lost comprehensive medical coverage, and Jermaine could not have a non-mandatory surgery. He kept playing basketball, and his surgical procedure was never rescheduled.

Jermaine recalled that problems between Monica and his father began when he was very young. They were separated for nearly ten years but were still legally married. His father lived nearby with another woman, and for the most part was absent from their lives.

> My dad, he wasn't really around. I mean, when I was born, that's when everything kinda dispersed like and he left, and whatever. They were [still] married. I would talk to him every day, but it was different. You ain't got that father figure around every day you can see [and talk to], when you got problems. I mean, you can talk straight to him. That's why my mom we got so close and stuff like that. She was like my mom and my dad, so all those boy troubles I had, I just told her, 'cause, I mean, I'd call him and tell him I want to see him and he be like, "all right," but he never came around, and that's how my big brother became sort of like my dad, 'cause he look

out for me and if I need something, he'll give it to me or he was always around and I could talk to him.

He [my father] moved in across Center Street around G Street. So it was like, he was with somebody else. It wasn't no kids, but it was a woman. But it seemed like he was making her more important than his family, his kids. So for a while, it was really, I don't want to say I hated him, but I wasn't really caring for him like I used to because he never had time to see me and my brother. So I'm feeling like we wasn't wanted no more, like he found a new family; he just want to settle down and be with them and forget all about us.

Jermaine felt betrayed and unloved. His father was not a dad and was not around to understand his "boy troubles" or to help guide him.[1] Boy trouble, for Jermaine, had to do with getting into fights, dealing with gangs, and the lure of the corner and street life, which he struggled with before he really got interested in basketball.

I mean, I was on that way, to go that road [to becoming a drug dealer] a couple of times, but they [his mom and brother] always kept me on track. Like, that wasn't for me. I'm on my way doing something good [now], and I'm different from everybody else.

Yeah, I wasn't selling, but they seen me outside, hanging out late, when I was young and like chilling with the drug dealers and talking to them or whatever. They [his mom and brother] was kind of getting scared. And I can see it myself; I was going that route too. Now that I look back and see everybody else doing it, I can see I was the same way; I was on the road to destruction, like.

'Cause that's not a good route to go. That's not for no kid, fourteen, fifteen, to stay out to one o'clock in the morning trying to sell weed. I mean, that's how you get killed. That's how bulls [young boys] get killed. I mean, if you fourteen and an old head come see you, he not gonna respect you.

[He imagines the conversation between an old head and

younger man:] "You ten years younger than me. I'm a take whatever you got. If you try to fight me, I'm a kill you. You wanna
be a man? I'm a treat you like a man." So, it's pointless.

Jermaine's father's absence was significant. Had his father
been around, it might have been more difficult for him to hang
out late and less appealing for him to associate with men who
were dealing drugs. Jermaine was grateful to Monica and Khalid. They were his support group and the main reason he turned
away from hanging on the corner with drug dealers. Still, their
efforts reminded him that his father had left and did not want
him. In the streets, older men paid attention to Jermaine and he
gained friends. Their lifestyle was "ghetto fabulous"—they had
money and respect. They acquired money from dealing drugs,
and plenty of young women were attracted to them. Some people deferred to them out of fear. Basketball was an activity that
took Jermaine out of the street and placed him in a different
context and group of peers and older men.

Ray

Ray and Jermaine were roadies or road dogs, close friends who
were often seen together. Their relationship developed because
they were neighbors, close in age, and they played basketball.
Ray lived next door to Jermaine in a bottom one-bedroom home
with his grandmother, Erica, and his brother, Byron.

Ray is a gangly, six-feet-one-inch-tall, light-skinned young
man with deceptive quickness and a deft shooting touch. A late
bloomer of sorts, his status grew at the end of his sophomore
year; his name began appearing in the rankings of the city's
best players, albeit low in the rankings. His grandmother, Erica,
spoke with great concern about her grandsons' futures.

Coaches come to me and say that he [Ray] one of the best in
the city. And I tell them it don't matter how good he is in basketball. If he don't take care of his schoolwork, he ain't going
nowhere. He needs an education and he needs some intense

counseling. I told his mother that kids can't go through what they did with her, without needing some counseling. Ray just holds it all in. He don't talk to nobody. I tell him he got to talk to somebody, ask for help.

Byron don't keep it in him. It bursts out of him. That's why he's always in trouble. But Ray don't say nothing. I told my daughter [Ray's mom] that you don't know how much them kids seen when you doing that stuff [drugs]. They seen and remember a whole lot more than you think.

Erica is protective. She wonders why men seem to want to help Ray. She wants people to help him, but she doesn't know whom to trust. Do these men know what they're talking about—will basketball help Ray? Are they creating false expectations that will ultimately hurt Ray? She is a firm believer in education, and most of the men speak only about basketball. She feels Ray needs more than basketball to be successful and worries that men who chase after young men are concerned about their own interests.

Ray's life has been unstable. When he was in the ninth grade, he moved between different family members' homes, changed schools, and learned that he had a brother, four years younger. At first, Ray and Byron struggled with living together and fought frequently. Ray usually won because he was bigger, but this did not prevent repeated fights. In basketball, Ray found a positive outlet for releasing his emotions, yet Erica remained concerned about Ray's and Byron's emotional well-being and what might become of them.

Erica was under great stress. Taking care of two teenage boys and being poor burdened her. She also had health problems—she is diabetic, on disability, and has not worked for over twenty years, after being diagnosed with blood clots in her legs. Erica reflected on their situation:

Having two boys is a handful. Byron is going to be placed [in the juvenile justice system] tomorrow because I can't handle it. The doctors took all these tests and none [of] them came back positive. They said it was all stress. I prayed to God for

help, and you know what He told me? He told me He was tired
for me and He didn't want me to go through this no more.
So when we was in front of the judge and he said that he was
going to place Byron, I was happy. It's the best thing for him.
I hope they place him for nine months. They need to make or
break him, 'cause six months [is] not enough.

Byron asked me, "Grandmom, can't they just put one of
those things on my leg?" And I said, "No, 'cause you just gonna
run around here and drive me crazy." He needs at least nine
months so that he gets his self together.

Byron had a reputation as a fighter, and he often got into
fights and won. He had learned that this was a powerful thing
because many kids feared him and older guys praised him. He
was considered "crazy," a good reputation for a fighter to have; it
implied that he might do anything because he was fearless and
did not follow rules or obey authority. He was suspended from
school a number of times for fighting, but Byron enjoyed his
reputation. Ray often scolded him and warned him that fighting
would lead to jail or being killed. One of Byron's responses was,
"I'm not like you. I'm thug life till I die," a reference to rapper
Tupac's mantra and lifestyle. Erica was hurt by having to deal
with Byron's frequent transgressions—in this instance he had
hurt someone badly. She was willing to give him to the juvenile
justice system, believing that it was God's will and hoping that
Byron's life trajectory might be changed.

Erica became Byron and Ray's guardian because she felt guilty
about what happened to their mother, Tamika, plus "it is family's job to take care of their own," she said. Erica is originally
from Virginia and moved to Philadelphia with her husband and
three children. Her husband left around the time Tamika, her
oldest daughter, entered high school, and it was difficult to provide for and raise three kids on her own. A bad winter and utility
problem was the turning point for Tamika.

It got real bad one winter when electricity went out, and they
[the city] didn't come fix it. I had to break up my family, and

I really didn't want to, to do that, because once you do that, you ain't got nothing.

I had always tried to keep all of us together, even though it was hard. But when that happened, I sent Tamika and Shelly to my sister's house, and I kept Junior with me at my friend's house because he was just a baby. I had to do it because I didn't want to overburden anybody.

Taking in four extra bodies was a lot and too much to ask. We all had it hard. But Tamika was the oldest, so I put her with my sister. She just went wild. She was out all the time, and I couldn't keep up with her. Then when the house got fixed, it was too late. She was too far gone.

Erica claims some responsibility for what happened to Tamika, who fell in deeply with drugs and the drug world. Erica was in a tough situation, facing dislocation alone, and being a single parent exacerbated this. She needed to work and could not keep track of multiple children when split up and in crisis.

Tamika, Byron and Ray's mother, is unforgettable. "It looks like she was in a knife fight but didn't have no knife," Chuck says, because she looks so bad. Her brown face is scarred with numerous pink marks that come from picking at scabs before wounds have healed and are typical of the long-term use of heavy drugs like crack cocaine. Her speech is slurred, and her pierced ears look like earrings were snatched from them, with the holes now slits. Tamika has been absent most of Ray's life, and his father was killed over drugs before he was born. When I first met Ray, he said he saw his mother once a year, but she was around much more as he advanced in high school and became a known basketball player. This improved their relationship and pleased him, but the damage of having a crack-addicted mother was evident. Ray stuttered badly, particularly when he spoke about his family.

Living in South Philly

Our players were often left to fend for themselves, pooling their cash together to purchase fast food, walking to save bus and train fare, and earning money through gambling and other illicit activities. Poverty, violence, incarceration, and death—usually all related to drugs—were normal. They were motivated by this reality and expected that their lives would be short and unfulfilling if they failed to escape the poverty and environment in which they lived.

Many South Philly residents blame younger men for the violence that occurs in their neighborhoods and schools. Parents and community folk talk a lot about "the corner." They tell stories about kids who are "out in the street, running wild," and the "bad" kids who worry their mothers. Being on the corner is synonymous with being a "gangsta" or a "thug" (or at least being mistaken for one) and with fighting and/or selling drugs. The corner is where older and younger men "hang," making open-air drug deals, strategizing about mischief or criminal activity, and where they are arrested and shot too.[2] People's status on the corner is tied to their ability to "handle" themselves and abide by the code of the street: individuals need to take care of matters of disrespect on their own because they can't depend on or trust police and civil authority to resolve interpersonal conflicts.[3] Parents and families are strongly committed to basketball and to keeping their kids off the corner; they consider a basketball player or an athlete to be the opposite of being a thug. Still, many athletes go back and forth between athlete and thug as they deem it necessary or useful. They hang out on the corner, run wild, and get into trouble. Plenty of athletes will settle on the corner, coming to grips with the reality of athletic mobility—very few make it as an elite player.

Jermaine and other kids who live on the block call themselves "Bankers," in reference to the name of their street, imitating how some real gangs take on names in their community. Bank Street is one block from Butler Avenue, a main street, and faces the housing project's parking lot. Bank Street functions as a one-way street because it is only wide enough for one car. The Bankers act as a small, loose-knit gang; they fight for each other against people from other neighborhoods when necessary. Like all other Bankers, Jermaine needed his friends for protection. Friendship depends on loyalty, mutual obligation, and reciprocation. But being a Banker may come with a cost, as Jermaine and Ray sometimes hung with "gangstas" (people who were unpredictable and often engaged in criminal activity) and did things they didn't want to do. Jermaine recounted a story of how this once happened:

> "I was in the store with Ray, and my bull [friend] John was gonna steal some phone cards. You know those prepaid cards. And we was gonna sell them and split the money up between the three of us."
>
> "Why would you steal phone cards?" I asked.
>
> "I didn't want to do it, but I had to, they . . . well, John was gonna do it anyways. We was just in the store and he was like, 'Yo, let's steal some phone cards and sell 'em.'
>
> "So I was the lookout, while he and Ray tried to take as much as they could. But then somebody came in the jahn [place], and so I told them, 'Let's go.' We almost got caught.
>
> "My bull John is gangsta; he be doing that kind of stuff all the time. That's why I told him I can't be with him all the time. Moms go crazy if I got caught. She'd kill me yo."

This might have jeopardized Jermaine's future, had they been caught stealing. But he felt obligated to be involved in the plot because of his group affiliation. Since Ray was "down" and was going along with John's plan, the majority decision was to steal the phone cards. In their peer group, majority rule is the norm. Jermaine could have decided to leave the store, rejecting the plan to steal, but he knew he would have been ridiculed for this and might even be beaten up by John and Ray. Involvement in "gangsta" activity was problematic and atypical for Jermaine and Ray because they were basketball players, and getting into trouble would decrease their chances for earning a college scholarship. Young men willing to be gangsta get asked to do more gangsta activities by peers, while being a ballplayer can offer freedom from participating in such activities. Ray and Jermaine got into less and less trouble as they continued on their basketball paths. It became known that they were not interested and that influential men wanted to see them succeed.

A Conversation with Jermaine, Ray, and Darrell

One evening after practice, I drove Jermaine, Ray, and a third kid named Darrell home. I asked them about some men standing on a corner.

> "Who are those guys on the corner?" I inquired.
>
> "Drug dealers," Darrell responded without much thought.
>
> "How do you know?" I questioned, wanting to know what he knew about these guys that clued him in to their being drug dealers as opposed to loafers, kids waiting for their parents to come home, or men who had just gotten off work.
>
> "Everybody know," he said matter-of-factly.
>
> "Do you *know* them?" I probed further.
>
> "Yeah. I mean, no. They know me, but I don't know them," he replied.
>
> "I know them, Scott," Ray said. "Well I don't *know* them know them. But I know them. One of them used to go to our school."
>
> Jermaine added, "Yeah, that Turk. But he don't go to school no more. He just hang out on the corner."
>
> "How do *they* know *you*, then? They know you from school or the neighborhood . . . ?" I asked.
>
> "Because we play ball," Darrell shot back.
>
> "Just because you play ball, they *know* you?" I asked with some disbelief.
>
> "Yeah, 'cause they seen me play," Darrell said.
>
> "They know us because we play ball and get girls, Scott," Jermaine added, giving further detail. Darrell grew frustrated with my questioning and tried to summarize his point.
>
> "Basically, you either a thug or an athlete. And if you an athlete, then you get respect, and girls like that. They [the thugs we saw] just wasting they lives."

Basketball is considered a niche opportunity. It is an acceptable means for our players to express themselves. It is a means
that is readily available and accessible, and one that has paid
off for many black Philadelphia boys. (This is a perception based
on the fact that most pro players are black and that Philadelphia is well represented.) Basketball is a transformational device
used to change young, poor, inner-city black men with no hope
into potentially upwardly mobile men. It can help steer them
from the inevitability of participation in drugs, violence, and
crime. Parents and boys have a firm grasp of the statistical im-
probability of succeeding, but this does not deter them. Instead,
they consider the positive short-term effects of playing and believe becoming a professional basketball player is a worthwhile
and viable possibility. They talk passionately about basketball's
perceived powers of influence. Basketball opens doors and saves
lives, both figuratively and literally.[4]

Jermaine says that his life changed dramatically when he decided to become a basketball player:

> I mean, I use my wisdom, I don't get into all that no more, I
> just tell 'em [drug dealers and others on the street] "no." They
> try to say, "You don't ride [hang out with us] like you used to.
> You changed."
>
> But I changed for the better, in my eyes. I don't want to
> live on Bank Street all my life; I want to make money. I don't
> want to stay here all my life. I want to finish experiencing the
> world . . .
>
> I mean, I talk to 'em [my neighborhood friends] whatever,
> I speak with 'em, but I don't really hang with 'em like I used
> to because we not really on the same path; we on different
> paths. They path, they want to get this money, sell drugs, or
> whatever. I wanna go to school, get my degree, do something
> with my life. And I look at it as if they not going to school, they
> gonna be back here doing the same thing. If they not dead or
> locked up, they gonna be doing the same thing.

Many young men feel compelled to enter the drug game because of their poverty and desire to make good money. Jermaine

thinks that because of the danger associated with this life-style, it is shortsighted and a dead end, even though he was on that track. He now emphasizes "decent" values, behavior, and possibilities: "experiencing the world," attending college, getting a degree, and doing "something with my life." Most importantly, he claims to use "wisdom" or maturity from understanding what was wrong about his past behavior. Now he is thinking long term, but this has required a change and belief that he could do something about living in poverty and its intractability. In this way, basketball gave him an identity, a different way of thinking about life, possibilities, and a bright future.

Ray and Jermaine felt indebted to their families. Sacrifices were being made on their behalf, and they spoke of showing their gratitude later. They dreamed of buying homes and cars for their mothers and grandmother and taking care of their brothers. There were other folks who supported them as well: extended family, friends, godfathers, coaches, and old heads. Jermaine called this his "support system." Support systems showed unconditional love and belief in them and pushed them to do the right things.

2

BECOMING A BASKETBALL PLAYER

Social connections and group affiliations—like family histories, race, class, and gender—are all very important to the aspirations of our players. Everything happens within a context. Thus the amount of attention that is given to basketball cannot be separated from place. Philadelphia creates a certain disposition: young black men learn early that their community values basketball, respects superior performance, and considers this integral to their masculinity.[1] This setting supports basketball as an identity, ambition, and career.

The Sociability and Legitimacy of Basketball

Boys play basketball as a way to be masculine and to earn respect. "'Cause everybody do it. My friends all play, and I ain't trying to get left out [of] the group. Plus, it's fun," Ray said. Greg, a fifteen-year-old who played four sports in high school, explained, "It's my first love. I don't know, I've just always played and liked playing ball. I remember my dad watching basketball, and I would watch it with him when I was little. Then he used to take me to the playground and teach me how to shoot." Greg was a subpar player at best, and his lack of ability ran in the family. Chuck had "fired" or cut his father from the South Philly team two decades earlier. Yet inability did not affect Greg's love for the game and consistency in coming to practice. He genuinely wanted to get better and worked hard to improve because he saw it as a masculine activity and he wanted to make his father proud.

Petey, also fifteen, was a good match for Greg. He had below-average skills and was ridiculed by other kids because he was not good. "I know that I'm not at the level of the other guys, but I'm practicing to get better. Next year, I'm gonna try out for JV [junior varsity]," Petey told me this after his sophomore year in high school. Showing little improvement, he continued to play because it allowed him to hang out with friends.[2] Petey expressed the hope that he would get better because basketball was one of the few ways he had available to earn more respect from others.

Our players feel a racial and gendered connection to basketball through the black men represented in the media—on television, online, and in magazines and newspapers.[3] These were their favorite players, idols and role models. They argued over who would wear the jersey with the number 23 (Michael Jordan's number). And they identified the basketball shoes they bought or wanted by calling the shoes "[Allen] Iversons," "Paul Pierces," or "KGs [Kevin Garnetts]"—naming the professional player who wore the shoes. Some called themselves by the names and nicknames of their favorite players, and they videotaped and watched college and professional games over and over. Jermaine told me that he even learned from watching basketball on television.

> "I learned from TV or whatever. I seen all the pros and the college players doing all these moves and whatever, and I just worked on it. I go to the park and just practice everything they was doing. It was frustrating at first 'cause I couldn't get it right."
>
> "How'd you learn the up-and-under [move]?" I asked.
>
> "Who was the big man that did it? Jermaine O'Neal. Yeah, he do the up-and-under. He get you up in the air, and then he go up under you and lay it down. That was my patented [move]; I used to get [fool] everybody with it. I just kept doing it. I was just playing five on five against the old heads; I used to do it and it used to work, so I took it to people my age in games and it was working."

Ray watched a videotape of Iverson playing in college[4] and knew what was going to happen as he watched the game. "Watch, Scott, watch. He gonna shoot the three[-point shot]." Ray paid close attention to Iverson's body movements and the movements of his defenders. Ray stopped and rewound the tape again and again to dissect certain moves, noting how Iverson held his head, how he faked out the other player, and how high he jumped. After watching the same move several times, Ray stood up and tried the move, imagining that someone was playing defense against him.

Ray said he believed he could become a professional basketball player because other young black men from the hood had done so before him. "Most of the [NBA] players come from the hood, Scott. MJ [Michael Jordan],[5] Iverson. They come from the same thing, bulls selling drugs, getting locked up." Our players felt that they had a lot in common with college and professional players. They were young black males, poor, from the inner city.

Some kids believe in their potential because their families have basketball histories and take pride in the successes of individual members. Family members borrow status from individuals who get recognized, win athletic awards, and have success. They talk about the achievement using "we," claiming some credit. The satisfaction is even greater when the success is made public.

I met the aunt of an up-and-coming player in West Philadelphia. Her name was Gneisha. When I told her about my interest in Philadelphia basketball, she later showed me a newspaper article that featured her family. The article covered her brother-in-law and two nephews. The older nephew had already earned an athletic scholarship to a Texas university, and the younger nephew, a senior who played for Tillman High, was playing for the city's high school public league championship.

Yeah, we already sent his brother to college, he playing ball. And now we got Bobby. He a player too. They wrote an article in the paper on him. My sister called me and told me. So I went online and printed a copy. They got a whole page and a half! That's too much for him. Now he really think he doing something.

He got a little brother, too, that play. My sister just said that now he got a trophy. He only fourteen and he came in last night with a trophy. She said she don't even know where he was playing, but he got one and she said it's nice too. That's the baby. But they want him to play football because he big. Not fat, but you know solid. But he got to keep his grades up. He don't play football, though. You know why? 'Cause he don't go to practice! I laugh because he always on punishment.

I'm gonna see the middle nephew play this weekend. On Saturday they playing for the championship at Big [University], at the Stanley Center. The oldest brother played at Tillman [High School] too, but he lost in the championship game a few years back. Their father played for Tillman too. And he was real good. He could've done something too, but he got into that street life. You know how it is. You've probably heard of him.

The men in Gneisha's family had basketball identities; and sports, particularly basketball, were important to them. The newspaper article was mainly about her middle nephew, but it mentioned her oldest nephew and brother-in-law briefly and listed their basketball achievements, proof that they were known. The oldest nephew was a "star guard for Tillman's 2001 semifinalists," and "in the mid-1970s, the boys' father, JJ, routinely torched high-profile foes on the playgrounds and schoolyards of West Philly."[6] For young and older men, being a basketball player was viewed as *doing something,* as was evident when the father later failed. "He could've *done something* too, but he got into that street life," said Gneisha. Clearly, basketball was important to Gneisha and her family as a way of "doing something" and earning status.[7]

A Basketball City

Jermaine and Ray have only lived in Philadelphia, so they cannot compare it to other cities. But they know that young black guys and Philadelphia guys "make it" based upon the number of professional players from Philadelphia. The city has resources and structures that help players to develop, gain attention, and play at the highest levels. The organization of basketball in Philadelphia and, most importantly, its networks of people work together to encourage, teach, and provide opportunities for young men to play and gain the exposure needed to be seen, promoted, and sought after by college recruiters. Philadelphia is home to a basketball social world inspired by a rich basketball history.

In 2002 Philadelphia hosted the NBA's All-Star Game. The *Daily News* dedicated an entire issue to basketball, "Hoops Heaven," on February 5, 2002. It highlighted Philadelphia's long-standing basketball history, local legends, places, and significance to basketball overall. Professional basketball in Philadelphia began in the 1890s. Legends, Hall of Fame players, and future Hall of Famers come from the city, such as John Chaney (via Florida), Dawn Staley, Wilt Chamberlain, Earl "the Pearl" Monroe, Tom Gola, Lionel "Train" Simmons, Rasheed Wallace, and Kobe Bryant (via Italy and the suburbs). There are local colleges with national reputations: La Salle (1954 national champions in the first nationally televised championship game), Villanova (1985 national champions, 2006 Final Four), Temple (ranked number one nationally in 1987–88 and five Elite Eight finishes), St. Joseph's (2004 undefeated conference season and Elite Eight finish), and Penn (perennial Ivy League champion).[8] These schools make up the "Big 5," an annual Philadelphia tournament between local universities, which is one of a kind. No other city has an annual nonconference tournament between local colleges and universities. And it's for one sport, basketball, not football, baseball, or hockey—more evidence of basketball's importance in Philadelphia.[9]

Philadelphia's basketball world is more than history. Women and men, young and old, are connected via basketball activities.

They form an extensive, interdependent network. Players begin playing at young ages and are helped by older players, former players, and close observers (kin and non-kin).

Chuck said to me, "If you got anything in you, if you show anything, you got a shot to do something with it, 'cause Philadelphia's a basketball town." His message is clear—Philadelphia is a space where players can be nurtured and promoted to higher levels of play. During a phone call, Chuck described a young man who was relocating to Philadelphia for the summer in order to take advantage of its basketball resources.

> "I got a call from this woman who said she used to watch me and Blade [Rodgers] and a bunch of other Philadelphia greats play. And she says to me that she got this boy from, from South Dakota or somewhere. He an Indian and she said that he an All-American but can't get no play [interest from colleges] because he in the middle of nowhere. But she say that he better than *all* our guys. What you think?
>
> "Now, I've got to give him a play and trust her a little bit because she sure enough know some basketball. She a coach herself and won a *great* many championships. I say I don't care if the boy is green and got one leg. If he can play, I'll take him. And if he can't [play well], but he willing to learn, we can make something out of him."
>
> I interrupted Chuck. "So she having this boy come all the way out here just to play in Blade Rodgers. She really think he gonna get a scholarship here?"
>
> "Yeah, you know she a Jewish lady, and I don't know how she know about him, but she say that he not getting the play [recognition and scouting by colleges] because he Indian and he in South Dakota. She know that if he come to Philly and play, if he can beat these niggers, then he can get a shot."

Both Chuck and Sarah (the woman who called him) believe that *place* is important. The kid's name was Jaywin and he was eighteen. If he could prove himself in Philadelphia, he would have a much better chance of earning a college scholarship because of the level of competition and exposure in Philadelphia. Sarah shared her feelings about the advantage of race and class in terms of basketball.

> Black kids from the ghetto get a look [by college coaches and scouts], no matter what, but an Indian kid in South Dakota doesn't have a chance. I want him [Jaywin] to come here so that he can get a look, because the kid can play. He can jump like [Michael] Jordan, shoot like [Reggie] Miller, and he's quick like Iverson. As a matter of fact, I think he's quicker than Iverson. And he's a great kid and a real leader. He's won two state titles and MVPs, but he still can't get recruited by good schools.

Jaywin needed to be in an environment where he could prove himself against tough, urban, poor, black young men, who normally get recognition from scouts and college recruiters. Philadelphia carries its own prestige and reputation, although based largely on black male athletes as products; thereby making it a hotbed for recruiting, particularly by local colleges and universities. Importantly, Jaywin's opportunity suggests that the context of Philadelphia did not just serve black kids, though Sarah felt that black kids from the ghetto had recruiting advantages. Teams from other cities in New Jersey and Delaware, as well as Philadelphia suburbs, brought black and white kids to "the city" to compete against the best.

Jaywin came to practice a few weeks later. He was not a big kid, only six feet tall and one hundred sixty pounds. We watched him closely and evaluated his ability. He was fast and jumped well enough to dunk a basketball. He played and worked hard, but he was not as skilled as our better players. He had to adjust to our players. They did not trust him as an unknown and did not pass the ball to him. He had very few opportunities to make a good impression and prove himself. He failed miserably early on, missing open layups and jump shots and losing the ball against tough defense. He was playing against much better competition than in South Dakota, and he found it difficult to earn status.

Still, Chuck and I grew fond of Jaywin; we liked his story and wanted to help him. Chuck enjoyed telling people about Jaywin's arrival. "This boy, Indian boy, graduate [from high school] in the morning and be here at four o'clock for practice, coming from halfway around the world. From North, South Dakota, somewhere. And we can't get guys to come for practice who live around the corner!" Jaywin had it as bad as our kids. He talked about his reservation and what young men did when they did not go to college—drug addiction, alcoholism, low-wage jobs, and unemployment. Jaywin developed a strong relationship with Chuck while in the league. They would watch games together, and Chuck talked about basketball theory and how Jaywin might improve as a player. After our season, Sarah asked if Chuck could help Jaywin get into college, since he hadn't gained the recognition or attention in the league. Chuck contacted a coach at a small local college, telling him about Jaywin's potential, and the coach agreed to let him try out for his team. Jaywin failed to provide his transcript and to enroll in the college on time and ultimately moved back to South Dakota. He attended a local community college there but dropped out after a year.

Jaywin had moved to Philadelphia to enter a better opportunity structure.[10] His sponsor, Sarah, assumed that what he had learned prepared him to play in Philadelphia and the Blade Rodgers League. Philadelphia was not simply a better opportunity for rewards and recognition; it was a better place for learning and becoming an elite player, if a young man had some ability and was willing to put in the work and make the right decisions. Hard work and the efforts of supporting casts, along with place (where one lives and plays)—all are important factors.

3

GETTING KNOWN THROUGH
NETWORKS AND EXPOSURE

Studies regarding how people get jobs have been limited to describing networks and how networks work. Coaching in Blade Rodgers, however, showed me that preparing and getting a job is not simply *who one knows*.[1] "Getting known" is a process and a career that requires significant work—both meritocratic and subjective. Young men have to perform in the presence of others. They *get known* as the result of being exposed to what a basketball player is and does, learning from and interacting with others in their community, and playing up to expectations.[2] The elite known players feel that they are successful because they receive accolades and praise; they are written about in newspapers, are asked to play for selective teams that travel, and are eventually sought after by college coaches. These players treat basketball as their career and seek to maximize their chances. They look for options, and they network and play as much as possible for a chance to build a lasting reputation. However, the career is not simply an individual enterprise. There are other people involved in the process. The social aspect of a career or the "politics," managing relationships, is as important as performance, especially for those without extraordinary ability or potential.

Although college coaches and professional scouts often claim to have *found* players who were previously hidden and unknown, there is a process for a player to catch the eye of these representatives. College recruiters rarely come to playgrounds or high schools without some introduction or prior knowledge of the players. Unlike old heads, recruiters don't provide money, rides, protection, advice, or early promotion until players have earned reputations. Networks alone are not enough to make one an elite player unless he is exceptional (or a seven footer). Players need exposure and must perform well to make names for themselves. Exposure is the opportunity to compete with high-status persons and play in settings where college coaches, recruiters, and scouts are present, and there are various paths to gain exposure.

A young man who plays in many settings, against or with better and known players, is seen by more people and can get recognized by those who can help him in his basketball career. Players are watched at early ages in year-round leagues, such as Blade Rodgers, City Youth Organization (CYO), and the Police Athletic League (PAL). Players are also watched through the numerous Amateur Athletic Union (AAU) teams that travel all over, to places like Baltimore, Washington, D.C., New York, Houston, Las Vegas, Orlando, and Los Angeles. Kids also play school basketball. The best players are recruited by coaches to schools, offered scholarships (to private schools), and promised playing time. Each year is a cycle: fall leagues and AAU tournaments lead into high school seasons in the winter; next comes spring leagues and more AAU tournaments, and then summer leagues and tournaments. Basketball is busiest during the summer when school is out and kids have free time. It is expected that kids improve most during this time because there are plenty of playground leagues throughout the city—high-profile summer leagues like Blade Rodgers and leagues for high schools, as well as the large and faraway AAU tournaments. Success in one season can run into the next season, creating positive impressions or buzz, getting "pub" (publicity), and gaining more exposure and new opportunities for up-and-coming players.

I met Ray and Jermaine when they showed up for our Blade Rodgers team practice. They had already finished their high school's season, were engrossed in playground play, and hoped that playing in Blade Rodgers would lead to their being asked to play for other teams and prepare them for their next high school season.

Blade Rodgers, a Career League

Boys came to play at Blade Rodgers for different reasons and with a range of goals. A considerable number of them played because of their desire to become elite basketball players. Players came for recreation or were sent by parents, relatives, or friends. A few players played six years for Chuck and me. Others disappeared, moving to different parts of the city because of changing family conditions, new guardianships, or leaving the city altogether. They stopped playing to work and help their families, and some quit after realizing that they were not achieving in basketball and were not gaining the public recognition they were seeking. Still others left to pursue better basketball opportunities on other teams.

Blade Rodgers League is representative of how basketball is played at the collegiate and professional levels. It is a big break from street ball and how basketball is played on the playground and in other leagues. Play is more formalized, requiring a different set of skills, discipline, and understanding of the rules. Games are structured, recorded, and regulated like college and professional basketball. Audiences include not only peers, but also high school and college coaches, as well as people from different parts of the city, suburbs, and beyond. People become known by playing in Blade Rodgers. Top players can be tracked in the *Daily News*, a local paper that reports the final scores of games and the leading scorers. Henry Ryan, the league's historian, discussed its mission:

> Blade [Rodgers] says the league began in '68, but the records began in '69. They developed the league to help the city get over gang wars and foster human relations. I think that basketball was related with good intentions to improve Philadelphia high school basketball.
>
> It was a big brother–little brother program that began with the Brown Leagues [the original adult league] and then graduating seniors [in high school] on down. The Varsity [eleventh- and twelfth-grade] League had teams to the Brown [adult] League teams, and guys would talk to the younger guys. Then

the Next Generation [ninth- and tenth-grade] League began because there were too many kids that wanted to play and not
enough teams.

Back then, Paul Jacks ran the mandatory tutoring program, and they kicked players out of the program for absence,
because producing great players with no education prevented
them from going to college.

In our league they [kids] learned to play *the right way*, to prepare them for college. The league was a feeding ground where
college coaches could see serious ball. You would see Denny
Crum [longtime coach at the University of Louisville], John
Thompson [Hall of Fame coach for Georgetown University],
[Dean] Smith assistants [Hall of Fame coach for the University
of North Carolina].

The Rodgers League was supposed to save people from the
most unscrupulous people [bad college coaches and agents].
Lower Division 1, Division 2, and Division 3 [collegiate competition levels, Division 1 being the highest and most competi-
tive] schools come to check out players too. Guys were being
discovered in the Blade Rodgers League.

There are so many [former] players who now have sons
coming up; they know what the league is all about. So it's
still pretty much known that this is *the* place to go if you're
serious. This is not a fun league. This is a career league. People
have stopped coming because they don't look as good. Instead,
they go where nobody is telling you tuck your shirt in and
watch your mouth. They [players in the Rodgers League] shoot
and score less and they have to play defense.

The league's mission is for kids to become successful basketball players, on and off the court. Over a forty-year span, Blade
Rodgers alumni have earned more than three hundred college
scholarships to play collegiate ball, and over thirty former players have played professionally.[3] This number may not be statisti-
cally significant—there is no éxact count of how many kids have
played in the league, nor is it known how many players have re-
jected scholarships (whether they accepted others or simply went
to another college without a scholarship or did not go to college

at all). What is most important is that the visibility of alumni in higher levels of basketball/basketball careers acts as proof that the league is special and that career mobility is possible. Notably, a number of Blade Rodgers League alumni, white and black, are professional players, college coaches, and a smaller number are NBA executives. The league endures and has a vast network that helps young men to advance to higher levels.

Blade Rodgers also prides itself on helping young men to have more opportunities for success and to become men who are good citizens. Men in the league are role models and act as father figures. In this way, Blade Rodgers operates as a big brother–little brother program. Older men work with young men to teach and enforce the necessary understandings of organized basketball. Kids are expected not only to learn how to play according to conventions to improve their basketball play, but to improve their personal character as well (i.e., responsibility, cooperation with others, management of anger).

The men who oversee and coordinate league activities have a history of working with young people. Chuck is a retired drug and gang counselor who worked for the city. A majority of the men are probation officers, including TD, the league's coordinator and Chuck's former longtime assistant coach, and one man is a retired police officer. These men are clear in their desire to break the cycle of young black male incarceration, drug addiction, and involvement in violence and crime. They believe that intervening early on might save a few young black men—that is why their discipline extends beyond basketball. They enforce broader social conventions regarding decorum and respect for authority and teamwork. They tell players to tuck in their shirts and to be neat, to listen to their coaches, and to respect their teammates, players on other teams, and calls made by referees. In addition, an hour-long session is mandatory on Saturdays for each participant in the sixth-, seventh-, and eighth-grade league, whether the youngster played that day or not. During these meetings, successful businesspersons and accomplished young persons are invited to give motivational and informational talks about what it takes to get ahead in society. One season, speakers ranged from a college student who grew up in poverty, to a

Rwandan refugee, a dentist, and a college basketball coach. All shared their experiences and serve as examples of how people can overcome difficult odds. Blade Rodgers uses basketball to bridge the inner city and broader society, and offers information to prepare young men for their adult lives.

For our kids, the Blade Rodgers League is now primarily symbolic, although it remains a place where the best kids play and college coaches recruit. However, AAU tournaments held in all parts of the country are regarded as the main sites for making a name and earning a scholarship. Kids enter a stage and perform in front of college coaches, some renown and others not. This speaks to a unique environment for earning a position or job. Exposure is the key. A résumé is not enough. Performances in the right venues validate status and position. Yet a kid must first get the opportunity to play on AAU teams, and this is not so easy. There is a glut of talent, and kids compete fiercely for spots.

4 PLAYING SCHOOL BALL

Jermaine couldn't wait to try out for his high school's varsity basketball team in the ninth grade. He was not guaranteed a place on the team and hoped that he could impress the coach. He had worked hard to get into shape by running around the neighborhood and practicing shooting and dribbling at a local playground. He thought about the upcoming season a lot and how many points he would score per game, how many rebounds he would grab, and the monstrous dunks and alley-oops he would get over other players.

Ray and Jermaine attended Thompson High School together, during Ray's sophomore and junior years and Jermaine's freshman and sophomore years. Ray had transferred to Thompson from a high school in West Philadelphia after his freshmen year when he lived with an uncle. He lost half a school year academically, and his whole basketball season, when he moved to South Philly with his grandmother. Jermaine, on the other hand, entered Thompson as part of his natural progression from middle school to high school. Ray made the varsity team in his sophomore year and played well. Jermaine failed to make the varsity team in his freshman year and was eventually kicked off the junior varsity team for fighting.

> I tried out or whatever, and they was saying they wasn't gonna to let no freshman play varsity 'cause they already had like ten seniors coming back and they only had two spots [open for new players]. And so I was against it [odds were against me], that was when Ray was there and Bryant was there, and they

was more known than me. So they already got the two spots. Bryant was known from middle school. 'Cause he played for Pressey [Middle School], and he was averaging thirty [points per game]. So that's how he got known. So everybody knew who he was. So we went to Thompson, and plus his uncle was assistant coach at Thompson, so they already knew he was getting a spot or whatever. So I just showed what I could do to get on the team. And I got on JV and I was crushing on JV. Then I got kicked off. It was at practice, and a bull from D Street or whatever he was saying that I wasn't passing the ball, and words became fists or whatever.

Making the varsity team as a freshman would have been a high compliment for Jermaine. It supposedly predicts a player's potential and highlights that a player is playing up or better than most players his age. Varsity teams are composed of the school's best players, who are primarily juniors and seniors. Jermaine's talent was still very raw, and there were only two available spots. Bryant was known and his uncle was a coach on the team, and Jermaine could not beat out Ray for the spot.

According to Petey, a schoolmate and friend of theirs, playing high school ball for Thompson helped both Ray and Jermaine to *get known* by their neighborhood peers and old heads and gain some attention.

"How did Jermaine and Ray become seen as good players?" I asked Petey.

"Jermaine got known 'cause he on JV [junior varsity]," Petey said.

"Did you play on JV?" I asked.

"No, because I was too late. But Jermaine was known first for street ball on the playground. Then he got known 'cause he dunked on this bull, an older bull who's bigger than him, Tommy [Handy], at Fields [High School]. And then the girls were all on him.[1] See, Jermaine got the ball and went up like he gonna do this. And then he just said, 'Forget it, I'm gonna dunk this,' and BAM! He dunked it on bull."

Jermaine had dunked on someone who was taller and bigger, in terms of size and status. Jermaine explained this event as a significant moment in his early career.

I got one on [dunked on] the bull Tommy Handy; he was one of the top-rated bulls in the city, and he went to Fields or whatever. Fields is a school, Stephen G. Fields. Their varsity [team] didn't have a game that day, so they tried to blow us out [win by a lot of points] so he [Tommy Handy] played [for the] JV [instead of the varsity]. I just went baseline and I dunked. I dunked before, but I didn't really have another dunk on anybody like that. So that's when everybody started saying "why am I playing JV" and stuff like that. Yeah, old heads came to see me play and started paying attention to me; it wasn't like Ray [had], but I had a couple [of old heads paying attention to me].

Dunking on another player is very impressive because it is a notable physical feat, jumping and slamming the ball through a basket that is ten feet high, and it is also a show of dominance over someone.[2] Jermaine could have been embarrassed if Tommy had somehow blocked or kept him from dunking. Jermaine got attention from old heads and became known to his schoolmates for his jumping ability.

Petey also talked about Ray's status and what he did to earn it.

And Ray known 'cause of his handle [dribbling ability] and jump shot. Can't nobody stick [guard] him. He and I won the three-on-three championship together, and he was like *wop wop* [Petey shoots two imaginary shots and the "*wop wop*" imitates the shots swishing the net], making bulls fall and stuff, and they ankles was hurt [embarrassing opposing defenders by faking them out with a dribble move].

And his [Ray's] [Thompson High School] coach didn't hardly play him at first 'cause Ray didn't play well in the tryout; he don't never play good in a tryout. So the coach sat him on the

bench and he'd go to sleep. That's how he got his nickname
Sleepy. 'Cause he'd fall asleep on the end of the bench and
then the coach would say, "Ray, Ray," and he be like, "Huh?"
And then he go for [score] like twenty [points] off the bench [as
a substitute player]. They just couldn't stick him.

Ray dominated in another way. By the end of the season, Ray was
the team's second leading scorer, and teammates and friends
saw him embarrass his opponents.

Petey taught me the term "known." Both cases, for Ray and
Jermaine, show that getting or being known is based on action,
involving what a person does to another person(s) or how they
dominate them, and is dependent upon the response and evalu-
ation by others. When kids play, they are potentially creating
stories that can be retold by others.

High school basketball is a context where many get known
because it is linked to the institution of school and, generally,
there are more spectators. Scores are reported in the newspaper, players and coaches are sometimes interviewed and written about, championship games are often televised locally, and
results are recorded as part of school and sports history. Ray's
scoring performances, that Petey remembers, were recorded in
the newspaper, and Ray kept many of the team's box scores that
told of the number of points, rebounds, assists, and turnovers he
made. A scout listed him as a "player to watch" in an end-of-the-
season ranking of players by grade level. Jermaine did not make
it into the newspaper. Newspapers did not report on junior varsity games, and he did not make the player rankings.

Playing for one's high school had limited reach though. One
local sportswriter claimed, "High school is not taken as seriously
because the teams are stacked, the coaches are terrible, and many
of the best guys don't play in school." The quality of many public high school programs has suffered since a rule change was
instituted and coaches had to be full-time teachers. Many good
coaches did not meet this requirement and had to be released.
This also hurt players. Lesser-qualified and lesser-known coaches
frustrate good players, who feel they know more about the sport
than the coach/teacher who is supposed to be guiding them.

Thompson High School's varsity coach was a math teacher. As I learned from another teacher at Thompson, he took the coaching job because no other teachers would and the job came with a stipend. After attending one game, I saw a problem. The coach was invisible. I had to ask someone who he was. He did not sit on the bench with the players and seemed completely detached from what was going on. Because of coaches like this, many star players, and those who follow their lead, lose respect for their coaches and sometimes quit or do not try out for their high school's team. Players come to understand that they need multiple men and to rely on old heads and coaches in other leagues as well to boost their careers.

5 OLD HEADS AND YOUNG BULLS

Ray and Jermaine learned that interactions with old heads were important. Marcus Jones, an old head at Espy playground, gave them their earliest opportunities to play with the weekend regulars. He "picked them up," selecting them as teammates, along with his son, as part of their rite of passage into more serious basketball and manhood. Their playing with men was necessary to their overall development. They would be challenged and toughened by playing against wiser, stronger, bigger, and more physically intimidating players than their peers.

The Role of Old Heads

Relationships formed on the playground often are distinctive and remarkable, most notably, relationships between older and younger men, "old heads" and "young bulls."[1] Old heads are important as supporters, role models, and/or coaches because they teach, encourage, praise, and provide support for younger players. Jermaine described old heads in this way: "It's like, it's like certain people like respect [an old head] . . . it's a respect thing. You call them an old head, it's like, nah'imean [you know what I mean] . . . you admire their game. Or you call them old head, they older than you, nah'imean." There are some instances where old heads perform different functions, as Jermaine explained in his relationships:

You got different ones, it depends, like, my old head, I still got the same one, but some of them come and go. Like, most of them, they get locked up or something, they stop playing basketball or whatever or they really don't care . . . they just there 'cause they think you gonna go to the League (NBA) or something like that. That's how most of them is.

But the whole thing about me is, where I'm from, I'm more like the underrated player. So I really don't have a lot of old heads like everybody else do. I only have like two old heads, and they really just play [with me] and they push me. But everybody else, I mean, they got like thousands and they get money [from them]. If they need something, they just buy something, they there for them. And I don't really got that [an old head relationship like this] and that's what pushed me real hard 'cause I'm trying to get where they at, like if I need sneaks or something, I call somebody and they give it to me, and I can't really do that right now. They mostly come and go, but there's different types of old heads.

You got a old head like you respect him, whatever, or the old head you just say it 'cause he older than you and show him respect, but you got a couple of old heads, they just there for you, no matter [what], whenever you need something, you in trouble, you need a ride to a game, they there for you. So there's different types. You use it [the term "old head"] in different meanings.

Old heads often become friends with younger men who show promise, "taking [them] on." "Taking a kid on" suggests that an old head is tied to a young bull and has a close relationship offering emotional, financial, or other types of support or resources when necessary. They come in different forms. Coaches, mentors, and instructors can be old heads, and their personal success and experience in basketball increases the amount of technical assistance they can give. But drug dealers can be old heads too,[2] attracted by being associated with a local celebrity who might later "make it." They can mentor through warning and turn younger men away from the street because of the potential to do something great and legitimate, or they can exploit players through gambling. They stage one-on-one games between play-ers or bet on games, choosing their young bull or his team to win. Money is often central to this relationship, as drug dealers can support and subsidize a young ballplayer. Repayment may be necessary and made explicit. After purchasing several pairs of basketball shoes for Ray, one old head asked him to sign a hand-written contract to be repaid $10,000 if he made it to the NBA.

Marcus

Marcus—also called Big Marcus, a thirty-something father of four boys and one daughter—is known throughout the city and even beyond. He is an old head. Ray and Jermaine got to know Marcus after befriending his son, Marcus Jr. or "Lil" Marcus. Big Marcus was a talented point guard at Buddy Strong High School in the 1980s, and his high school reputation as one of the best players in the city still garners respect. Local scouting services make references to him when writing about his son, who was rated one of the top high school juniors. A quarterly ranking of high school players reads, "Marcus Jones, Jr. [son of Buddy Strong High School great Marcus Jones, Sr.] . . ."

Chuck vouches for Marcus's past talent and skill, because he coached him briefly, but says that Marcus was conflicted. He did not take advantage of what basketball could have done for him. Marcus came to Chuck's practices for a short while and then stopped attending. Marcus wanted to be a basketball player but also to hang with his buddies who were thugs. He ended up getting into trouble and now teaches others from his youthful struggles.

Marcus acts as a mentor and role model for his sons as well as Ray and Jermaine, advising them to stay out of trouble and not do what he did. He was a good college player, but perhaps he could have done even more with his ability. Jermaine recounted what kept Marcus from being successful:

> What he told me was, he started smoking and getting into the streets and he had a baby [Marcus Jr.] and he had to support

his family. He spent two years at Texas Southern; he [first] went to Southwest [College] for a year, [and] he got the assist record there, and the . . . , he was like second in steals there; and then he went to . . . Texas Southern, [and] he [was] like third in assists and fifth in steals. Like dag. Like he told me he didn't make it [to the pros] because he started smoking, getting into the streets, drinking, whatever. . . . He stopped working out like that [hard], 'cause he said the baby was stressing him out; he just had the baby, so he had to get a job and all that.

Marcus grew up in South Philly and considered Espy his home court because he played there as a young bull. He felt obligated to help when he saw Ray's and Jermaine's raw talent.

And it was like, so he said, he said he didn't have the people around him so he could have made it, like Steve, like Harold and all them [old heads in the neighborhood], they wasn't the type of person[s] that just come and work out with him and all that.

He said, he just want us to have what he didn't have. He want to give it to other people. Like he didn't have, like he do his own workouts and whatever, and like he wasn't invited to workouts, it was a North Philly thing. He was from South Philly. If you was from South Philly, you wasn't going to no big-time workouts in North Philly. He was like, he just want to give back, like, the opportunities he didn't have; he want to give to other people so they could have.

He, like, he ain't even into that—money. He don't care about the money like that. Like, if you just chilling around him, he don't say nothing about it. Like, you got those old heads they say, "If you go to the league [NBA], I want this, I want that." He never say nothing like that ever since I knew him. He just like, "It'd make me happy, if you just go to school, get your degree, and do something with your life. Whether it's basketball or not."

Marcus works full-time for the city as a social services coordinator and is back in school working toward his bachelor's

degree. At the playground he serves young men who play basketball, hoping that they will be successful, go to college, get
a degree, and be upwardly mobile. He is not looking for what
he might get materially from his relationship with younger
players. Marcus imparts wisdom and creates opportunities for
players to play more and gain skills. Yet this example illustrates
a sad fact. Old heads are available to affect the lives of young
bulls because they have failed to become upwardly mobile and
they remain in the same poor communities in which they were
raised. Old heads generally have no direct experience with being
an elite player, or they have experienced both success and trag-
edy. Therefore, teaching is usually focused on what *not* to do and
perceptions/speculations of what *to* do.

Marcus offered advice and encouragement to many younger
boys, but his relationship with Ray was special. Usually, the bond
between a young bull and old head with status is formed because
an old head is drawn to those he perceives as being like himself.
Ray was considered the best in his neighborhood. Marcus saw
him play, in between playing his own games, and thought Ray
had a lot of potential. "Ray remind me of me when I was a young
bull, except for the drinking." In return, Ray claimed that he
wanted to be like Marcus. "Marcus is my main role model, Scott.
I mean, he nice [good]. He be cooking [beating] young bulls, so
I know he was nice when he was young. I want to be like that
when I get old, still schooling young bulls." Ray respected Marcus's status and hoped to be like him someday.

Marcus created opportunities for Ray and increased his networks. He sponsored Ray, Jermaine, and his oldest son at Espy.
He had influence as one of the oldest and best players at the
playground.[3] Marcus often played on the same team with Ray
and Jermaine, ensuring they got a chance to participate and play
well. They worked hard to validate his letting them play with
older regulars.

> They didn't used to let us play. They told us we was too young
> and all that. But we kept asking them—me, Ray, and Lil Mar-
> cus—and when some of the old heads left, we would get our
> squad and play and we'd beat 'em. We knew we had to shut

them up. And then Big Marcus started telling them that we could play and that was it. We've been playing ever since. You still got some of them old heads who say we can't play, but they stupid.

Marcus also introduced Ray to other good older players who could advise and encourage him. One such man was Jackson, who played every Saturday and during the week. This relationship carried expectations. On one occasion Ray, Jermaine, and I were headed back to their homes after shooting baskets at Espy. Ray spotted Jackson at a far-off corner of the playground, stopped in his tracks, and said:

> "Yo, I can't go home right now. I'll get with you later."
> "Why?" I asked.
> "Because I gotta play with my old head," Ray replied.
> "Whatcha mean you *gotta* play?" I shot back.
> "I *gotta* play. He be teaching me stuff, and whenever I see him, he want to play me. I'll be down later."

Ray was obligated to play Jackson. Jermaine explained, "That's how it is with some old heads. When they see you, they want to play you, to school you and make you better." On Saturdays Ray, along with Jermaine, often played on Jackson and Marcus's team. During games Jackson and Marcus kept a watchful eye on Ray and instructed him.

Marcus and other old heads from Espy also attended Ray's and Jermaine's games away from the playground, particularly high school games. Marcus spoke with coaches from high schools, traveling teams, and junior colleges. Jermaine believed that he benefited from Marcus's reputation and influence.

> His [Marcus's] reputation help[s] him a lot because everybody know who he is. They take his word for everything. So that helped me somewhat, for the simple fact that is, for a couple of teams I really didn't get no time on, and he called the coach and told them I could play, and they put me in—I start starting afterward. Marcus, he helped a lot of people get into college,

like a lot of people that can't go straight to college, he got a lot of junior college connects [contacts]. Like two summers ago, he had two coaches from two different junior colleges come down and see a couple of us play. And he was trying to get us in school or whatever.

Many young men in South Philly considered Marcus their old head because of his local status and generosity with his time, instruction, and advice. He was known for providing "workouts," or informal sessions consisting of drills and conditioning. He mentored young players on the court, teaching them skills and basketball theory. He would push them emotionally to work harder and play tougher. Marcus was a gatekeeper of sorts, as well. He knew a lot of coaches in and around the city, particularly at the high school level, and could vouch for players. He also had relationships that bridged kids and colleges (albeit junior colleges). However, this rarely panned out because low-level coaches were given and followed a lot of recruiting leads. Marcus usually met these coaches while watching games in which they were recruiting or via weak ties—the friends of friends.

Jermaine was rarely "that guy" or the person with highest status. At Espy, Ray and Lil Marcus carried higher status. Jermaine wanted to be considered a star and to have the amount of respect and attention that Ray and Lil Marcus received. He worked much harder than he probably would have if he had attained their status level. This began on the playground. He learned what it took to become a star, from current and former stars, old heads, and peers. He also learned the different statuses and accompanying treatment of players and how to use old heads.

6

A SATURDAY MORNING AT ESPY

Jermaine and Ray's relationship developed because they were neighbors close in age, but intensified with their shared basketball experiences and dedication to becoming known basketball players. They went to their local playground, Espy, daily to practice shooting, play games, and check in with others. Playing in their neighborhood, on courts they considered their home courts, was where they felt safest and could play with familiarity. Jermaine and Ray knew who would be there, the rules of the court, when the regulars played, and their status position among friends. They played on the same team whenever possible, feeling that their friendship and knowledge of each other was a definite advantage. They pushed each other to improve and to earn local reputations as players.

One spring Saturday morning, I watched Jermaine and Ray play at Espy playground. They were warming up with others, trying their best to take turns shooting. It was important to make shots because players return the ball to a shooter after a made shot, but misses are rebounded and shot by whoever gets the rebound. Jermaine practiced jump shots and "finger roll" layups. He looked to see if it was clear for him to shoot, to avoid his ball hitting another ball being shot at the same time. Jermaine would dribble hard to the basket, lunge, and then jump up toward the basket, one leg leading, while cradling the ball in his right arm. As he rose in the air and neared the rim, he lifted the ball up in one fell swoop until it was just above the rim. Jermaine rolled the ball down his hand, and with a light flip of his wrist, the ball hopped from his fingertips and through the rim. These moves were rehearsals for his eventual performance. Jermaine was considered a jumper, and it was important for him to test his legs and show his jumping ability, that he had "ups" or "bunnies," just as Ray practiced jump shots because he was known as a shooter. These shows could intimidate opposing players and encourage teammates.

Someone yelled, "Let's go," and the players moved into their positions. Those who were about to play in the first game took their last practice shots and went through their stretching and warm-up rituals: running in place, jumping up and down, touching their toes, and standing on one leg, while grabbing and pulling their other leg behind them. Those who were not playing sat down or moved to a side court.

Ray and Jermaine were playing with Marcus, Jackson, and one other man. Ray had missed on "shooting for firsts [or outs]"—the shot that is taken to determine which team gets the first offensive possession—so the other team started with the ball. Marcus directed Ray and Jermaine on defense by pointing to spots on the court where they should be. Marcus had two goals—to win and for the boys to learn something they would need for high school basketball.

At Espy the regulars play a two-three zone defense, which means that the defenders guard a specific area of the court. Two players are set about ten feet in front of the basket they are defending, and their other three teammates are in positions three feet in front of the basket. Both sets of defenders form horizontal lines parallel to the basket. Playing zone defense is not typical playground basketball. On most other playgrounds in the city, man-to-man defense is the rule. In man-to-man defense, each player guards a particular individual on the opposing team, one that they choose or are instructed to guard. This prevents confusion, because each player is only responsible for defending one competitor. A zone defense, however, requires awareness, coordination, trust, and players who share an understanding of what their teammates are going to do in certain situations. Zone defenses are territorial, and individuals are expected to cover a range that is constantly in flux. Marcus's special directions to Jermaine and Ray illustrate this: "Jermaine, you got down low, the center. Don't let them pass the ball in the middle. [Then looking to Ray] Ray, you play up top with me. If a man has the ball, you got to guard him until he give it up [passes the ball], then you rotate back, all right?"

Ray was supposed to move with the player as long as they had the ball, Marcus said, and then he was to move back to his spot when the player gave up the ball. While Ray guarded the player that was out of his spot, Marcus would be covering Ray's spot, and when Ray moved back, Marcus would return to his own spot. They had to trust each other to move to the right place at the right time, and they had to be aware of any movement by opposing players. Jermaine was told to be in the center of the court close to the basket, and to make sure that players on the opposing team did not get the ball in the middle of the zone. Marcus's directions aligned the team's efforts. If each person was clear on his role, there would be no confusion among teammates or breakdowns in communication that would allow the other team to get an open shot or easy basket.

Jermaine was tested as soon as the game began. An opposing player darted to the center of the zone defense, and Jermaine moved to prevent the pass into the player. He was too late and the player caught the ball. Jermaine crowded the player with his arms outstretched to deter him from trying to shoot or drive to the basket. Jermaine's actions worked; the player passed the ball.

Marcus coached Jermaine and Ray on offense, as well. When Jermaine grabbed a rebound after the opposing team missed a shot, Marcus yelled, "Look up!" Jermaine looked up the court and threw the ball to Ray, who out-sprinted the opposing team down to the other basket and scored.

On this particular Saturday, their team won four games in a row, before losing one. They played well and Marcus had guided Ray and Jermaine throughout, telling them where they should be, what they should do, and encouraging them (mostly Ray) to shoot and be tougher.

Marcus and Jackson shot the most, and they scored most of the team's points. Jackson was a gunner, meaning he shot a lot and rarely passed. He took shots while two people guarded him.

He drove to the basket, where the other team had their three players in a zone, and tried to shoot over the bigger guys. Jackson also had breakdowns on defense. Instead of being in a good position to prevent easy scores, he reached after the ball a few times to jar it loose from an opposing player's hands, often letting the opposing player drive for an easy basket when he was unable to steal the ball. None of his teammates said anything, and no one seemed upset that he had played poor defense or had not passed the ball. Jackson was respected for his scoring ability, and therefore his teammates deferred to him, allowing him to shoot the ball whenever he pleased and to play poor defense with no backlash. The silence from other teammates when Jackson played poorly illustrated the team's hierarchy, the roles of different individuals, and that they all understood the code of conduct.

On the other hand, Jackson criticized Jermaine for taking a difficult shot and missing it. The score was tied eleven to eleven—the game ends when one team scores twelve. Up to that point, Jermaine had not taken a lot of shots. He was set up near the basket and Ray passed him the ball. Jermaine received the pass with his back to the basket, quickly jumped, and shot the ball without seeing the basket, turning 180 degrees in the air as he shot. Unfortunately, his defender jumped at the same time and blocked the shot.

"What are you *doing*? I was open. Damn!" Jackson said as he trotted back on defense. Jermaine pouted and said, "That's the only shot I took all game." It was a costly shot. The other team scored the go-ahead basket and won. Jermaine's shot was inappropriate, according to Jackson, and no one challenged Jackson's view. Jermaine did not have the status to take a shot *and miss* when it could mean winning or losing the game. By taking his shot at that moment, he defied convention and the hierarchy that the team had been following. Had Jermaine made the basket, Jackson most likely would not have criticized him. Instead, he may have given Jermaine "props" (praise or respect) for taking the shot at such an important time and making it. The last shot is an important shot, usually reserved for those of high status.

The team had to sit down to wait for another opportunity to play, which usually was a long wait.

The team was organized according to how much each player's scoring ability was recognized. Essentially, it was predetermined who should shoot. Jackson and Marcus had the "green light," or freedom to shoot whenever they wanted, without suffering any repercussions or upsetting the others. Ray was allowed some freedom to shoot because he was known for his age and was considered a good shooter. Jermaine and the other teammate—five on five is played at Espy—were lowest on the totem pole. They knew that they were expected to assume supporting roles. One had to have a preexisting status (as a known player or thug) or had to work hard to gain the respect of others before being given the right to shoot freely. Higher-status individuals are expected by others to monopolize the ball and get the most shots; therefore they are typically the leading scorers even when they shoot a low percentage.[1] Moreover, they typically receive little blame, relative to their amount of responsibility. Importantly though, a person's status is not simply a static label that, once achieved, requires no further effort. Rather, achieving and retaining status are part of a dynamic process[2] that demands constant attention because status differences between people inform expectations and interactions. This is not always settled—there are people with ambition, hoping to improve their status.

7 THE HEART OF THE PLAYGROUND

Ray, at sixteen, was atop the local hierarchy for young men playing at Espy. He received deference from teammates and could shoot freely. Ray had high status because of his prior experience as a varsity player on Thompson's team, and because of his reputation for embarrassing and outplaying local boys and men. He and Jermaine considered playground ball important to their careers because of their relationships with others and what they learned. At Espy and other playgrounds, they were tested physically and mentally, and friends and others in their community could watch them play because of proximity.

Playground ball overlaps with the culture of the street.[1] Boys learn that aggressiveness, toughness, and fearlessness are valued.[2] Players tell each other "don't be afraid" when one seems hesitant to shoot. Or "go strong [to the basket]" when nervous while holding or handling the ball. "Show some heart" and "don't be soft" are other phrases that are used. "Heart" is an overused term that is not clearly defined. It is always a compliment used to describe a player's competitiveness, will, and personal drive.

I asked a successful coach at one of the local universities to explain what heart meant and how he identified it when watching players.

> It is an intangible that is often hard to spot, but we look for it in kids because it's what makes all the difference. If the kid gets on the floor when the ball is loose, and how he "gets after" folks [plays without fear and guards an opposing player

closely giving little room]. It's mental toughness and persever-
ance. That's what you want, and some kids just have it.

Heart is something that is seen; you see it in how some kids
play. The coach spoke about it as natural—"some kids just have
it"—while Jermaine considered it a style that he learned on the
playground.

> The playground, that's where everybody get they heart from.
> [If] you can't play in the playgrounds; you can't play nowhere.
> That's how I feel. You can get fifty [points] in the league, but
> if you play in the playground leagues, you gonna get handled
> by old heads—they know that you better than them, you not
> gonna embarrass them, so they gonna bump you, he gonna
> push you, elbow you; you got to take it and still play. So that's
> how you get your heart.

Jermaine links toughness and heart to adaptability and being a
good player. Players need to show that they are tough and have
heart as a sign of masculinity and mental strength because
weakness is a character flaw that is ridiculed by others and taken
advantage of both on the playground and in their community.
It also prepares them for higher-level competition, where it is
expected that the best players can take physical punishment
without backing down and even make baskets and plays when
fouled. Heart can sometimes lead to conflict and violence when
young men seek to show that they are tough and refuse to back
down from possible conflict. This is especially relevant to playground play, where boys and men play as a show of masculinity
and to gain respect.

Bandit Leagues

Playground ball increases in frequency and intensity in the
summer. Chuck says that playground leagues are "bandit"
leagues, because they effectively steal players' attention from

more serious leagues, like Blade Rodgers. In his view, playground basketball is corrupt. Bandit leagues host a range of players: from kids who are serious about basketball, play for their school team, and hope to earn an athletic scholarship to college; to kids and men who have never played organized basketball (such as for their high school or in the Blade Rodgers League).

A league's prestige can be enhanced or diminished based on the reputation of the local network operating it, as well as how many locally known players participate or have participated in it. Community support is key, measured by the number of spectators that attend the games. Older men begin some of the leagues from the neighborhood and typically get money and the place to play by applying for grants from the city.

Marcus started a league at Espy named Athletics and Academics (A and A), which was funded by the city. Marcus applied for a grant that paid for referees, T-shirts, an electronic clock, and an awards banquet. There were three leagues divided by age groups: sixteen-and-under, thirteen-and-under, and ten-and-under. Jermaine and Ray played in the sixteen-and-under league. Marcus's explicit goal was for the league to provide academic tutoring and a place for kids to play. However, Jermaine and Ray said that they were not aware that tutoring was offered; they simply played basketball. It was just a recreational league for them.

Fathers and other men from the community volunteer to coach and pay the league fee to insure that a particular kid, their son or young bull, plays a lot and gets the opportunity to impress others. The participants, players, coordinators, coaches, referees, and spectators are very familiar with one another. There can be much at stake, in terms of local and personal pride, linked to everyday experiences and confrontations people may have had with each other on and off the court. There is potential for great recognition and embarrassment in front of the people whom participants know and care about. All of this leads to flashy play and exaggerated behavior, highlighting individual efforts and abilities rather than team goals.

During an A and A playoff game, a male spectator said that the kid shooting a free throw was going to "choke," or miss the free throw, because he was feeling the peer pressure to succeed. It

was the end of a close game. "He gonna choke; he ain't nothin'."
The young man heard this and challenged the man: "What? You
crazy! Wanna put something on this?" The young man was cocky
and asked the older man to make a wager. The older man accepted: "I've got five on it." The young man stepped up to the
free-throw line and shot the ball. "Marcus, collect my money," he
said, as the ball swished through the net and the free throw was
made. Folks laughed and cheered the shooter, giving him high
fives as he ran down the court.

Playing is a performance and an opportunity to be evaluated.
Players participate in local games to showcase their talent and
gain recognition in their communities. At the beginning of another game, a kid yelled out, "Steve, I know why you starting . . .
your *uncle* is the coach." Several people laughed out loud; this
discovery was an insult. Steve apparently had been bragging
before the game about being "a starter." Those who play at the
start of any game are considered the team's best players. Coaches
typically begin games with their most talented guys in order to
establish the team's momentum. The spectator claimed that
nepotism was at work. Steve's uncle was probably coaching to
give him an opportunity to start and play.

How Status Travels

In Marcus's A and A league, Jermaine and Ray were the stars of
their team and both enjoyed great freedom when playing. With
few exceptions, A and A players were regulars at Espy and lived
nearby. However, Jermaine and Ray also played for another team
in a different league, just blocks away, at the Tracks, another
playground. The league at the Tracks was loaded; there were a
number of known players from different parts of the city. Here
Jermaine did not have high status and was susceptible to challenges from others and even teammates. Ray, in contrast, was
the star of their team and shot as much as he wanted.

Once while I was driving Ray and Jermaine to their game at
the Tracks, Jermaine began to complain about his low status and
treatment by some teammates.

"Scott, I don't even really want to go," Jermaine said.

"Why?" I asked.

"'Cause they all be hating [jealous], 'cause everybody want to show out [show off]. Last time Ray throws me an oop [a pass above the rim to a teammate for a slam dunk] off the glass, and I miss it, and they [the other teammates] yelling at me. We up [winning] by twenty-three though, Scott! It's not like I tried to miss. When I make the dunk, they don't say nothin'. And I ain't said shit about Nate's shooting. He's an uzi," Jermaine whined.

"What's an 'uzi'?" I asked.

"A gunner, a black hole,"[3] Ray chimed in before Jermaine continued.

"You know . . . someone that shoots every time they get the ball. I ain't said nothing about his shooting, but he gonna get on me about missing an [alley-]oop. I swear, I hate him."

"Why you playing with him?" I inquired further.

Ray giggled and responded, "He put the team together and paid most of the money, so we can't fire him."

For Jermaine, his conflict with Nate and other teammates existed because he did not agree with the team's status hierarchy and how the team operated. Ray was the star, the number-one guy, and Jermaine was competing with Nate for a secondary "star" spot that he believed should have been his naturally. But Jermaine's level of play was inconsistent. He did not play high school varsity and was not written about in the newspaper, nor was he known for some spectacular game where he scored an extremely high amount of points. Still, Jermaine believed that he was a good high school player, on his way up the ranks, and better than his teammates, except for Ray. His jumping ability distinguished him from teammates, and he was playing to prove himself, but so were they. His play threatened to overshadow their performances.

Ray said very little because he did not have the same problem as Jermaine. When I asked Ray about his relationship with Nate, he responded, "He don't say nothing to me. I get my shots up [shoot a lot]." Ray's elevated status in this setting meant that others criticized him for *not* shooting when he could have, a benefit for being known as a shooter and the team's star.

During a game I attended, Nate took shots constantly, rarely passing the ball to other teammates, except Ray. He was not just an "uzi"; he intimidated his teammates. Jermaine did not shoot a lot. Nate had yelled at him previously, and he did not like being embarrassed in front of a crowd. So, he passed the ball, mostly to Ray.

The game was close in the end, and a time-out was called. Ray and Jermaine's team led by three points, but the other team seemed to be gaining momentum after trailing by nine points. Jermaine was wearing his emotions on his sleeve. He was frustrated, as evidenced by his fussing, blaming, and frowning since he had received only a few passes. Nate had taken a number of extravagant shots from at least twenty feet or so, making a few, but missing most of them. In addition, Nate had been "talking shit" to the other team and to the crowd. Some of his friends and acquaintances, who were watching from the sidelines, yelled criticisms and expletives at him about his shooting, and he retaliated by guaranteeing that he would make the next shot he took. "Shut up, bitch! That's why your punk ass ain't playing. I bet I make the next one."

The situation reached a climax when a teammate tried to enter the game as a substitute. At halftime this teammate had complained that he had not been given the chance to play much in the first half. Nate had said that he could substitute for him with six minutes left in the game. Just before the substitute was supposed to enter the game, Nate took a wild shot and missed, then fouled an opposing player in frustration. Jermaine raised both arms and threw them down dramatically, with a look of disgust. "Come on!" he whined. Nate was embarrassed by his shot and was upset with Jermaine's complaining.[4]

While the opponent took the first of two free throws resulting from Nate's foul, the substituting teammate waited at the scorer's table. The referee motioned for the young man to enter the game after the first free throw, but Nate waved him back, causing confusion. The teammate hesitated and stayed at the scorer's table. After the second free throw was taken and made, the scorer's table hit the horn for the substitution to be made. The teammate ran onto the court, calling to Nate, who then reneged on his word: "Fuck that, I'm not going out. I paid the most money in this bitch." He did not want to be replaced at that moment because it would spotlight his mistake and look like a punishment for his bad play, which was a threat to his self-esteem. Instead, he stayed in the game to try to regain some of his credibility.[5]

Play began and the opposing team yelled to a referee about the violation: Ray and Jermaine's team had six players on the court, when only five from each team are allowed. The referees stopped the game and called a technical foul. Jermaine stomped off the court, complaining, "You said he could sub [for] you."

"No, I didn't," Nate shot back. "He didn't say nothing to me. . . . Shut up and stop being a bitch."[6]

Jermaine mumbled something inaudible and paced the sideline with his arms tightly crossed. Nate believed he could say and do as he pleased because Jermaine could not beat him up. Jermaine was insulted but did not respond, and both looked bad publicly; Nate had played poorly and out of control, and Jermaine had been "punked" or bullied. The game had been close but the clock continued to run during this whole ordeal. When the smoke had cleared, only three minutes remained. Ray took several quick three point shots, but it was too late. They lost by twelve.

After the game Jermaine complained more about the absence of shooting opportunities and Nate's selfishness. "I only touched the ball *four* times in the second half," he said.

Nate heard Jermaine and responded, "Shut up, I lost money!" Nate continued, "Stop complaining. You know I'm gonna shoot when I get the ball. So fuck it, play around it."

Nate directed the order of the team with impunity. He could tell others not to shoot, not to enter the game, and limit others' criticisms of him in public. He had the power to influence and to resist. Jermaine whined some more but did not confront Nate face-to-face, since that would have been a sign that he wanted to fight. Jermaine was sure that he would lose. Nate was a few years older and had a reputation. He sold drugs, which is how he had the money to pay most of the league fee. Nate also had "backup," friends and family who would fight for him if he got into trouble.

In the next game, Jermaine didn't shoot much. Instead he passed the ball to Ray and others to avoid conflict. Jermaine was frustrated by the social order that gave him lower status than Nate and the consequences of this—he could be yelled at and he did not shoot when he could have. For Jermaine, the status hierarchy was ill considered, and the team's loss validated this. Nate had been able to usurp Jermaine's position because of Nate's tough reputation off the court, not because of his basketball ability. What was more important to Jermaine, however, was that he had been "taken out of his game" and was unable to draw positive attention to his skills.

In playground ball, particularly in playground leagues, people focus on individual talent. It is very important for players to entertain spectators, who are exhilarated by fancy moves and grandstanding. Audiences are vocal in their approval or disapproval of individual efforts, and the stories they tell about what they see at these games can serve to build or maintain a player's reputation. Nate knew this. He and many others, old heads and young bulls, have only the playground as a venue for playing ball and earning kudos and praise from spectators. Nate was older than most of the players (nineteen or so), who were predominantly high school aged (sixteen to eighteen), but still felt that much was at stake after being talked about negatively.

For Jermaine, building a basketball reputation was challenging, exciting, and frustrating. The local status game is neighborhood based and affected everyday life. He had to compete with a range of players, in front of people he (and those he competed with) knew well. Community norms and statuses, like being a thug and drug dealer, sometimes superseded basketball status and ability. And so being known on a playground or a couple of playgrounds was important locally. Status from playground ball and high school ball overlapped and could be used together. However, there was a broader basketball world that Ray and Jermaine needed to enter and appeal to.

8

CHUCK BREAKS THEM DOWN

South Philly Blade Rodgers practice began in April after the high school season, and league play ran from June to August. Jermaine and Ray were advised by Marcus Sr. to try out for our team. He told them that Blade Rodgers' high level of competition and prestige would give them exposure to new audiences and that they would learn a different style of play. That was not all. New kids were generally in for a big surprise; Chuck was different from any coach they had had (and probably would ever have). He was primarily concerned with establishing a certain order and set of expectations.

South Philly Practice

Practice is where kids learn our expectations and norms and where they become a team. The Nicole Redmond Recreational Center covers a city block, and standard gray metal fencing encloses most of the property. There are three short steps that lead to the entrance and two heavy aluminum-sided doors. The aluminum is unpolished chrome that gives off a glare when sunlight hits it. Immediately inside, the foyer has high ceilings and there is a cold and dull gray linoleum-tiled floor. A modest-size glass trophy case stands to the left. There are pictures and a worn basketball net hanging on one picture (symbolic of the cutting down of nets after winning a championship), a clean baseball, and worn boxing gloves placed and hung around trophies recognizing several championship teams: a nine-and-under Little

League team, a girls' soccer team, two boys' basketball teams, and a few "Golden Gloves" (city boxing championships). To the right is the boxing gym and a classroom that is regularly used by young grammar school–aged kids and women for tutoring and after-school care. The center's office is straight back and to the left. It is cluttered and messy with papers, clothes, and sports equipment that seem to date back a number of years. There are five staff persons who are generally on the phone or watching television: three women (two over the age of forty and the other in her mid-twenties who frequently wears furry lion slippers), one thirty-something white man, and one forty-plus man (who is an African immigrant). Except for the two older women, this is the staff that coaches and runs specific programs. The white man runs baseball, softball, and soccer; the younger woman runs dance classes; and the African man runs the martial arts and boxing programs. Continuing through the foyer, one comes to another set of double doors that lead to the outside recreational areas: an emptied pool (that stays empty), three basketball rims without nets, and a manicured baseball diamond. The baseball field, which rarely hosts games, looks official, with the number of yards from home plate to the three different sections of the outfield painted on the outfield wall in large white print, accompanied by local sponsor logos and slogans.

The gymnasium is located upstairs via a winding stairwell. The doors, at the top of the stairs, are often locked to keep kids from entering the gym or the other rooms upstairs. One wall in the hallway has a sign that reads "TANF [Temporary Assistance for Needy Families]—the clock is running, come find out what you need to know." The gym is guarded by its own double doors. Many basketball games are played in this gym: the recreational center here has its own basketball league; local schools ask for gym time to play games and hold physical education classes; a church league plays its games here; and a few other basketball programs hold practices here.

Our teams practiced Monday through Friday, beginning at 5:00 p.m. and running anywhere from two to three-plus hours, depending upon when kids arrived and when Chuck got there. After my first year of coaching under Chuck, I would lead the first hour or so, and then he would arrive and take over. My job, although never explicitly discussed, was to put them through their warm-up, drills, and conditioning. If Chuck had not arrived by this time, then I would teach our offensive and defensive plays. Upon arrival, Chuck would survey the practice. Who was in attendance? Who was new? What drill were they doing? Were they doing it right? And why weren't they doing it right? For Chuck, these questions were not only about basketball. He watched for this as an opening to talk about much broader things.

After surveying the practice, Chuck would yell, "On the line." The kids had to line up single file facing us, with their feet on the court's baseline or sideline. As a rule, when a player's feet (both of their feet) were not on the line, for any reason, they would have to do five push-ups or more. Push-ups were a punishment for not standing still, and the number of push-ups given was based on the number of violations a player had incurred. A number of kids found it difficult to stay on the line, particularly at the younger ages. They might dance, shifting their weight from side to side and doing a bounce with their shoulders or fidget with their hands, or they might spin around on the line on one foot or just shuffle their feet.

Doing the same thing day after day in practice could be monotonous, but each practice for the high school–aged kids was new because of the lack of consistent attendance by players. Very few kids attended enough to memorize our plays and learn nuances, which impacted our play and performance during league games, as well as frustrated Chuck. Chuck perceived our poor attendance as a sign of mixed or little loyalty. He knew that kids were playing somewhere; several players who were not at practice were choosing to play elsewhere. He also felt that they were not taking themselves seriously enough. They were not focused on learning and improving their skills, only on "playing." Chuck considered this backward. "Why are you going all over the earth to play, when you can't play?" He would say this to kids who were absent because they were playing on traveling teams or had games with another team. Moreover, their habits and attitude while at practice often reflected their low regard for it. Basketball as a career, as considered by Chuck, was not just "recreating" or playing; it was serious, requiring learning and an understanding of roles and authority.

Family Connections

Chuck has been coaching Blade Rodgers' South Philly team since the league began, and kids often came with some knowledge of him. Their mothers and fathers, uncles and aunts, and grandmothers and grandfathers know him, and some are former players. One kid said, "My uncle told me to come down here." Another one told Chuck and me, "My father said that he used to play for you and you're the best coach." And a father said, "I brought my son down here because I know you can teach him. You cut me, but I learned a whole lot from you and TD [the league's coordinator and Chuck's former assistant]. So I brought my son down here to learn. I figured maybe if he listened to you, he could be a good player."

Chuck enjoys his reputation and these ties and relationships. He has helped people and developed lifelong bonds because he cares about what they have become and feels obligated to help their children. Omar, a father of two young boys and uncle to two other players, researched coaches and leagues and brought his sons to us.

"Now, tell Scott what you told me," said Chuck to Omar.

"Huh? When?" Omar asked.

"The other day, after the game, about little Rob and Jason and high school. Scott said that he thought they [Rob and Jason] had quit us because we hadn't seen you in a while. Tell him what you told me after the game."

"Oh. I said to Mr. Chuck that Rob and Jay were gonna be with him [play for Chuck], with you [me and Chuck] guys, all the way through high school [they were in seventh and sixth grade at the time]. 'Cause I like what you doing with the kids. Y'all teach them. I did my homework and I checked around before I brought them up here. Y'all the best for them."

Chuck was known for what he had done in the past, for helping players to make it. Also, he was a trusted man who cared
about kids and did more than other coaches. Former players and
friends "give" their kids to Chuck, giving him authority and supporting his coaching style. These kids often become "my guys,"
as Chuck says, and are like extended family members, fictive
sons.[1]

> I would fire [kick off the team] your ass [speaking to Kashif, a
> member of our sixth-, seventh-, and eighth-grade team], but
> I'm afraid your mom might set my car on fire. [The kids, in-
> cluding Kashif, began laughing.] That's right, that's right. She
> told me he was mine forever and if I didn't take him, she'd
> blow up my car, and I believe her, so I'm stuck.

Chuck uses family ties to push kids emotionally, to criticize,
raise expectations, and threaten them with repercussions.

> Are you afraid of me? You not? You not afraid of me, Charles?
> That's all right 'cause I'm not gonna hurt you, but you see that
> black motherfucker down there and that little teeny one right
> there, and him, him right there [pointing out three kids]. I
> will bust they ASS! That's right, 'cause they like family to me.
> D-D, how long you been with us? [D responds.] Three years.
> And you still ain't grown none. [Chuck shakes his head feign-
> ing disgust. All of the kids giggle.] I know they mothers, they
> fathers, they uncles, they brothers. If I told they fathers and
> mothers [that they did not do what I told them to do], they'd
> tell me to bust they ASS![2]

Chuck challenges the boys by asking if they're afraid of him. This
style reinforces traditional masculinity, fearlessness, and toughness, and instates a masculine order—men over boys—maintained
through joking that pokes fun and by using physical messages.
He slaps them on the arms and cheek, and holds kids' faces in his
hands to look deeply into their eyes. Sometimes the slaps hurt,
but they are playful, like what an older sibling might do to their
younger sibling (or vice versa) before dashing away. Chuck also

believes that class is important; boys from poorer backgrounds are tougher and socialized into understanding physical expressions as something that boys and men do, usually learned via harsh parental discipline, peer interaction, and local violence, as well as by the broader culture of violence and symbolic masculinity.[3]

Calling Them Out and Breaking Them Down

Chuck practiced "psych rituals" to counteract many players' belief that they did not need to practice and their inflated sense of self and their ability.[4] He wanted to inspire them to hope for and earn a better life. He also wanted to teach them deference. Chuck says that "you have to 'break 'em down' and 'call 'em out,'" for kids to understand who is in charge and that they have to respect us as coaches. "Bullshit," according to Chuck, is a summation of the excuses that kids offer regarding why they did not attend practice or why they were late or why their grades were poor or why they did not play for their school's team. Most often these excuses redirect the blame for their behavior to someone else or something beyond their control. It is a denial of responsibility, explains Chuck, and it is one of, if not the first, thing that he attempts to set straight. He does this by asking a young man very basic questions. He assumes that they are not telling the truth and so scrutinizes their replies with further questions, smirking, and posturing. His goal is to "break the kid down," to let them know that they cannot put things past him because he is wise to them and their bullshitting.

> "Come here, man. You. Come here. What's the matter? You don't understand English?" Chuck says to a kid who is attending practice for the first time. The young man nods "yes" as he walks up to Chuck.
>
> "Then why didn't you come when I first asked you? You didn't know who I was talking to?" Chuck asks.
>
> The kid scrunches his lips, raises his eyebrows, and shrugs his shoulders, while shaking his head "no."

"What is you saying, man? Who else would I be speaking to? I pointed directly at you. Come on . . . Where are you from?" Chuck asks as he looks the boy over and then nods up and down, with his lips poked as though he has figured out something.

The kid pauses and then speaks with uncertainty. "Where am I from? . . . I am from here," he says, with his eyebrows raised and eyes squinted, confused by what seems an obvious answer.

Some other kids begin to giggle, and Chuck smirks and shakes his head as though disappointed. Growing embarrassed, the kid tries to figure what Chuck wants to know.

"You mean where I live?" the kid says, and Chuck nods "yes" and makes his lips into a straight line by tucking in his bottom lip tightly. "Oh, I live on . . ."

Chuck interrupts him. "See, you guys got plenty to say until it's TIME for you to talk, and then you start stumbling over words and don't have nothing to say. [Raising his voice] Where do you live, man? What street?"

"Fifth and Levi."

"Fifth and Levi, huh?" Chuck confirms calmly, and the boy nods. "What school you go to?" Chuck continues.

"St. Bart's." The young man says this with certainty.

"How come you just now coming to us? You just heard about our practice?" Chuck continues to pace back and forth in front of the young man.

"Yeah, I just found out. Quincy told me."

"Quincy? You mean my man Quincy, who got the [barber] shop down there on E Street?"

"Yeah. He told me."

"When did he tell you? 'Cause I talked to him some time ago and we've been up here for two months and the rest of these guys, they knew, but you just hearing about it."

The boy shrugs his shoulders. Chuck nods again, seemingly taking in all of the information, and then gradually he erupts.

"Where you been, under a FUCKING ROCK?" Chuck raises his voice and asks harshly.

"I mean, he told me before, but I couldn't come because I was in trouble and my mom wouldn't let me out." The boy panics and speaks quickly before dropping his head.

"Oh, you heard about it, but you couldn't come because you was in trouble. Now listen to what you saying, man! You's a FUCKING LIE! You're a liar!" Chuck replies.

The boy looks at him sideways, with his head tilted, and then shakes his head and crosses his arms. He seems upset and embarrassed by Chuck's questioning and cursing. He does not know what to do. The other kids are standing on the line, and some are giggling, which might have alerted the victim that Chuck was behaving normally and this was not to be taken too seriously. But Chuck continues.

"You *not*? [The kid shakes his head 'no.'] Now stop. Just stop. Don't bullshit me, MAN [Chuck hangs on the 'a' sound and whines so that it sounds like 'maaaaaann']. A minute ago you just said that you didn't come because you *didn't know*. And now you saying you couldn't come because you *was in trouble*. What is you saying to me? Does that sound right, Bank Street?"

Chuck looks over at Ray, who is smiling. Bank Street is Chuck's nickname for Ray because he lives on Bank Street. Chuck starts up again.

"You all think I'm a fool. You think I'm a fool, right? [Ray and others giggle and laugh more.] That's right [Chuck chuckles]. You all think that you can just come down here when you wanna come down here. But ain't none of you any good. None of you's *that* guy. You all need work and need to listen. That's why you guys get into trouble. And that's what we down here for, to teach you. But don't bullshit us.

"Get back on the line, man. It's all right. You ain't no different than the rest of them. You *all* liars. New niggas! N-O-O Niggas."

Breaking them down is another exercise in masculinity and order. Chuck makes explicit the social order, coaches over players, by being a dominant male. He cuts kids off and yells. Chuck routinely spends thirty minutes at each basketball practice talking and asking questions in which he "calls them out," push-ing the kids to defer to his authority and submit themselves to him and the team. His point is made through interrogation. The contradictions in the story are significant—they show that some kids get rattled by being questioned and others are used to get-ting over on people. This, however, is not the kids' fault, says Chuck. They are immature, not adults. Players must understand and be willing to accept responsibility for their mistakes, at the same time recognizing their dependence on others for success.[5] Even with warning, there was little that a kid could do to pre-pare for Chuck.

Coachability

Jermaine showed one day for our practice and then disappeared. This was not uncommon. Marcus warned Ray and Jermaine about Chuck's old-school, authoritarian style of coaching, but Jermaine was scared off. He returned a few weeks later, more prepared to deal with Chuck and committed to learning our plays and playing in Blade Rodgers.

> Marcus hooked me up with the team. He brought me up to the gym to meet Chuck and you. So I'm playing or whatever and I wasn't really that good, but I thought I was better than I was. I just went up there, I made the team, but after the first practice I didn't come back for a while. 'Cause I wasn't used to getting a coach yelling at me, like spazzing and smacking me. I couldn't really handle all that. But I came back because I wanted that. I needed that 'cause I knew that if I wanted to go to college, the coach wasn't gonna be easy on me. So I just had to take it. I could tell the coaches, they had faith in me. They wouldn't yell at me if they knew I could do some-thin'. So I had to just take it as a compliment, and [we] started winning.

Jermaine considered practice part of his growth and learning. Chuck's style was something to get used to because he might meet other coaches in the same vein. Ray didn't grapple with Chuck's style. Instead, he quickly became a favorite of Chuck's and mine because of his work ethic, consistency, positive attitude, and willingness to learn. So Chuck made a promising deal with Ray, after Ray had shown dedication by coming to practice for over two months and learning our plays.

> Bank Street, I'll tell you what. You keep coming and sticking by us, and I'll get you a scholarship. That's right. 'Cause you got a little something in you. That dog in you. And I know just what to do with you. You stick with us and I'll get you in a school. What you think about that? [Ray was visibly excited and encouraged by Chuck's offer.]

Chuck liked Ray early on because Ray came to practice and didn't complain. He worked hard and did what we asked. We saw that Ray was very talented. He was a pure jump shooter and very quick. His best quality, though, was his competitiveness. He had heart and hated to lose. Chuck was very critical and saved his praise for few players, so this talk with Ray was special. Too much praise could mislead a player and nurture false confidence and big-headedness. Chuck's style demanded deference, and players needed to learn and have a coachable mind-set. Young players had often been heaped with praise by family, old heads, and others, but Chuck stressed that they were still "learning," they were not "that guy" or stars yet. And so they needed to accept his authority and be open to what he had to say.

> I am a guru. Don't nobody in the world know as much about basketball as I do. That's right, Antwan [playing to one of the kids]. And I know from my own experience as a player and coach and referee. So there ain't nothing you can teach me. I was a very good basketball player. Better than all of you could dream to be, put together. Plus, I have coached for over thirty years at all levels. We start with little kids, sixth, seventh, eighth graders, and go all the way up to the pros. So you ain't gonna tell me nothing. Nathan [nothing]! That's right! I am the teacher and you the student. But you can learn a whole lot

from me, Scott, and Ali [an older man who sometimes helped out], if you willing to listen and work hard and get what we trying to teach you.

Chuck pushed kids to seek his approval and seemed very rigid. Yet he was quick to forgive a kid who quit but apologized and wanted to rejoin the team. Kids were malleable and would make mistakes, which we had to accept, but they needed to respect us as legitimate authorities because we were knowledgeable and were trying to help them. Chuck maintained that kids who did not come back were not committed and would probably quit regardless of our rules and expectations. Quitting was a character flaw that a person might or might not grow out of.

9

GOTTA WANT *IT* "LIKE THAT"

From afar Jermaine's and Ray's basketball schedule might seem carefree. But they were in fact taking risks and playing under pressure. Playing for different teams and formal and informal basketball was not easy: managing multiple reputations and opportunities was political, and they had to be concerned with their scheduling and relationships with coaches and other players; competition increased because the number of people increased as one entered more settings to play, and the stakes rose with the seriousness/prestige of the basketball; possibilities for failure, rejection, and disappointment were high when they were not picked to play for a team, not given playing time, or played poorly against higher-status players.

Bryant was one of our core players who made Thompson's varsity team as a freshmen because he was known. As an eighth grader, he scored forty-one points in an AAU game, and as Jermaine said, Bryant's uncle was the assistant coach of Thompson, ensuring that Bryant would make the team. Bryant was a "tweener," or a player who was in between two positions, based upon skill set or height/size or both—he was between being a big guard and forward.[1] He did not handle the ball or shoot well as a guard, but could guard anyone on the court and sometimes score in bunches. He was strong willed and wanted to win, but he took risks to look good. Sometimes the risks hurt the team, particularly when he was called for fouls and took bad shots while being defended by more than one player. Bryant didn't worry about "looking a fool" and was an exciting player in this way; you never knew exactly what he would do, although you knew he would play hard.

During a close game, Bryant stole an errant pass and sprinted ahead with the ball for what should have been an easy layup and score. He tried to dunk the ball. This was a natural and expected move for Jermaine, but Bryant's move was a struggle that he lost. His attempt was not even close. He slowed as he neared the basket, to gather himself and explode, but he was not a strong jumper and did not even get the ball over the rim. He was "rim blocked," blocked by the rim, and his body buckled in the air against the immovable force of the rim. Gravity brought him down awkwardly, and he stumbled and fell to the ground; the small crowd burst into laughter. All I could do was shake my head in disgust and disbelief. We won the game, but after the game I had to ask Bryant about what I considered to be a really dumb and unnecessary play.

"Bryant, what was that?" I asked.

"What," he said, pretending that he did not know what I was talking about.

"You got hung!" I said, referring to the rim block. I continued, "Have you ever dunked?"

"Not in a game. But I'm getting bunnies, Scott. I almost made it, huh?" Bryant said with a smile.

"Naw, you wasn't even close, man. And we needed the basket." I shook my head and chuckled. "Next time just lay it up, please. Why would you try to dunk when you've never made it before?"

"I got the breakaway and was hyped," Bryant explained. "I thought maybe the game would make me make it. How I'm gonna know if I can make it if I don't try? If I had made it, it would have been hyped."

Bryant was right: how can a person know what they are capable of if they don't try to do things? It was not that Bryant threw all caution to the wind to try and dunk the ball; rather, he reasoned, when asked for an explanation, that he hoped the circumstance would lift him to great achievement and new ground.

Success would have earned him something; he would have been talked about and could talk about what he had done. It was not the right thing to do if winning was the priority, but it was appropriate for him personally. Bryant was not afraid to make the mistake. He was the type of player who played aggressively throughout the game, regardless of the moment. Not because he could not do otherwise, but because it was his strength—he had become known for his passion and will. This was a sign of self-confidence and belief in his ability, which enabled him to play even when he was overmatched.

In contrast, Jermaine's older brother Khalid played and made his reputation only on the playground. This was not because Khalid was not talented. He was taller than Jermaine and a much better ball handler and shooter. But Khalid lacked confidence, and this limited his opportunities to play. He tried out for his high school's basketball team during his freshman year but did not make the team. He believed that there were politics working against him. Similar to what happened to Jermaine in his first year at Thompson, Khalid understood that there were limited spots on varsity and junior varsity because the coach had his team in mind before tryouts, others had seniority, and the few available spots were given to new players who were known. Jermaine used his experience as motivation; he came out for our Blade Rodgers League team and worked to improve and gain more recognition and exposure. Khalid took a less effective approach. He simply continued to play and practice at Espy. Khalid told me that he was not ready for Blade Rodgers and needed to work on his game. He also said that he would be ready the next year after his school's season. But he did not try out for the school team the following year and only showed for one or two of our practices before disappearing.

To be sure, Khalid had different concerns than Jermaine. Khalid was worried about how the family would stay afloat while their mother, Monica, struggled to secure stable employment. He worked after school as a tutor and coordinator at one local recreational center, and during the summer he would double this with a low-wage service job. As Jermaine reflected in an earlier chapter, Khalid was a father figure of sorts because he worried about Jermaine, supported and encouraged him, and gave him money.

Still, Khalid often participated in workouts given by Big Marcus when he was not working and focused more and more time playing and thinking about basketball as he got older. But he never got known outside of the neighborhood as a basketball player. After graduating from high school, he continued to work out and practice his play. Eventually, he tried out for the team at his college but failed to earn a spot. His stories about not making this team sounded similar to his high school stories: he was better than most of the players but the coach had favorites; and at his final practice, the coach cursed him and they nearly fought. Jermaine explained that Khalid "didn't want it like that [wasn't willing to do whatever it takes]" and lacked the confidence and heart to really stand out.

Players who attain status at the citywide level and beyond do more than just work hard to develop the appropriate skill set. They must make good decisions as well and play in different settings, putting up with and dealing with peers, old heads, coaches, and others, and come to understand what it takes to succeed in different situations and settings. Most importantly, the decision making occurs within a certain orientation. Players take risks and adapt to become successful. Khalid's biggest fear was that he would look bad, not play well, and that others would talk badly about him. And so he never played for us, even after Chuck and I visited with him, Jermaine, and Monica. Blade Rodgers offered high visibility and the possibility for success *and* failure.

10 PLAYING UPTOWN

To many people, Blade Rodgers is *the* way to solidify one's reputation in Philadelphia as an "elite" basketball player. Throughout the city, young men wear Blade Rodgers League T-shirts, jerseys, and shorts as proof that they are, or once were, real basketball players. Clothing from other leagues is worn as well, no doubt, but an association with Blade Rodgers warrants great prestige in Philadelphia, Delaware, and southern New Jersey. Its strong reputation draws a variety of people to its games and, as a result, nurtures greater expectations from its spectators. This challenges the players to do their best, to give audiences what they came to see, and to gain legitimacy in the minds of those watching.[1]

Art, a former high school All-American and player for Chuck, offered some words of inspiration to our team before a big game.

> Man, I'm excited to see you all up here. This is a big deal, man, nah'imean. These was the kind of games I lived for: playing in a big ol' nice gym, with all those people [in the audience]. This is *up*town and *this* is where you bring it. All that playing down at the Tracks and Espy and D Street, that don't mean shit! When you come UPTOWN . . . to the big gym, with all of those people and scouts and the best ballplayers, THIS is where it's at. THIS is where you make your name. Man, I used to make my living up here. I loved playing here. It's better than all that playground shit. Uptown is playing on the big stage, under the bright lights.

Setting is very important to understanding the impact of specific performances on a player's reputation because of league differences in competition, audiences, and quality of facilities. Blade Rodgers is more prestigious than the playgrounds, and, most importantly, it is where influential people go to watch players.[2]

Blade Rodgers League is made up of three youth leagues and a college league. They include the Rookie league for sixth, seventh, and eighth graders (which runs from April through May); the Next Generation league for ninth and tenth graders (running from June to August); the Varsity league for eleventh and twelfth graders (which runs from June to August); and the All-Star league for collegiate basketball players (from July to August). The league also staffs and manages a housing project league separately. League games are played throughout the city, primarily in college gymnasiums. Kids come from Philadelphia and its surrounding areas, both inside and outside the state. In addition, different racial and ethnic groups are represented: black, Asian, Latino, and white, but teams are largely either black/predominantly black or white/predominantly white, and the league is overwhelmingly black.

Each league in Rodgers has been named after a prominent national figure and Philadelphia native. On Blade Rodgers game days, a banner is hung at floor level to advertise the sponsors for the day. The names of the leagues that will be playing are shown as well: "Red Cola & Second Federal Bank present the 2001 Butch Jackson Next Generation League [ninth and tenth grades]."[3] Butch Jackson is a nationally recognized black entertainer. He is not a basketball player but he knows Chuck, Blade (the league's namesake), and others in the league because they all grew up during the same era and have overlapping networks and experiences.

The high school league is named after a deceased player who also grew up with three men in the league's network and then went on to play in college and professionally. The college league is named after a former Rodgers League player whose death received national attention when he died during a college game in his senior year. He was one of the nation's leading scorers and was projected to be a high pick in the NBA draft.

Foundations and companies sponsor the teams. Some of the foundations represent the charitable efforts of former players who are now on professional teams. Other backers include local mom-and-pop businesses and regional banks. Teams have the name of their sponsors on the back of their jerseys, above the numbers. By displaying its sponsorships so visibly, the league presents itself as a "money" league, a serious enterprise that is worthy of private funding from local and national sources.

There are many advantages to being part of Blade Rodgers that players can't get from other affiliations. By playing in gymnasiums on campuses of major universities, young men catch a glimpse of college life. These colleges are in different parts of the city, which ensures that young men travel and get to know about places outside their neighborhoods. Teams get to use the amenities in well-designed facilities: locker rooms to change in; full bathrooms, including showers; and benches to sit on. This is very different from playing on a neighborhood playground.

Blade Rodgers summer league games for high school and college players were held at Big University most of the time. It is an old, "official" basketball arena located on one of the city's main thoroughfares, making it easily accessible by many forms of transportation. Once inside the facility, there is a student security officer or a full-time security officer. A large trophy case in the middle of the foyer displays numerous team plaques, ribbons, trophies, and mementos. Steps on the left and right lead downstairs to locker rooms and the basketball court. Halls off to the left and right of the trophy case lead to the stands above the court. Around the corner, the hallway opens up into an enormous space: the gym is a 15,000-square-foot arena with very few interior walls and an elevated ceiling. During Philadelphia's hot and muggy summers, the vast space creates natural cooling. There are two large scoreboards on opposite ends of the gym, and two walls lined with painted portraits lacquered onto plaques—showing the school's athletic history and excellence. The plaques commemorate former athletes who have been inducted into the university's sports hall of fame. The seating in the gym is unique because the bleachers do not begin at floor level; instead, they begin much higher up, looking down from a distance at the court. This serves as a distinct boundary between the ballplayers and the audience, reducing the amount of interference from spectators during the game.

There are several other venue distinctions between Blade Rodgers and playground leagues. The most obvious difference is the courts themselves, which have hardwood floors rather than asphalt. The arena floor has the name of the university at the center and both ends of the court, which adds to the prestige and sense of professionalism. The courts are much bigger than at any playground; everything is regulation and in line with the conventions of collegiate and professional basketball. A young man is proud when he can say that he played at Big University's arena, rather than at Espy or the Tracks. The games are often broadcast over the public announcement system, and the score is kept via the large electronic scoreboards on the walls. Playing on regulation courts with uniforms, coaches, and referees, amidst the pageantry of competition, reinforces the message that one is "uptown" and this is *real basketball* played by serious ballplayers.

Our First Game

Before our first game of each season, Chuck warns kids who are new to the league about the difference between Blade Rodgers and other leagues.

> This is our last practice, and tomorrow we go to war, gentlemen. And that's what it's gonna be. War. Other teams are coming, and they gonna be after you. Well, not you, they gonna be after South Philly and Chuck Green! 'Cause all of them want to beat ME. But we have prepared you. You know the plays: "open," "double-down," "on the roll." [And] you know how we play defense. So you're prepared; we've given you the armor. That's right. Our stuff, our plays, that's your armor.

'Cause there's gonna be some big ol' long monsters up there, and some of you's gonna look up and your mouth gonna be like this here [wide open] and you gonna say "*oh my God.*" And that's okay. I expect that, because Blade Rodgers is different than all them other leagues and the playgrounds you been playing at. You go around to Tenth and Rhodes [Espy] or the Tracks, or the AAU or the PAL, and you think you *that guy.* But you take your little hiney up THERE [pointing north] and do all that dribbling behind your back and through your legs and up yo' ass, and here's what's gonna happen. They gonna grab the ball, take it away from you, and dribble right down and lay it up. [And say] Thank you very much. That's right.

I'm telling ya *right now.* I know exactly what's gonna happen 'cause you can't bring that playground, baby basketball up there! Not up THERE [pointing north again]! They disciplined and bigger up there. But we equipped you and we not gonna let nobody hurt you, so you ain't got to worry. Just do what we say and you'll be all right. We're not going to put you in a situation that's gonna hurt you.

Chuck addresses the guys to show that we are a "we." He says "we have prepared you," "we've given you the armor," and "we equipped you." Our teaching brings them together; it is their shared culture. They have run laps and suicides, done push-ups, and endured Chuck's lectures and criticism. Together. Solidarity is important, and our guys know that a gang beats a kid all by himself. We have to work as a team to be successful. Chuck gives a twist on Booker T. Washington's "Fingers of the Hand" metaphor. "Individually, we just fingers and can't cause much damage. But if we work together [he balls his hand into a fist and presses his lips together], like that, we can *knock a motherfucker out!*" Most importantly, Chuck says, "We not gonna let nobody hurt you." They are not going to battle alone. Chuck and I are omnipresent and will make sure that basketball doesn't turn into fighting. Chuck's word on this is believed because of his intimidating presence. If he acts crazy to his players, how might he act to strangers or opponents!

Still many appear to be like "a deer in headlights" when they play in Blade Rodgers for the first time because it is so highly competitive, organized, and team oriented. The best of the city play here, and the speed, intensity, and skill of many of its players are surprising when one is more used to the self-centered mentality and unevenness of talent found in street ball. Jermaine struggled in his first season at the Rodgers League.

> It was different 'cause, number one, you had to play man-to-man [defense], and it was real organized. Like in all other leagues we played in, they wasn't really that organized, like you could do what you wanted to do and get your little twenty [points] or whatever. But in Rodgers [League], it was real hard to get twenty, because even though it was man-to-man, there was a lot of help defense. So I had to make the adjustment. Plus I had to get used to playing against all the top players in the city. The competition was a lot better [than in other leagues] 'cause every team was basically stacked—they had their best players in they neighborhoods or whatever, so you had to bring it every night.

Players—who were accustomed to playing on playgrounds, in playground leagues, and even for their high schools—had to learn how to play well in this league. In addition, they had to learn how to play "help defense," how to score against better defenses, and how to compete against the best players in the city. The league is organized, meaning people play according to norms and rituals not found in playground and neighborhood leagues or in school leagues. Teamwork is key: a player who tries to do too much on his own—dribbling a lot or taking on more than one defender—is going to lose the ball. He will become embarrassed trying to gain attention by performing an outstanding move. This is unlike the playground, where individual success and style, difficulty of a move, and faking out an opponent count for as much status points, if not more, than actually scoring a basket.

Miles, another one of our guys, was interviewed and written about in one of the large local newspapers after playing well during a high school game. Miles talked about his transformation under Chuck and how it prepared him for success. The article read:

> By his own admission, Miles Richey was formerly a "gunner." "When I was maybe 12 [or] 13, I almost never passed the ball," he said. "It was to the point, in a way, where my teammates didn't like me. I always played hard defense, so I figured I deserved to shoot when I wanted. When I started playing for Chuck Green in Blade Rodgers, he taught me real basketball. Now, I shoot if I'm open, but if not, I drop it off to somebody else."

Miles had been an "uzi" but learned to become a team player. This worked in his favor, and his high school coach played him significantly more with each season. By his senior year, he led them in scoring without his teammates resenting him.

Another kid, Jamal, struggled with our interpretations and evaluations of his play. His problem was confounded because he was six feet two inches tall and weighed 240 pounds. Jamal wanted to dribble the ball and take long shots. However, we needed him to take advantage of his size by playing close to the basket, rebounding, shooting close shots, and pushing opponents around. His mother highlighted the problem:

> "He [Jamal] think he a guard. He wants to dribble on everybody. But I used to play ball. [And] I tell him that he needs to stop [dribbling] and go down low where he can take advantage of his size. He a big guy."
>
> "Yeah, but that's what they all want to do. They all dribble. They think that's the way you suppose to play because they see it all the time on TV and in those And 1 [basketball] videos,"[4] I said.
>
> "That's what he tells me," she added.

Being criticized by his mother, and even Chuck and me, was not enough for Jamal to reconsider how he played. Playing bad or "baby basketball," as Chuck called it, meant Jamal would not adapt because he did not believe that he lacked ability or skills. He justified his self-perception by referring to games where he scored a number of points against good competition, as well as his exploits of smaller kids in practice. From a coach's standpoint, Jamal was putting himself, and ultimately the team, at a disadvantage because he did not play in a way that took advantage of his size. He was also unwilling to do what was right, determined by what we told him. Chuck and I wanted him to stay near the basket and rebound, but he stubbornly continued to dribble and shoot away from the basket.

Players need to learn their coach's expectations, structure, and team concepts or risk having poor performances, conflict, even a loss of playing time. Physical characteristics, such as height and body type, generally create competitive advantages. Playing as a guard, typically done by short and quick players, requires good decision making, skill in passing and dribbling, and the ability to shoot and make mid- and long-range shots. In the league, guards also need to understand their limitations due to the level of competition and how other teams play. Moves and shots that players claim they make regularly on the playground and in other leagues often become errors in this league.

11 SOME FALL OFF

Many kids fell out of our program. Chuck never "cut" players or told anyone that they had not made the team because they were not good enough.[1] However, some were "fired" if they behaved disrespectfully. Many quit because they didn't play enough in games, couldn't put up with Chuck, or they could get more playing time elsewhere. A number of these players who "fell off" were very talented and even played for their high schools. They found it difficult to adjust to Chuck's style, our expectations for how basketball was to be played, and specifically their role on our team. Ultimately, players interested in "making it" had to decide if they were willing to change and really "wanted *it* like that."

Donald was a tall, athletic left-hander and a good player. In practice, he looked to be much older than he was, outplaying some other kids who were one and two years older. He made a number of jump shots and played aggressively on defense, harassing guys, rebounding, and stealing the ball. But in his first game with our team, he looked very passive. He no longer used his instinctive sense of knowing where the ball was. Donald did not grab any rebounds or have a single steal. He lost the ball a few times and missed layups that he should have made. Admittedly, he was not himself. The setting and expectations were very different from practice and what he was used to. He grew frustrated with trying to learn our plays, and when he failed to quickly grasp the new style of play, he became unsure of himself. Sensing Donald's frustration, I approached him after his second game with the team. He complained:

"I'm tired of this. I keep getting yelled at because I don't know the plays."

"I know it's frustrating, but you've only been to three practices and two games. It's gonna take some time. Just keep coming and you'll get it. You can't expect to learn it all at once," I said to him.

"Yeah, but it makes me seem dumb and I ain't no dummy, but I just can't remember all of the plays. I know some like 'open' and the other one, but . . ." Donald's voice trailed off.

His friend Tracey added, "It's frustrating to me too, but I understand now. I don't always remember all the plays, but you can do it. You just got to go to practice. My grandfather told me about Chuck. So it [his yelling] don't bother me no more. He told me what to do."

I continued, "Yeah, man. Think [about it], you [have] only been here a few days and he [Chuck] already calling plays for you. There's a lot of other kids that don't even get much burn [playing time]. If he didn't think you had some talent, he wouldn't yell at you. We're not upset with you about not knowing the plays. We get upset when you don't do what you supposed to. You should make layups [referring to an easy shot he missed]."

Donald sank his head. "I know. I know. But I'm not gonna be able to make practice tomorrow. I don't know."

Donald appeared dejected because he wanted to play well and be a part of the team. A few of his friends played on our team, and he felt that he was more than able, athletically, to play in the league. Donald's main frustration was in feeling like he was starting over. Learning "real" basketball made him feel dumb—like he didn't know anything. This affected his confidence and hurt his performance. Things that he may have done naturally and that Chuck and I expected him to do he was unable to do because he was thinking too much.

Chuck was a contributing factor to Donald's frustration, but Chuck's style was not a complete surprise to him. Donald knew how tough Chuck was firsthand because he had come to tryouts the year before. He only lasted a day or so because he spoke disrespectfully to one of the young women who played on the team that year. He was flirting and went too far, saying something specifically about her body. Chuck immediately told him to get out of the gym and was adamant in letting everyone know that young women were not to be talked to like that. Donald's return this year showed that he was not thwarted by Chuck's coaching style (or was at least willing to put up with it) and that he really wanted to play in Blade Rodgers.

Donald was learning something new and at the same time would be giving up something, even if only partially. He would have to give up street ball and the less organized style of basketball that he was used to playing. Chuck and I demanded it, but giving up street ball was not easy to do. Like most of the kids on the team, Donald was still spending a lot of time with his friends who played street ball. He played with them in school, after school, and on weekends.

Commitment to street ball was a problem. Specifically, playing how one wanted to with little regard for the structure of plays, match-ups between teammates and the opposing team, good shot selection, and the game clock. Playing in places with low exposure and low competition is how kids remain "unknown" even when they are talented. They may be able to beat known players in one-on-one contests or in informal settings, but a player needs to be able to play organized ball by its rules in order to get the opportunity to compete in spaces with wider exposure. It takes a delicate balance to manage the two styles. And how would Donald remember the plays if he was not fully committed to learning "real" basketball and team basketball? Without this commitment, Donald was destined to remain unknown at the city level. His only hope would be to play well in high school, learning team ball or showing exceptional individual ability, and then compete in leagues like Blade Rodgers later.

Having plays is a symbol of organization and formal basketball. For Chuck, the role of plays is both symbolic and practical. Plays give direction and are learned so that individuals know to be at a certain spot on the floor at a specific time. Players are assigned tasks and take on certain roles to be in positions to do what we'd like for them to do, as opposed to making their own decisions. This shows organization and deference. Plays also serve as a means for us to control and regulate our players. When we run a play, we exert some control over the game by deciding who should get the ball and who should shoot. Thus, players give up their own freedom of sorts, to run a play that has been thought of and directed by someone else. They have to run the play correctly, or they risk being yelled at and even kept from playing. The system is not neutral; it demands deference to Chuck and me.

Chuck had a "do what I say or don't play" policy, which I also adopted. We decided which players would be in the game. They didn't play simply because they had status or thought they should. Players had to contribute positively to stay on the floor. Chuck's customary response to players who complained about not playing a lot of minutes was "If you play for two minutes and do nothing, why should I let you stay in the game? If you don't show me nothing in two minutes, why would I expect you to do something with four minutes. It don't make sense. I'll try somebody else." Each player had something to do. We didn't expect the same from everyone, but we did expect maximum effort. A player with little skills could get more minutes if they played hard and were productive. Conversely, a player like Aaron, one of our kids with great potential and skills, could sit on the bench a lot if he gave less. Talented players had the advantage because Chuck and I wanted to win. Chuck believed in finding a way to get the most out of players, rather than sitting them on the bench. If they didn't want to cooperate, then they could leave and he would ask them to do so.

Aaron, who played three years for us, was a kid who never seemed to fully accept our instructions. Instead he tried to impress others with his individual play. Chuck reminisced about Aaron:

> . . . That boy, that yellow boy [of light skin complexion] Aaron. He could have been a good player for us, very, very good. But he had all that shit in his head. Everybody telling him he was *that* guy, but he never showed it with us. He tried dribbling on two and three guys and threw that wild shit up. He fucked up

the ball all the time, man. It killed us. But he sure could play defense. WHOO, could he get up in they ass! He was a tough kid. But just wild and outta control.

Aaron was a great athlete, quick, strong, and could jump well, though he was only about five feet nine inches tall. He began attending basketball camps at nine years of age and played in leagues and on traveling teams from the age of ten. But he was firmly set in his ideas of how to play. Aaron believed that he was a "star" and therefore did not pass the ball to other players very often, even when more than one defender attempted to guard him. Trying to dribble around and between three defenders was a typical performance for him, and this was unacceptable in our team framework. Not only was this type of performance indicative of his playground orientation; it also showed disrespect for his teammates and for Chuck and me as coaches.

I would substitute for Aaron during games when he was selfish. He would roll his eyes and talk back to me. "Scott, Scott, why'd you take me out? 'Cause I lost the ball? I was fouled; the ref didn't call it." Once he figured out that the issue was his selfishness, he began to blame teammates for his over-dribbling. "Nobody came to the ball," he would say. He began our season as a starter and our star player, but I decided to replace him as a starter with another ball handler who I knew would put the team's agenda first. Eventually, Aaron made some changes but not until we had an argument after one game.

"Scott, I don't understand why you don't give me no burn [playing time]. I'm the best player on the team, and you got me sitting on the bench. Why is that?" Aaron said in a whiny, singsongy tone.

"First of all, you're *not* the best player on our team. Maybe you could be, but you're not *that* guy with the way you play. I tell you every game the same thing, Aaron. You have to stop trying to dribble on everybody. Every time you touch the ball, it's a turnover waiting to happen. You don't pass the ball, and your teammates don't want to play with you. You got tripled-teamed [guarded by three defenders all at once] and still didn't pass the ball! That means that we were playing four on two and you didn't pass the ball [if three people guard him, our other four players are being guarded by only two opposing players, leaving somebody open]."[2]

"Yeah. Why is that?" he asked. "Somebody should've come to the ball."

"No. You should have passed the ball! But you dribble with your head down so you can't see that there are defenders coming to trap you. And then when you run into them, you can't pass and you lose the ball. You hurt the team when you out there [in the game]," I said.

"I can dribble through three guys, Scott." He said this with total confidence, and I shook my head in disbelief. Now he was fessing up.

"You only play because I think you've got potential, but potential don't mean nothin'. If you can't do what I need you to do, you're not going to play. I don't need you," I said.

"You don't need me, Scott. You don't *need* me? . . . Wow, it's like that, Scott. You don't *need* me?"[3]

"Yeah, it's like that. I *don't* need you."

I walked off, leaving him behind, and I heard him repeat, "Wow. That's messed up."

Aaron showed surprise and pain when I said, "I don't need you"; he was hurt because he thought that he was the best player and an indispensable part of the team. His response, "It's like that?" and then repeating my statement, "You don't need me?" showed his hurt. I had expressed that he was not really that important to me and the team, and in his eyes I had disrespected him. How could I treat him like a scrub, a bad player? Some kids refer to the act of being disrespected in this way as being "done dirty." Being "done dirty" suggests that the player is not being given a fair shake, a real opportunity to show how good they are, and this denies them the possibility of increasing their status.

I was somewhat surprised that Aaron showed up to the next game, but he was definitely in a more pliable mind-set. I did not start him again and heard no complaints, as I had in the past, and when I put him into the game, he passed the ball and played much more within our system. During the rest of the season, however, he struggled trying to play within our conventions, and in his next two seasons with our team he reverted to his primary basketball socialization. One night's event summed up his attitude.

Aaron arrived to a game late because I had given him the wrong starting time (a Freudian slip?). The game was almost over, but I pointed to the bag with uniforms and told him to get dressed. He did so and sat on the bench with the other players who were watching and waiting to get into the game. Then he asked me if he could go into the game, and I told him to wait a minute. He then leaned over to his friend and said, "Watch when I get in, I'm a drop [score] sixteen in three minutes." His friend laughed, nodded, and gave him "dap," bumping fists approvingly. Seeing this, I shook my head and refused to put him in. His comment showed that he intended to monopolize the ball and shoot with little regard for his teammates or winning.

Aaron quit in his twelfth-grade season. He felt that he should have had more of a "starring" role on our teams and grew to resent Chuck and me as coaches. Younger players were playing more than he was, and he asked me why he was being treated unfairly. "Scott, why do you always pull me [substitute for me]? When Keith make a mistake or Ray, you don't pull them." It was a valid question. Aaron did not share the same status as the star players, Keith and Ray. His time had passed, and he was no longer the most talented or the most known player on our team. He pressed and took risks and wanted the opportunity to be the hero, but his play was too erratic. Aaron was having a similar problem on his high school team. He had been recruited out of a public middle school to play at North Catholic. His play and attitude upset the coach, who decided not to use him much. This experience echoed what we had been telling him. His playing time and status plummeted each year in high school, and he did not get the opportunity to play ball in college.

12 BRINGING 'EM BACK AND PUTTING IT ALL TOGETHER

Chuck took a lot of responsibility for how our teams played. In postgame talks, he would curse, ask guys why they don't listen, and only give kudos to those who played as well as they could. He would reiterate what we had done at practice and shake his head in disgust. He accused guys who didn't show or were late of disloyalty and being "basketball bums," going everywhere to play, and playing for anybody. These postgame talks dragged on and on, usually lasting thirty to forty-five minutes. The kids would try different things to escape. "I got to go, my moms is outside waiting." Or, "I got another game." Or they would huddle up and put their hands in, as we did to break huddles. After this he would go outside of the gym to a bench and smoke a cigarette. He wanted and expected me to sit with him, and he would go over the game some more. He could remember the game in great detail, like what the score was when a guy made a mistake.

After winning the first five games of the season, our team lost four in a row. Then we won a game and a second one by forfeit to clinch a spot in the playoffs. It was a very disappointing finish. We had fewer players in each of the last four games. Ray, Keith, and Bryant had missed games due to traveling and playing for other teams. Chuck felt betrayed: if kids were going to play for other teams, they must not appreciate us as coaches nor care about their teammates. We were saved by a couple of new players given to us by the league. The new players were bodies, so that we did not have to forfeit, but they were not good players.

They were not serious or had been cut by other teams because of their lesser abilities. Chuck was frustrated by how the season had turned out, and we talked about whether or not our team should be in the playoffs.

"Man, I know we made the playoffs, but I don't think these unloyal motherfuckers deserve to play. It's an honor, a privilege. But these guys act like it's owed them. They don't show for games, but they expect us to do for them! Fuck 'em. What you think?"

I listened to his disappointment, and I was also frustrated. "Well, I understand what you saying, but I think we should still let 'em play."

"How could you say that? They treat us like this, and we doing all we can. We riding them here and there, and you tutoring them. And they don't show no appreciation. And that's all right, but then they do this and they show up when they want to, and we suppose to accept that? Naw, man. FUCK THAT! You couldn't get enough of them lazy niggas to the game no way."

"I hear you, I hear you. But we can do it. Let's not do it for them; let's do it for us."

"For *us*? Scott, you crazy."

"Yeah, I know. What if I can get seven or eight guys?"

"Who?"

"Keith, Bryant, Jermaine, Ray, Miles, Justin, Tyrone, plus we got the new guys."

"You think you can get those guys to show for the game?"

"Yeah, I think *we* can. If you talk to Keith, I'll get Ray and Jermaine, and I can call the others."

There was a long silence.

"Okay, Scott. I'll do it. But for you, not for those motherfuckers. I'll go down to Keith's house and talk to him and his family, but if they give me some bullshit, Scott, I'M A FUCK ALL OF THEM UP! I'll go down to Bryant's house too. You try and catch up with the other guys and call me and let me know who you got."

And with this, I had convinced Chuck to let our team compete in the playoffs. He knew that my talk about "doing it for us" was just a way to keep our season going. I believed that we had a good team and could compete with the other teams if we played well. But I didn't know how the playoffs would be "for us." Instead, I was willing to give our players another chance and opportunity to play.

We divided the task of talking to players because of efficiency but also based upon relationships. I had spent a lot of time with Ray and Jermaine and knew where to find them. The team was *our* team, but Jermaine and Ray were more my guys. Similarly, Chuck had to talk to Keith because he had a long relationship with Keith's family; he coached four or five of Keith's uncles and Keith's mom. Keith was our cog—he "made everything go." Chuck valued his heart, attitude, competitiveness, and work ethic. When Keith lost the ball, he busted his butt to get it back. He did not quit or run from challenges. He played until the game ended, whether we were winning or losing, and regardless of how big we were winning or losing. He wanted to win and did whatever he could; making big plays, wanting the ball and an opportunity to make an important contribution. His jersey was always drenched at the end of games, much wetter than any-body else's. Keith exhausted himself and was fearless.

The trouble was that we didn't have a big guy, a center, who was dominant or simply sufficient. Our team was undersized, and sometimes I'd look at the opposing team and say to Chuck, "I'd take the big guys that they don't even play. I know they could help us." Our opponents got a lot of rebounds because of their size advantage, which Chuck and I constantly harped on. "Block out! Block out! Get the rebound!"

In one close game during the season, we called a time-out to strategize. Our big guys had given up several rebounds, but we could still win the game if we got the ball and scored a basket. The other team was shooting a free throw, and we were in the low block (spots closest to the basket) with a chance to rebound. If the shooter missed, we had to block out and secure the re-bound. This was not a given. The shooter was on the foul line because we had not gotten the rebound and then had fouled him when he was trying to score. I asked, "Who gonna grab the rebound? Somebody's got to block their big man out." Keith looked around and shook his head, disappointed with his bigger teammates. "I'll do it," he said. "I'll get the ball. Fuck that." And he did. We were tough to beat when Keith took on responsibility and led by his actions.

The Job of a Coach

Coaches create a framework and plan for winning. Their players are components, and good coaches are skilled in assessing each player's capabilities. Coaches determine what their team can do as a whole and how each player fits into the collective team effort. The team will suffer if the coach is weak in any of his jobs or if the players refuse to accept their roles or cannot do their jobs/tasks.

Our team had finished seventh in regular league play and would have to compete against the defending champions for our first playoff game. The winner of that game would face the third-place team two days later and then play for the championship, or "chip," as the players called it, early the following week. We won our first game, upsetting the defending champions after being behind by fourteen points! In the first half, our team looked as they had in our losing games, but they worked well together in the second half. They passed the ball to one another and played pressure defense, forcing the defending champions into several turnovers that we converted into easy scores. This was impressive. Our players had finally "put it all together," Chuck said, doing what we had been asking and expecting them to do all along. Next, we easily defeated the third-place team and advanced to the championship.

Chuck used a lot of psych and handled each player according to their ability and how he felt they might best respond to him. After games, Chuck and I usually told players what they had done well and what we expected them to do in the next game, clarifying their roles on the team, and how each role fit into the collective effort required to win. Chuck liked to use stew as an analogy:

"We're making stew and everybody got to bring something to put in the pot." Jermaine had performed very well in the first two playoff games, but Chuck didn't want to let him know how well he was playing. Instead, Chuck asked Jermaine to do more. Chuck believed Jermaine's desire to get known and to impress us had driven him to play well, and he was afraid that praise would throw Jermaine off balance. Jermaine might not play well if he knew that he was pleasing us and impressing others. He might grow complacent or, worse, become full of himself. He was doing what we knew and expected he could do: grabbing rebounds; passing the ball to Keith, Bryant, and Ray unless he had a layup or dunk; and playing aggressively on defense. Chuck's psych was in withholding his praise for Jermaine's performance and setting even higher expectations and goals for him.

Keith had averaged over twenty points for the first two playoff games and was undoubtedly our MVP. He needed to work within the team framework and not independently, except when a play required him to do so. Chuck rarely yelled at Keith because Keith generally knew when he made a mistake and was better left to self-management and being instinctive; over-coaching would frustrate Keith, and he would react by trying to do too much or rebelling. Bryant needed to score and be instinctual, taking risks, and playing strong defense. He had been a good defensive player the prior year, when he was a lesser known player, but with his advance in status, he focused more on offense and less on defense to gain more attention. Chuck felt that Bryant needed to be talked to directly and reminded of what the team needed from him. When he was frustrated or engrossed in a personal challenge with an opposing player, we sat him down to regain control of his emotions and refocus. Chuck came to handle Ray with the most delicate approach because Ray had the most potential to impact a game but needed to feel comfortable. Early in the season, Chuck's yelling and chiding distracted Ray. He would become nervous, play poorly, and worry too much, and Chuck would yell and take him out of the game. In the playoffs, both Ray and Chuck made adjustments. Ray felt that he understood what Chuck wanted from him. Chuck lessened and softened his criticism. Because of Ray's practice record, Chuck was confident that Ray would work hard to correct his mistakes.

I learned my role on the fly, by Chuck's cues and responses, and from TD, Chuck's former assistant coach of about twenty years. TD told me that my job was to cool out the players when Chuck cursed them out. Chuck said that he was the "hard pedal" and I was the "soft pedal." I learned to counterbalance Chuck because I felt that he was too tough sometimes. He let me do it most of the time. The exception was when a player believed that he was better than he was and wasn't willing to listen. "You can only tell them so many times, and either they gonna do what we ask or they not." If Chuck did not want me to talk to a player, he would yell, "Leave him alone, Scott. Let him go. Fuck him. He don't want to listen. He ain't never gonna listen." His yelling at me was difficult, but I knew that it was not directed at me. We would talk about this later. He would put his arm around me and say, "I'm sorry for yelling at you, but you know I wasn't yelling at you. That nigga just make me so mad. Whew . . . You know you my man."

Chuck was managing a lot of people, himself, players, me, as well as parents, referees, and the league's table staff. I was learning by being with him and through our discussions before and after games. I rarely disagreed with Chuck openly because I was learning from him. I raised questions one-on-one or simply let them go. He insisted that we were partners, but I knew that we were not equal partners and accepted my lower position. He was the president, and I had become his vice president. This was not simply about personal style. Chuck was known as a guru—he was "the man." If I cared anything about winning, and I did, Chuck had proven himself, others vouched for him, and the players responded to him and played harder when he was around.

13 THE CHIP

We were excited about the chip (championship) but were clearly the underdogs. Jackson Management, our opponent, had giants. Other teams had maybe one or two guys that were six feet five and taller; this team had four guys over that height. Their tallest player was a tenth grader who stood six feet eight inches. Our tallest player, Justin, was six feet four. Would someone play extraordinarily well because it was the championship game? Would their effort be enough for us to continue our Cinderella run and upset the best team in the league? Jermaine and Ray hoped that they would play well, knowing that doing so would increase their status tremendously. Chips were great for pub (publicity) and making lasting impressions; people remember champions and how players perform in championships, whether good or bad.

The game was scheduled for six o'clock. A large crowd came and expected a good show. All but two of our players arrived early, dressed, and were beginning to warm up with twenty minutes before tip-off. Ray was one of the two who were absent, and I asked Jermaine where his "roadie" was. "He at a wedding, he called me though, and said he on his way. He'll be here."

I set out Ray's uniform so that he could grab it and dress quickly when he arrived. Then the referees asked for a team captain and Chuck responded, "Captain? All my guys are captains. Go on up there," and he waved to the kids and pointed to the center of the floor where captains speak with the referees before a game.

Our players were confused, unsure if Chuck was serious. "Go," he said, assuring them of his sincerity. The referees picked up on Chuck's directions and asked both teams to the middle of the floor for last-minute instructions, warnings, and clarifications. The talk ended and players went to their respective team's bench and sat for the introduction of players. Over the loudspeaker a man with a polished voice began the introductions:

Welcome to the 2002 Ray Jackson Next Generation League Championship Game sponsored by Robinson's Bank. Tonight's match-up is between the visitors, Jackson Management in black, and the home team, McDonald's . . . I'm sorry, Steve Johns [our team's name], in red, named in honor of the late Steve Johns. And now the player introductions.

For Jackson, number twelve, a tenth grader at Philadelphia Saint Christian Academy, [name] . . .

The announcer read the names of Jackson Management's players. As their names were called, the players got up from their seats, trotted past their coaches and in front of the scorer's table, shook my hand and Chuck's, and then ran to shake and slap the hands of their teammates who had gathered in the middle of the floor. The crowd of about three hundred people, split on both sides of the arena, applauded. Certain players received louder applause and yells according to their varying status levels. The coaches for Jackson were introduced, and they also walked over and shook our hands.

Next, our team was introduced and followed the same routine. I had written down the names, jersey numbers, and schools attended for all of our players. As they trotted out, I put out a fist to each of my players, who matched my knuckles with theirs.

The referees called for the starting players to begin the game. Chuck looked for Ray one last time and then called the names of the starters, "Keith, Bryant, Jermaine, Miles, and . . . Justin. Let's go get 'em, gentleman. All right let me hear it."

Our team gathered in a small circle and raised one or both of their arms in the middle of the circle, putting their hands in a pile on top of Chuck's hand. Jermaine led the cheer, "One, two, three," and in unison we all called out, "South Philly."

The game started quickly. Jackson scored first when one of their big guys made an easy post move. This was going to be the biggest problem for us: their big guys could overpower our smaller big guys. Jermaine made a basket and the game was tied 2–2. Then they jumped to an 8–4 lead with more easy scores from the bigger players, who were having their way. There was not much that we could do. They simply passed the ball to one of their big guys, who would turn around, face the basket, and shoot over our guys or drop step, pivot, and score a layup. The game was close for a while, and then Jackson's lead grew to eight points.

Chuck asked for a time-out. Bryant was out of breath. Miles was playing tough but was very slow because he was tired. Justin was trying to be strong but was simply overmatched. Jermaine was scoring well but was not as strong as the player he guarded. And Keith had committed two fouls and was frustrated.

Keith's status preceded him, and Jackson was playing good defense to shut him down. Jackson's players and coaches had observed and made note of Keith's strengths and weaknesses to determine how they should guard him. Jackson wanted him to drive and challenge their big guys, and when he did, they instructed one of their smaller, quick guys to run the other way (cherry picking). Their big guy blocked Keith's shots or grabbed rebounds and passed the ball down court to the small, quick guys in hopes of getting an easy score. Keith had missed on at least five drives to the basket, having been fouled on three of the plays, but the referees did not agree. The missed drives resulted in easy buckets for the other team because our players were not running back to protect our basket. We did not panic. Chuck and I understood that, as the star of the team, Keith felt extra pressure and was trying to do what he felt the team needed.

Bryant was upset because Keith was not passing. He would stand in an open spot hoping for Keith to pass the ball so he could shoot. Bryant should have played defense to stop the other team's scoring. If the other team rebounded the ball and ran out to a fast break, Bryant should have been running to make their attempt difficult, regardless of what Keith did.

Jackson's lead grew to twelve points by the end of the first half, 35–23, and Ray still had not arrived. At halftime Chuck spoke as he usually did: asking players, "What the fuck is you doing?" and "Is you scared?" And he scolded them for not doing what we had practiced and urged them to play the way that we had taught them. Still, there was no Ray.

Jackson Management began the second half much the way they had ended the first half. Keith dribbled down, passed the ball to Bryant, who tried to dribble drive down the middle and shoot over Jackson's giants. His shot was blocked, and he fell to the ground dramatically. No foul was called. Instead, one of Jackson's big guys snared the ball and threw it down the court. Their point guard had leaked out. He caught the pass and jogged easily to the basket for a finger-roll layup. Jackson stretched their lead to fourteen.

The game appeared out of reach, and Keith continued having a tough time scoring. Jermaine, however, was playing his best basketball. He had scored a number of baskets and was grabbing rebounds and playing tough defense against a known and bigger, stronger, and better player—Hanif Martin, whom everyone called "Neef." Jermaine's best defense was not enough though; Neef was scoring fairly easily against Jermaine and had scored most of his team's points.

Neef was Jermaine's archrival. He was one of Jermaine's middle school mates who was ranked in the city as an eighth grader, and he often reminded Jermaine of their status differences. Hanif had been given a scholarship to one of the predominantly white and affluent Catholic high schools in the city that regularly recruited poor black kids for basketball. This game was highlighting their differences in ability. Hanif had scored twenty points in the first half, while Jermaine, at his best, had scored only eight.

Finally, Ray arrived with seven and a half minutes remaining in the game and Jackson's lead at fifteen. He was wearing a peach-colored tuxedo rental with all of the accessories, including a ruffled-front tuxedo shirt, peach tie and cummerbund, and white patent-leather dress shoes. I quickly gave Ray his uniform and told him to get dressed. He was ready in a flash and returned to our bench. Chuck put him in the game right away. Ray substituted for Miles and made an instant impact on the game.

Keith drove to the basket and took a wild shot that was blocked by one of Jackson's big guys. The ball was tipped again in the air, as players jumped to grab it, and it fell into the hands of a Jackson guard, who started to dribble for another easy score. Ray and Keith chased the guard down, and Ray tapped the ball from behind. The guard lost control, and Keith tracked the ball down, spun, and passed it to Ray. He dribbled up the court, heading straight toward Jackson's two biggest guys, with Jermaine running on his right side. Ray passed the ball to Jermaine, who took two steps and leaped; Jermaine raised the ball over his head with one hand and slammed the ball forcefully through the rim over the six-feet-eight-inch player. It was a tremendous individual play. The crowd went wild with applause, *oohs*, *aahs*, and yells. Jackson's coach called a time-out.

Our guys were excited, slapping Jermaine's hands and yelling encouragement to each other. Chuck told the guys that we were going to run our press (pressure defense) against Jackson. When the time-out ended, our guys got into their positions, as designated by the play. Hanif threw the ball into a Jackson guard, and we doubled him, sending two guys at him. He turned his back and couldn't see his teammates. He panicked, and Keith stripped the ball loose. Ray scooped it up and dribbled for an easy layup. Jackson was confused by our press. Neef yelled at his teammate and told someone else to take the ball out; he wanted to receive the pass and try to dribble the ball against our press because he thought he'd do a better job. He received the pass and dribbled past Ray and Keith as quickly as he could, but Jermaine got set in front of the basket and Neef could not slow down to avoid him. Neef attempted to jump over Jermaine and lay the ball up but ran him over instead. The refs called an offensive foul. Charge! Neef jumped up after the collision and ran over to a ref, arguing the call. We took the ball out, Keith passed the ball up to Ray, who passed to Jermaine, and he quickly passed the ball back to Ray. Ray took a ten-foot jump shot. *Whap!* It swished through the net. Jackson called another time-out.

The game resumed and Jackson had a new plan. Their smallest guard took the ball out and passed the ball to the other small guard, who passed the ball to Neef in the middle of the floor. He turned and started to dribble. But Ray was right behind him and tapped the ball forward to our big guy, Justin. Justin passed the ball back to Ray, and we were off to score another basket. Neef struggled, making bad passes and losing the ball dribbling, and we quickly cut their lead to seven points.

Jackson's coach called another time-out with four minutes left to play in the game. Our guys were even more excited and could sense that we had a real chance to win the chip. The momentum had obviously shifted, and the crowd was abuzz. Keith pumped his fist in celebration, and then Bryant did the same. As the guys came to huddle for our time-out, I slapped hands with them and offered praise and instruction: "good defense," "way to get back," "keep rebounding," "grab everything with two hands." Chuck was yelling emphatically at the referees, and I waited to see if he was coming to say something to the team. But he kept yelling, waving his hands, and making a big scene. I herded the guys into a huddle and talked about what we needed to do to win. His tactic kept pressure on the referees; he was not happy and asked for more calls to go our way. Referees sometimes become lax, naturally adjusting to momentum.

I looked up again to see if Chuck was coming to say something, but he was still going off. I ended the huddle. "Nice job, nice job. Now be careful with the reaching, Bryant. You and Keith got three fouls. We in this game, but they not going to give it to us; *we've got to take it!* LET'S GO!"

The guys nodded their heads. Jermaine led the team cheer, "One, two, three . . . South Philly." The game resumed, and we kept pressing and playing hard. Jackson continued to lose the ball and play out of control, and we overtook them when Ray made a long jump shot with sixteen seconds remaining. We had the lead for the first time, 56–55. A Jackson guard threw the ball to Neef for him to take the last shot. Ray and Keith closed in to double-team him, and Neef tried a spin move, turning backward on his right side to avoid Keith but running right into Ray. Ray tapped the ball away, but the ball rolled out of bounds. Jackson took the ball out. Jermaine and Ray doubled Neef, and Bryant and Keith each guarded another player closely. They couldn't pass the ball in because of our great team defense, and the ref called five seconds (a team has five seconds to inbound the ball). We got the ball.

Jackson tried a pressure defense of its own but fouled Ray. He was given two free throws because they had committed too many fouls. Ray made both and we returned to defense with eight seconds left, now ahead by three points. A Jackson guard passed the ball to Neef. He faked and then tried to dribble past Ray and Keith again. He nearly lost the ball but jumped to pass the ball to a teammate down the court. His teammate could not catch the ball, and it went out of bounds under our basket (the basket that we defend).

It was our ball, with two seconds remaining in the game, and Chuck called for a time-out. The referee granted it, and Chuck set up a play: "Keith, you take the ball out, and Bank Street [Ray], you and Miles run elbow [a screen-and-roll play] for you to get the ball. Then let them foul you so you can take the free throws and win this game. All right, who do we got in the game?" Bryant, Keith, Justin, Jermaine, and Ray raised their hands.

"Okay, how much time left?" We all turned and looked up at the score clock on the wall at the far end of the court to see 00:02. "Okay, we only got two seconds left. Scott, what you think?" He pulled me aside and asked me quietly, "Should I give the other guys a little taste?"

I looked up at him and gave a confused look. This was a rhetorical question—Chuck would do what he wanted. He wanted to let everyone play because it was a championship game, and they could later say they played in the game, but I did not think that this was the time to play scrubs (poor players). He continued, "We'll be all right; it's only two seconds. Keith passes the ball to Ray, [the other team will foul him,] he go to the foul [line], make free throws, and it's over."

I shrugged my shoulders and shook my head, biting my lower lip, not confident with his plan.

A referee blew his whistle, signaling it was time for play to resume, and Chuck yelled, "Jackie, Greg, and uh, uh, Joey get in. Keith and Bank Street, you stay in, and, Keith, you know what to do." The referee held the ball for Keith to put the ball into play, and Ray and Greg ran the elbow play. Ray got open. But Keith looked past Ray and threw a one-handed baseball pass. The ball traveled half the length of the floor toward Jackie. Jackie is five feet six inches tall and does not jump well. The ball flew over his head, going out of bounds without anyone touching it. Jackson called their last time-out. Keith's errant pass gave the ball over to Jackson under the basket in which they needed to score! Chuck was beside himself and had no words. He took off his hat with one hand and raised it over his head to throw it down but stopped himself. He looked at Keith and shook his head, with his arms hanging by his sides. Why didn't Keith run the play? Why didn't he pass the ball to Ray?

Chuck was in shock. I quickly yelled for Bryant, Jermaine, and Justin to go back into the game for the scrubs. I told the guys to guard against anyone who might shoot a three-point shot because we were up by three points and a three-point shot could tie the game. The clock had not changed; there were still two seconds left, and the score was 58–55.

Chuck regained his composure and spoke to the team: "Well, we can still win this game. I don't know what the fuck THIS MAN [pointing to Keith, who looked dejected] just did! But we all right, we all right. Everyone back in. Wait. Miles, you get Justin. We just can't let them shoot no threes. Whoever guarding the man with the ball [out of bounds] has got to step off and guard the shooters. We don't care about the man out of bounds. He can't hurt us."

Jackson ran a play where their smallest player went from one corner of the floor through players to the other corner of the floor. The player caught the ball, twenty feet from the basket, and threw up a desperation shot. It hit the back of the rim, bounced way up to the top of the backboard, fell back down to the rim, rolled around the rim a little bit, and then dropped into the net as the final seconds of the game clock ran out and the clock buzzer went off! Jackson had tied the game, 58–58, and forced overtime.

The crowd was screaming, and Jackson's players jumped on their hero. Our players came to our bench. Keith had his head down. Bryant looked tired. Ray and Miles trotted and sat down. But Jermaine was upbeat. "Yo, it's all right. Come on. It ain't over. We got this. That was just a lucky shot."

Chuck threw his hat down this time. And he bit his bottom lip hard, shaking his head, his hands on his hips. He couldn't believe it. I huddled the guys again, urging them some more. "Come on, come on. It ain't over. We still got this game."

Chuck came to the huddle and lit into Keith. "YOU DIRTY ROTTEN SONOFABITCH. I OUTTA KILL YOU. YOU STINKIN' . . ."

Chuck leaned into the huddle and spoke under his breath, "Don't listen to me," and started to back up.

"I CAN'T BELIEVE YOU DID THAT, MAN! WHAT IN THE FUCK WERE YOU THINKING?"

The guys were confused. Again, he throws his voice to us, "We all right, let's play smart and go get 'em." And he backed away, shaking his head in feigned disgust.

Some of the guys snickered and then we broke the huddle. "One, two, three . . . South Philly."

Chuck's actions were a needed distraction. He took our minds off of the game for a moment and made us laugh. Overtime began with a tip-off. Jermaine outjumped their center and tapped the ball to Miles. But Miles held the ball casually, and one of Jackson's guards hit the ball out of his hands and stole it. He passed the ball to Hanif, who had smartly run toward our basket. Hanif gathered the ball and laid it up. Chuck yelled, "MILES! DAMN!" And threw his arms up, put his head down, and shook his head. I cheered the team. "It's all right. It's all right. Come on. Let's play." Keith made a jump shot. But then Bryant fouled out on a stupid attempt to steal the ball. Ray took over and carried us, scoring five consecutive points, two layups and one free throw. And Jermaine added a layup. Jackson only scored two more points. We won the game by five points, 67–62!

We rushed the floor. Chuck slapped Keith on the shoulder, saying, "I oughta kill ya." Keith grinned widely, and Chuck laughed and hugged him.

I found Ray. "You saved us. I'm glad you decided to show up," I said sarcastically, and we high-fived.

Jermaine hugged me from behind. "We did it, Scott! We won the chip!"

"You did it!" I shot back. "You was a monster! I told you how to go to the rack!"

Jermaine was all smiles. The crowd was on its feet, clapping. We looked up and waved. A few folks had come downstairs to the floor from the stands and were hugging and high-fiving players.

The game was a coming-out party of sorts for Ray and Jermaine, who performed great individually and within their team-assigned roles. Jermaine scored twenty-one points and gathered eight rebounds, to go with his dramatic dunk, and Keith ended the game with twenty-five points. Ray scored fourteen points and made several assists and steals in the short time he played. Jackson's star, Neef, had scored thirty-two points but did not win an individual award because he was on the losing team.

Keith's and Jermaine's individual achievements were a part of our team game. We taught Jermaine to go to the basket strong, especially when a bigger guy was defending him. If he had tried to make a finesse shot, like a finger roll, he most likely would have missed, or the big defender may have blocked the shot and kept the momentum in Jackson's favor. Jermaine's dunk changed the game's momentum, and it was not simply an individual accomplishment, since Ray and Keith both played a role in getting the ball to him. Though Keith missed his first five shots, we expected him to make some shots later, which he did, scoring when we really needed baskets. Keith was our star and shot a lot, but if he had stopped shooting, Jackson's defense would be under less pressure. They were doubling Keith, which gave other players scoring opportunities when Keith passed the ball. Ultimately, Jermaine was the biggest beneficiary in this game. Keith was awarded MVP for the league, but Jermaine earned the MVP (Most Valuable Player) award for the chip.

14
THE GLOW *BUT* REALITY OF SUCCESS

Ray and Jermaine were able to see and feel that others knew of their success away from the league.[1] However, they still had a long way to go to become elite players. They were young and this was only one achievement—it could be a fluke.

The *Daily News* gave nightly reports of league play, and this time the paper showed the championship score and indicated that Jermaine had earned game MVP and Keith, the league MVP. Ray had played well, but because he was not present for the whole game, he did not score as much as Jermaine or Keith. Therefore, his impact was not reported in the paper. The absence of recognition was not lost on Ray's mother, who asked me why Ray had not been named the MVP. I told her the obvious reason, "Ray wasn't even there the whole game. But he did well. Jermaine played his best, though. He had a real good game." She did not like hearing about Jermaine; it seemed that she felt Jermaine's performance threatened Ray's standing.

Ray and Jermaine were featured separately in their small, black-owned neighborhood newspaper as "up and comers." Jermaine's surprising standout performance in Blade Rodgers was the story's primary focus. He had failed to make the varsity basketball team for his school, but played well against the city's best players, and would certainly be ready for varsity next year. The article also discussed Ray's past success at Thompson and his future plans.

People from recruiting and scouting services also attended

the playoff games to rank and compare players. Here are two ex-
cerpts of one scout's report after visiting Blade Rodgers and Blade
Rodgers Rising Stars (postsummer league) regional tournament.

> On the summer league scene, there were three that I fre-
> quented in Girard College, Blade Rodgers and True Ball Greater
> Philadelphia. At Rodgers, there's always some new uprisings.
> Guys like *Keith Mann*, *Ray Webster*, David Summer, Jack Henson,
> Hanif "Neef" Martin, Stevie Lewis, *Jermaine Perkins* stood out
> this summer [my emphasis added to highlight the names of
> our players].
>
> Last weekend's Blade Rodgers Rising Stars Tournament
> brought about impressive performances from some city kids.
> Here are a few profiles: Ray Webster 6'1+ W/PG Thompson—
> showed up for the playoffs with the Phoenix and was a huge
> reason why they upset the tourney favorite Cecil Kirk, from
> East Baltimore, by not backing down from their bullying tac-
> tics and nailing 5-for-9 from deep. There is talk of Webster
> transferring this fall, so stay tuned.

The person conducting these rankings attended only three
summer leagues, none of which were playground bandit leagues.
He was attracted to Blade Rodgers and the other two leagues
based on their reputations for competitive play and their legitimacy tied to history and/or high schools. Blade Rodgers teams
were primarily neighborhood/area based while the other leagues
were school leagues where high school teams played against
other high schools. Chuck reflected on the effect of winning the
championship.

> I'm so proud of what we done with them no-counts! We done
> it. And you should have seen them down at the league [post-
> league, end of summer tournament]. They walking around
> like they own the motherfucker. And that's great. Because
> they done it. They champions. Bryant and Jermaine and Ray
> and Keith, they walking around with they chests puffed out
> like peacocks, but they used to be chickens! They on top of the

world. That's good shit and can't nobody take that from them. They'll remember this for the rest of they lives.

A few days later, the word had traveled. Reese, a neighborhood friend, saw Jermaine and Ray at the Tracks and made fun of Ray. Reese said to Ray, "You didn't do shit. What happened, I thought you was a baller." He was referring to the chip and Ray's fourteen points, which had not been reported. Jermaine responded, "We won the chip, though. Did you see it in the paper?" Reese replied, "Yeah, J, I saw [the paper]. *You* was representin' [representing South Philly well]." Reese gave Jermaine dap (put his fist to Jermaine's) and shook his head at Ray, feigning disappointment.

Another friend, Teddy, overheard the discussion and congratulated Jermaine. "That's good, man. That's where it's at." Ray played to Teddy's interest and told him about Jermaine's dunk.

> Keith passed me the ball on the fast break, and I looked up and saw that big motherfucker in the middle, and I said, "Shit, he's big." I passed the ball to J. I thought he was gonna finger roll it or something, but then he, he cocked it back. I said, "Aw, shit." He wolfed it on him [laughing and giving Jermaine dap].
>
> Then I was going to give him a soft pat on his butt or hip or something, and he slapped me on my hand and that shit hurt. It hurt so bad and I was shaking my hand trying to play it off, but that jahn [thing] hurt, yo. Jermaine was so hyped.

Ray and Jermaine had made some changes in their style of playing. They had learned to play organized ball according to the conventions and norms Chuck and I taught. Winning as a team helped them to receive the kind of recognition they were enjoying. The victory itself, and the subsequent reports of Jermaine's performance, solidified his and Ray's standing in their neighborhood.

Jermaine and Ray were far busier and more confident in their abilities after winning the league championship. They, and four other players from our team, were asked to play on teams that competed in Rodgers' Rising Stars tournament that began after the league's regular summer season. Our players may not have been as talented as those on several other teams, but they were selected because we won the championship. Although things had definitely taken a positive turn, Ray and Jermaine learned that even winning the championship did not give them more status than the city's elite players.

The Harsh Reality

A few days after the chip, I went with Jermaine and Ray to a bandit league game at the Tracks. While watching games and awaiting their own game, Jermaine and Ray were hit with the harsh reality that they were low-rung players and relatively unknown at a citywide level. We noticed Hanif Martin, or Neef, the star of the team we beat in the chip. Neef saw Jermaine and came over to us. They shook hands and began talking about playing at the Tracks. They avoided talk about the obvious—our championship and Neef's team's defeat.

> "You playing down here?" I asked Neef.
> He nodded his head "yes."
> "Who you playing with?"
> "Strong [High School]."
> "Oh, you play with Denny," I responded. Denny played for Strong High School and was one of the best players in the city. I had only heard of him and was piqued by the possibility of seeing him play that night.
> Jermaine tried to ease into talking about the chip.
> "Why haven't you been to Rising Stars?" he asked, referring to the Rodger's League all-star team created after the championship. Neef said that he hadn't been around since the chip because he was out of town with a traveling team.
> "You gonna make the team?" he asked Jermaine.
> Jermaine responded quickly, "Yeah!" as though the answer was obvious. Neef looked at Jermaine squarely and with warning.

"Don't act like you *all that* now, just because you won a lit-tle cheap trophy." Neef referred directly to the championship trophy.

Jermaine fired back happily, "What are you saying, them jahns is big. But it don't matter, I got the MVP and we won the chip!"

"That bullshit trophy. That's probably the only one you got."

"Shut up! You know I got all them trophies from Brown."

"Yeah and who was the MVP of them games?"

"Whatcha mean? You got cooked for sixty-seven [someone he defended scored sixty-seven points]!"

"I'll kill you [in basketball]. You couldn't stop me. How much I cook you for [score on you]? The only reason we lost was because I didn't have nobody else. If I had someone who could just score ten points, we would have beat you."

"You didn't score that all on me, though."

"You're right," I said to Neef. "You didn't have no help. But whose fault is that? You guys didn't go down to those big boys you got on your team. Y'all would've had us. Jermaine is the second biggest guy on our team, and our center is only an inch taller. You had three guys six [feet] six [inches] or taller. You should've killed us."

"But they suck. Every time they get the ball, they shootin' up bad shots. I had to carry the team, and they couldn't stop me. I did whatever I wanted."

"Well, if that's the case, I guess you guys should've been working with your big guys. All you had to do was throw the ball into them. We don't even have a big man. It doesn't mat-ter how many *you* scored. You should have scored fifty, maybe then you would have won," I countered smugly.

"Yeah, *we* won the chip," Jermaine added proudly.

"I wouldn't have wanted that cheap trophy no way. I would've been mad. I worked hard and all I got was that cheap shit."

"Yeah, right," I agreed with Neef, returning his earlier sar-casm. "You would've been *real upset* to win the chip! It ain't about no trophy; it's about winning."

He didn't like what I was saying, and so he inquired, "Who are you?" looking sideways at Jermaine and motioning to me.

"That's our coach," Jermaine responded. Neef looked back at me, with raised eyebrows and his head slightly tilted toward me.

"That's right, we told them what to do *to you*, and that's how we won the game."

"Whaaat?" Neef interrupted in disbelief.

"Yeah, *you* did just what we wanted you to do. How you think we came back from fifteen down? Ask them what we told 'em."

"What he tell you?" Neef asked Ray and Jermaine.

Ray stuttered badly. "They, they told us to, to double-team and tr-tr-trap you."

"It didn't work." Neef smirked and shook his head, rejecting my claim. He continued, "What happened was this motherfucker [pointing to Ray] came in the game, and we didn't know who he was. And he was hitting jump shots and he killed us. And then J dunked on Ab and that set everything off." Ray smiled. He was getting props from Neef, who had status. And Jermaine was happy with the recognition of his dunk.

"Y'all didn't know about Ray, huh? Well, he did put his thing down in the second half, but he didn't make a lot of jump shots; he made layups off of steals. Y'all couldn't get the ball over half-court. You tried dribbling the ball and that was just what we wanted."

"Whatever. This guy killed us, and I didn't have NO help. You still ain't on my level [he said to Jermaine]. You think you can play wit' me?"

Jermaine nodded his head emphatically. Neef waved him off and rolled his eyes.

"I still don't know who *you* are. What's your name?" Neef questioned Ray.

"Ray Webster."

"What school you go to?"

"Thompson. I averaged a quiet sixteen."

"I didn't ask how much *you scored*. You proud of playing for Thompson and only averaging sixteen."

"So, so, I-I told you."

"It ain't like Thompson is shit."

"It's gonna be this year," Jermaine chimed in.

"You didn't even play last year," Neef said, laughing and talking down to Jermaine.

"Yes, I did. I did so play *a* game!" He looked to a friend a few yards away. "Petey, Petey, did I play in *a* game at Thompson?" Petey looked and shook his head "no."

"Petey, I didn't play on JV?" Petey nodded "yes."

"In *a* game? What's *one* game?" Neef asked.

Jermaine shot back, "I played in six games, and they asked me to come up at the end of the year to play varsity."

"You didn't even play varsity."

"Yeah, 'cause I got kicked off, but I was the star on JV. I was cooking them. I dunked in every game."

"You talk about dunks like you just starting dunking," Neef arrogantly blasted Jermaine. "So what if you dunked. You got kicked off varsity for a stupid-ass reason."

"I was fighting. You was ineligible. Who's stupid?" Jermaine shot back.

"I'm not stupid. St. Dom's is a hard school. I had to get used to it; you were just fighting."

"So we won the chip. And we gonna win public [league] this year."

"You gonna win pub[lic] [league]," Neef echoed, dripping with sarcasm.

"Yeah," Ray confirmed.

Hanif had higher status than Ray and Jermaine. He had a basketball history already and had been known since middle school before becoming a young star at St. Dominic's, one of the best basketball teams in the city each year. This gave him the credibility to question the status of others. If he didn't know someone, they weren't known. Jermaine knew Neef because they played at Brown Middle School together, where Neef was the star. Jermaine wasn't a star at Brown and didn't play on varsity at Thompson. Ray played for varsity, but Thompson was a bad team and therefore he would have had to play extraordinarily well to draw even a little attention.

Success Breeds More Success

Even with Hanif's comments, Ray and Jermaine carried confidence into their next year and their performances. Winning the championship brought them more attention and opportunities to play than they had before. They began playing on AAU traveling teams. Travel games at the end of the summer took them out of town to tournaments along the eastern seaboard: Massachusetts, Maryland, New York, Washington, D.C., and to national tournaments in Florida. Playing in other cities and larger tournaments also increased their respect at home. Jermaine commented about how the championship game had created new opportunities.

> "My first AAU team was after Blade Rodgers chip when I got a baseline dunk and I got MVP. Then the AAU coach, named Ken Long, from Philly Ballhawks came and he put me on his team."
>
> "Had you tried to play with him before Blade Rodgers, before this game and your dunk?" I asked.
>
> "Yeah, he said I wasn't good enough. I went to a practice with John-John, so I was playing, and I thought I played good, but he [Ken Long] said he ain't got room. He got his team or whatever.
>
> "So the person I dunked on in the chip was his big man. So once I did that and got MVP, he just told his big man, 'You got to find another team' and took me on [put me on the team]."

Summer and summer ball ended. Playing in Blade Rodgers had exceeded Ray's and Jermaine's hopes. They had won a championship and earned more respect and recognition. The effect was dramatic and set the tone for their next high school year. But they were hoping for more than just momentary success.

Being known and elite required consistency and strong performances against the best high schoolers overall. So far, Jermaine and Ray had only beaten other ninth and tenth graders. Ray had two years and Jermaine had three years left in high school. They were still young and needed to continue building their career portfolios.

15   RAY VS. GREEN

Jermaine and Ray returned to school with confidence, high hopes for success, and having learned a lot. Jermaine's tenth-grade experience was very different from his ninth, when he failed to make Thompson's varsity team. In his tenth-grade year, the seniors had graduated, Bryant transferred to Buddy Strong High School, and Jermaine had the second highest status behind Ray. The problem was that Thompson's team was terrible and did not win a lot of games even when Ray and Jermaine played extremely well. This hurt their chances of becoming elite players, and they were reminded throughout the season that there was always someone better with more status.

The Philadelphia high school basketball scene is fifty-plus schools in three leagues/conferences: a Catholic schools league; the Inter-Academic Athletic Association (Inter-Ac), a conference mix of private and religious-affiliated schools; and the Philadelphia public schools league. One public school has a national reputation and a number of professional ballplayers as alumni and a former coach who also coached at the college level is now in the Basketball Hall of Fame. Other schools have remained at the bottom of the league standings, and their players rarely earn athletic scholarships to college. Thompson is one of these schools, a low-performing public high school, academically and athletically.

I went to Thompson's biggest game of the year to see how my guys would do. The game was played at Carter High School, situated on a slanted corner in neither the worst nor the best part of North Philly. It had a brownstone facade and two entrances, the main entrance and one for students with children needing day care. I entered the front doors with my six-year-old son, and we walked down a hallway looking for the gym.

Though we were inside the school, we had difficulty finding our way to the gym and into the game. Special procedures were in place on game days to assist in crowd control and lessen the probability of fights or violence. In fact, I called the school for information about the game and was told that the game was not open to the public because of the real threat of violence. I had missed an earlier game at Thompson because I heeded this same message, but Jermaine had told me that this was just a deterrent used by all of the public schools. Eventually after walking around and around, we found ourselves back at the front door.

Along the hallway walls were newspaper articles about Ronnie Green, blown up and placed in glass cases. One article stood out, titled "Carter's Green Is the Best Thing Since Wilt." At the beginning of his senior year, Green had broken Wilt Chamberlain's high school scoring record, averaging more than thirty-two points per game for three years. The article compared the two: Wilt Chamberlain, who had held the scoring record for nearly fifty years, since 1955, was seven feet tall in high school. Green is only five feet ten inches tall (this is being generous). Green was a phenomenal talent because of his ability to score, made even more impressive by his small stature.

I figured out where the gym was and avoided a security guard to reach the gym. A well-dressed man in a suit greeted us gruffly and took my money. He ushered us in behind a number of men who appeared to be in their twenties and thirties but blended in with the students on hand to watch the game. They wore baggy jeans, sweat suits, headbands, fitted baseball caps, and team jerseys. Footwear included Timberland boots, Nike, Air Jordan, And 1, Reebok, and Adidas.

My son and I sat in the middle of the bleachers, in the center of what seemed to be the student section. I warned my son that the crowd might be loud and rambunctious. The bleachers were open on one side to limit the fans. They filled quickly. The other side looked disorganized. Fifteen or so chairs per team were put out with an island in between as the scorer's table. The chairs had been carelessly placed on the dingy, dusty floor. After a short while, the teams came out of the locker rooms to begin warming up. I pointed out Ray and Jermaine to my son as they ran by. My son nodded in acknowledgment; he had seen them countless times at practice and during games. They were serious and intense, showing no smiles or expressions as they spoke quietly to teammates and got ready to play. My son commented that they looked mad. It was an important game for them, and they had their game faces on.

The game began and Thompson jumped to an early lead behind Ray's accurate and frequent shooting. Jermaine started slowly, missing a couple of easy shots. The real game, however, was not on the court. Instead, the spectacle was in the stands, where the old heads verbally sparred. The crowd was all black, predominantly high school girls and boys, with a few women and men. Four old heads from South Philly had come to the game, including Marcus. They all knew Ray and Jermaine but seemed only to be there for Ray. Three of them were very conspicuous because they urged him on so loudly. From the moment they entered, they began their campaign. They were not there to simply watch Ray, but to campaign for his respect, promote his reputation, and draw public attention. They yelled and incited the home-team crowd. Marcus did not say much. The Carter High fans around these men were relatively quiet until Ray's old heads really got going. As Ray played better and better, his old heads became more demonstrative.

When Ray had the ball and was guarded by Green, they yelled, "He can't hold you"; "He can't stick you, Ray"; "He ain't got no D [defense]." They stood, pumped fists, and cheered when Ray scored—and he scored a lot. "That's my young bull"; "You the star"; "He don't know you. But he will." They encouraged and criticized Ray's teammates, too, because they wanted to see Thompson beat Carter. This would be a huge upset and could possibly make newspaper headlines in the sports section. Ray would be a star for sure, they hoped.

Ray missed a long shot that was rebounded by one of Carter's taller guys. The ball was passed out quickly to Green, who took two dribbles, looked ahead, and lunged, throwing a one-handed ɔball pass to another Carter player. The ball bounced into the ʾerʾs hands, and he took two steps before leaping and rising quickly to throw the ball through the rim for a dunk. One of Ray's old heads spoke to Jermaine, who was the nearest defender on the play. "Don't let him do that to you—block it next time!" Jermaine threw his hands up and put his head down, angry and embarrassed by the comment. He could not have stopped the play and had done little in the game thus far.

Carter's crowd grew tired of Ray's old heads. One man turned around to ask them, "Who is he?" Two old heads responded, "Ray Webster." The man turned back to the game, faking boredom, "Never heard of 'im." They shot back, "You will. He averages twenty-five a game." Green's old head replied, "Green is the leading scorer in history," and swatted at them, while smirking.

Ray's old heads had talked up Ray, signaling a challenge. Yet it was clear that Green's old heads did not feel threatened by Ray's performance. They questioned who he was because they did not know his name and had not heard of him. Everyone knew Green, but Ray was still a high school nobody at the city level.

Ray's old heads tried to take some air out of the crowd. During a time-out, they reminded Green's supporters of a game Green played one month earlier. One of Ray's old heads asked, "What happened against LeBron James?" Green's leading old head (he talked the most and seemed to be the oldest of his group) shrugged his shoulders and said, "He [LeBron] the best in the country, Ronnie [Green] the best in the state." The discrediting failed. LeBron James was the best in high school, the best amateur in the world, first pick of that year's NBA draft, skipping college altogether. Green and his team got the opportunity to compete against James because of Green's reputation. The game was scheduled and televised locally as a match between the two stars. This was enough to reinforce Green's status.

Carter's crowd began to get more involved, yelling and feeding off the energy of Ray's old heads and his superior play. They urged Green and Carter's team to play better. The game had taken on more significance. Ray was trying to overshadow Green. His old heads were insinuating that Green's reputation was more hype than substance. There was also a territorial issue,

North Philly versus South Philly. I overheard an older man, one of Green's supporters, say to another man, "When they come from downtown, they always get a little full of themselves."

At halftime the score was still relatively close; fewer than twelve points separated the two teams. One kid, who appeared to be a Carter student, said to another kid that he was going to talk to Green. He yelled to Green, "They think other bull is better than you." Green looked up and smirked, looking for who would think this. The kid pointed to Ray's old heads. One of Green's old heads called Green over and said something to him. Green shook his head understandingly and went back to the court to start the second half. The old head looked over to Ray's old heads and said, "Now, we'll see what your young bull got."

It became clear, early on, that this half of the game would be different. Carter began pressing Thompson full court, forcing the ball out of Ray's hands by sending two guys at him and making it very tough for him to score. They stole passes, blocked the shots of Thompson's players, and grabbed rebounds after Ray's teammates missed shots. They got plenty of easy, uncontested baskets. One of Carter's big guys blocked a shot inside, grabbed the ball, and threw it to Green, who was at half-court. Green drove hard to the basket, with only Ray in front of him, and then spun back on his left foot, flipping the ball up and over the rim with his left hand. Some of his old heads and the crowd jumped up and clapped their hands. Green stopped and looked up at Ray's old heads and stared them down, letting them know that he was now playing to embarrass them. Ray came right back, with a quick dribble move and jump shot. *Swish!* He made the basket and his old heads stood up, all but Marcus, slapped high fives, and yelled praise to Ray. Quickly, a Carter player took the ball out of the net and threw a long pass. Green had leaked out, running toward the opposite basket. Green tracked down the long pass and dribbled three or four times, gathering his legs under him and dunking the ball with two hands! Again, he looked over to the corner where Ray's old heads sat. He raised his right hand to his left shoulder and then quickly swiped it across his throat, as though he was cutting his throat. The gesture meant that the contest was over. The crowd roared. One of Green's old heads looked over to Ray's guys and put a finger over his mouth, shushing them. Green drove to the basket again and was fouled while shooting the ball and making the basket. Someone in the crowd shouted, "He shootin'. Made you look." Others in the crowd adopted the phrase, since it was the chorus of a current hit rap song, and they kept it going for a few choruses.[1]

Carter's lead over Thompson grew quickly to twenty points. Green had responded to the call of his old heads. He scored in bunches and ended the game with twenty-nine points. Thompson lost the game; they were clearly overmatched. Still, Ray was the game's leading scorer with thirty-seven points. Even Green's old heads acknowledged this.

After the game, one of Ray's old heads made his way down the bleachers and approached Green's old heads. They shook hands and talked a little about the game. Ray's old head mentioned that Ray was Marcus's young bull. "You [re]member Marcus Jones, from Strong [High School]." Green's old head responded, "Yeah," and the man pointed to Marcus, who nodded his head to identify himself. Green's old head commented on Ray.

> "I like him, I'm gonna look for him. What grade he in?"
> "Eleventh. He going D1 [Division 1, the highest competitive level in collegiate athletics]."
> "D1?"
> "D1."
> "You better take him outta *that* school. Ain't nobody gonna recruit him from *Thompson*."
> "I got connections."
> Another person said, "I heard that! He [Ray's old head] said he got connections to get him into D1."
> "You better get on it then. I want him to do good. I'm gonna look for him."

Even though Ray had played well, Green's old heads and supporters questioned Ray's status, in relation to Green. Ray had been listed in the public league's midseason rankings as one of the best juniors in the city. Yet Green's old heads had not heard of Ray before this game. Thompson High and Ray were a non-threat because Green's status exceeded Ray's and Carter was the best team in the city, while Thompson stunk. The game was important for Thompson but not important for Carter. Carter's crowd came to see a show, but they did not take Ray and Thompson seriously. In this light, Green's old head could sincerely give praise for Ray's performance because Ray was relatively "unknown" and good basketball players are always something to watch, no matter what part of the city they come from.

The game and individual performances were overshadowed by the interaction of the crowd and the old heads. Ray needed the help of his old heads because Thompson was an underdog and Ray was relatively unknown outside his neighborhood. His old heads acted as public relations representatives, working to create a buzz around his name.[2] They supported him and campaigned for him in hostile territory. They had sacrificed and taken off early from work to follow him to this game. They also risked a potential fight by urging Ray loudly in the midst of a partisan crowd. Their actions were necessary because Ray's scoring was not enough, and people needed to know Ray's name for him to become known. Their talking and instigating made him and his performance memorable. They also provided information and statistics to validate their claims about Ray's ability. Ray had impressed some, and hopefully Green's old heads and students at Carter High would talk about Ray later, increasing his recognition and publicity. Jermaine, on the other hand, had gained little with no old-head support.

16 PLAYING EVERYWHERE

Thompson's season ended without much fanfare. The team won only five games and did not make the playoffs. Ray's scoring output against Green was a great accomplishment. However, nothing was written about the game, and Ray's performance gained little public attention. At the end of the year, he was only named to the Third Team All-Public (and citywide honorable mention) after being the league's second leading scorer. Still, Ray had "given" (scored) Carter High and Green thirty-seven points and could list this on his growing basketball résumé. More than anything, Ray's confidence grew even more, and he used the Carter game as validation that he had improved and could play against the best high schoolers at all grade levels.

Jermaine ended the season as Thompson's leader in rebounding and second leader in scoring and minutes per game behind Ray. But he painfully recounted feeling less recognized than Ray and that he had been treated unfairly. The old heads paid a lot of attention to Ray and Marcus Jr., who played well at a Catholic school. Jermaine said the old heads that went to Thompson's games only cheered for Ray and often blamed him when the team lost. Ray was the team's star and was beyond criticism.

Their high school season was over and something was missing. Ray and Jermaine would need to continue to improve; play on a better team and for traveling teams, where competition is stiffer as a whole; and play in front of scouts and recruiters. As other coaches learned about their abilities following our championship and their junior and sophomore seasons at Thompson, Ray and Jermaine were asked to play on more teams. At times they found themselves in a quandary because they were on multiple teams and had to manage an all-year basketball career. They played in gyms and on asphalt playgrounds. They were on their high school's team, bandit league teams, Blade Rodgers, and traveling teams. They traveled from game to game via trains and buses, walking, and getting rides from friends' parents and me.

Which game would Ray and Jermaine attend if two games were scheduled at the same time? Both of them made decisions based upon the advice of their growing support networks (which sometimes created conflict), their goals of getting known, and their understanding of what it would take to gain more publicity, buzz, and attention. They considered exposure—where they were playing and for whom (team), with whom (teammates and competitors), and in front of whom (audience) they were playing—and opportunity: how much they would play and how well they might do (see appendix 2). These were not independent factors. The exposure and opportunity that each team or game might bring added to the possibility of building their reputations and stories beyond their neighborhood.

Playing AAU Ball

Two of Chuck's former players, Alvin and Bobby, started a high school AAU team that traveled to tournaments on the East Coast that spring. Ray and Jermaine (and Keith) attended a number of tournaments around the region with Alvin and Bobby's team. Alvin reported on Ray's showing after a tournament in New Jersey. "He showed his *ass* [played well]. They couldn't stick him. He was killing; he went for like twenty-five [points] a game." Ray had played well against known players outside of the city, and Alvin believed that Ray could earn a scholarship if he continued to play well. Jermaine did not stand out as much but bragged about playing for the team because they had a sneaker contract (an exclusivity deal that ensured that the team would only wear the company's apparel and shoes). These were signs of their upward mobility in the basketball ranks, as well as their expanding networks.

Bobby and Alvin are young black males. Bobby is Keith's uncle. He loved coaching basketball and got a thrill from helping kids improve and seeing them thrive. He worked at a local high school as a NTA (non-teaching assistant), which meant that he acted as a male figure providing guidance, counseling, and security. He especially helped young men who were having trouble in school.

Alvin was a basketball entrepreneur. He used his networks to create a three-tiered system made up of his and Bobby's AAU team, our Blade Rodgers team, and St. Dominic's high school team. Alvin volunteered with his high school alma mater, St. Dominic's, and acted as a scout and recruiter. He attended middle school basketball games and tournaments and spoke with kids about attending the high school. Later he started the AAU traveling team to give select kids an opportunity to play outside of school. The team was essentially a recruiting class for the school—containing all of Alvin's recruits and whomever else the school's coach was interested in. Consequently, Alvin could watch the kids play closely and assess their ability. The high level of competition and practices prepared younger players for high school. His efforts might eventually help him to become a high school or college coach. When the AAU team won games, he was perceived as a great coach and coordinator for organizing the team and bringing all of the players together. When St. Dominic's had success, he was praised for his recruiting. He was developing relationships with good players, and using and expanding his networks and influence.

Our relationship with Alvin was mutually beneficial. He found and brought us good, younger players (usually eighth graders). We trained them and "broke them down," and he observed their play with us and with his AAU team before passing them to St. Dominic's coaching staff.

The feather in Alvin's cap, in terms of recruiting players, was his relationship with a shoe and apparel company. Alvin would talk to the young players about the sneakers and jerseys that the team got.[1] This excited kids and was a huge incentive. The sneakers were "testers," "exclusives," and "unreleased" merchandise. Testers are "concept" shoes that a sneaker company has developed but not mass-produced. Select athletes are given the shoes to wear, "test," and then give feedback on whether or not the shoe is good and will sell. Exclusives are shoes that are produced in limited number and are therefore hard to find and are priced higher (simple supply and demand). These shoes typically will be made of some special material, such as patent leather instead of the typical rawhide leather, or made in some special color(s). Unreleased shoes are shoes that are not yet available in stores. As a result, kids who wear them before they are released help to build the anticipation and increase the demand. Of course, only special kids can wear shoes that few others have and before others can buy them. This carries high status, particularly when the kids and their peers are poor but live in a society where clothes and other material goods are used as status symbols.

AAU basketball is considered essential for those players who want to *look* known. But it did something else too. AAU play is part of the regional and national recruiting machine. College coaches go to AAU tournaments to see players in centralized places. Players go to tournaments to gain exposure, to be seen by college coaches, and to be ranked by scouts. There are countless tournaments that vary in size, numbers, quality of participating teams, and prestige. There are three major sneaker companies—Nike, Adidas, and Reebok—that dominate the AAU scene by sponsoring teams and running most of the biggest tournaments. They make money by selling apparel and shoes, and from gate revenues. Most importantly, college coaches attend the big tournaments and buy programs for as much as $200. The program includes team pictures, rosters (with name, height, position, and jersey number), personal profiles, and interviews of the best players.

I attended an August tournament in Las Vegas to see Jermaine play and watch the AAU action. There were three national high school tournaments on this particular weekend, with hundreds of teams from across the country. They were ranked and put into categories based upon skill level. Jermaine's team was in one of the highest divisions and playing in a Reebok-sponsored tournament.[2] Nike and Adidas had tournaments going on at the same time. One of Jermaine's teammates was playing in two tournaments, although he traveled with Jermaine's team to the Reebok tournament. Reebok's tournament was hosted by seven area high schools with games played from 9 a.m. to 9 p.m.

I went to a few games at the main site, a new, large suburban high school. The school was several one-story buildings sprawled across a few acres with two modern gyms. Each gym had a snack bar, with high bleachers on both sides and large digital score clocks on the far walls. I went to one of the ticket windows to purchase a ticket. "Admission $5" was written in ink on white paper. I watched Jermaine's team play and then chatted with coaches from Temple, Drexel, and La Salle afterward. They were present at a game between a Philly team and a team from the Midwest. They could see non-Philly players and Philly players they had seen many times. It was an ideal event for making player comparisons and evaluations because players (and teams) are ranked and matched against each other in order to provide a good show and true test of ability.

International Ballers

In spring, just months after their high school season, Jermaine and Ray got the opportunity to join another traveling team that brought even more exposure and attention. Jermaine called me one evening with very exciting news.

> "I'm going to Italy, Scott," Jermaine said.
> "Italy?" I asked in total amazement.
> "Yeah," he said coolly.
> "How you gonna do that?" I asked.
> "You know Steve Adams?" he said.
> "Yeah, he played for Green University," I answered.
> "And in Italy. He got a junior team he taking to Italy," he said.
> "How'd you get on the team?" I asked.
> "He saw me play and thought I was nice," he said with enormous pride.

"But how'd he see you play?" I asked.

"Alvin knew him, and he took us, me and Ray, and a few other bulls down where the team was practicing. We was just supposed to be scrimmaging, but me and Ray was killing them. So he asked if we wanted to play for him. He gonna get us summer jobs, tutoring, and sneaks!"

Ray and Jermaine played their way on to Steve Adams's team, upstaging some of his selected players. They began practicing with Adams's team, and their families had to cover the passport application fee and get the necessary paperwork together for the trip. They also missed the last two weeks of school. Upon his return, Jermaine told me about the trip.

"How did you do?" I asked.

"I did cool. I was killing them, Scott," he said, and then continued, "They asked me if I wanted to stay there. They was loving me! I was rebounding, and I got some nasty dunks on some big bulls. After the game, kids was asking me for autographs. It felt like I was a superstar."

"Did you all have jerseys?" I asked.

"Yeah, home and away [jerseys in different colors to easily distinguish one team from another]; they was hot [nice looking]. We got to keep our warm-up shirts. And we got And 1s [a brand of basketball shoes]."

Regardless of whether Jermaine and Ray would continue to be successful in basketball, this trip had expanded their world. They could say that they had traveled overseas to play basketball. They were talented enough to play outside their neighborhood, playground, and school with other good players throughout the city. Someone outside their local world, respected in the basketball community, had been impressed by their play and asked them to join his traveling team. Moreover, Ray and Jermaine were given a paid summer job opportunity (as day-camp counselors) as part of playing for this team, and the *Daily News* wrote a story about Steve Adams and the team's experience.

This was rewarding and something to be proud of. The jerseys, shorts, T-shirts, and basketball shoes were tangible proof of how far their status had risen as well. Ray's grandma Erica and Jermaine's mom, Monica, organized a "welcome back" block party to recognize their achievement; blocking off the street, they barbecued and had music blasting.

17 CAN'T LOOK POOR

Life didn't just change in terms of school and basketball for Ray and Jermaine. They believed that they were becoming stars, and non-basketball activities became very important in how they lived up to this identity. They developed certain expectations for how others should treat them and how they should present themselves. Known players were not simply playing ball and being "good kids"; they were also local celebrities and should act and look the part. How they approached school, dating, and dress became important in their quest for being elite players.

Jermaine had earned a 1.8 GPA for his freshman year but said to me, "I'm really smart, Scott. I just don't do my homework, and so I get B's and C's mostly." I responded, "That's the dumbest thing you could say to me. A smart person doesn't say stupid things like that." B's and C's didn't equate to a 1.8 GPA, so he wasn't completely honest with me. He told me that he would turn it around the next year, and his first-semester sophomore report card was dramatically improved. He earned a 3.7 GPA, mostly A's and a couple of B's. The city gave him a low-income student fellowship, and he got bus tokens each month and a cash prize.

Jermaine's success in basketball was the main impetus for his academic achievement change as he began to believe that he might be in a position to earn a college scholarship. He considered what Chuck and I told him—that his grades could make the difference between going to college and having to stay at home and find a job. His mother's feelings also motivated him.

I messed up my freshman year and went to summer school for math. My ninth-grade year, I failed one class. I was a C, B student (otherwise). But my sophomore year, I improved a lot. I mean, I started doing more work. I started knowing how much it really meant, and how much I [had] disappointed my mom. 'Cause she wanted me to get good grades, and now it was making her happy. Like she knew I could play basketball, but she wanted the books too. She wanted the diploma, and she didn't ever want me to not graduate on time. So that pushed me more, 'cause I felt like I was hurting her or whatever and she was getting mad. And she stopped believing in me or whatever, and she didn't think I was going to achieve.

Jermaine found joy in making his mom happy and living up to her hopes and expectations. He earned the highest GPA on Thompson's team but admitted that he had less fun in class because most of his peers weren't as focused. He also grew to lose respect for teachers who seemed to have little faith in students' ability or who were not clear in their instructions and grading. His change made him more critical of the low quality of education he received at Thompson. Jermaine maintained his focus through the year, but his GPA suffered when he missed the last two weeks of school to play basketball in Italy.

Conversely, Ray had made very little improvement academically. Although he did not fail courses, he was satisfied with C's and doing just enough to remain academically eligible to play. He entered a serious relationship and was teased when he spent "paper" (money) on a ring. "She's my heart, my boo; and what my boo wants, my boo gets," he said. The relationship was short-lived though. Ray talked about having a great number of young women chasing him and wanting to "give" him sex. Ray also shared stories of receiving oral sex and engaging in other sexual activities at school. He became "the man" and a self-proclaimed "pimp," managing sexual relationships with multiple young women all at once, and even receiving money and gifts in exchange for his time and attention.

Jermaine, on the other hand, began a relationship during his freshman year that lasted three years, with some breakups due to immaturity and silly spats. For one anniversary, Jermaine took his girlfriend out to dinner at a Chinese restaurant. On another occasion he bought her a name-brand jacket. He liked having a "wifie," or serious girlfriend, and expressed that "smuts" and "hos" were just good for one thing—sex. He held on to the sense of stability that a long-term relationship guaranteed and the feeling of belonging, being loved, supported, and encouraged faithfully. Of course, he did not have to reciprocate his girlfriend's fidelity. As he explained, he was a young man with desires and needs, plus a lot of opportunities. He felt that he was still a good boyfriend because he bought her things and never intended to leave her. The other girls that he "messed with" were "just sex."

Ray and Jermaine felt successful because they got more attention from young women. Jermaine summed this up: "I ain't even gonna lie to you, Scott. It's been pretty nice. More girls talk to me; I got more pub [public recognition] and juice [status and attention] now." They began to receive elite treatment as a result of all the public recognition they got for being good basketball players.[1]

Jermaine and Ray also dressed with special effort to look like they had money or were "making" it. Ray explained, "You can't look poor, Scott. It's not cool." I asked Clarence, a ninth grader who played for our team, why he spent so much money on clothes and why he bought his particular clothes. "Because it's cool," he told me. Another kid reiterated Ray's point, "to look like you got money"; and a fourth claimed, "Girls like it [for boys to dress well]." Dressing was for others; it created the impression of success and wealth. Dressing, like dating, had a social value. People paid attention to how the ballplayers dressed, and this affected how others treated them and thought about them.

Dress and basketball status were complementary and symbols of manhood. Ray explained that young men who dressed well could "get" girls. I asked him if being a ballplayer was enough. Could a ballplayer who didn't dress well "get girls"? He and Jermaine laughed, and Ray said, "No." They laughed about a high school teammate who wore the same jacket and old-looking sneakers every day. "He don't get no girls, Scott," Ray said. In a sense, dressing and getting girls were part of being a good ballplayer, and dressing poorly and not being able to attract girls lessened one's status as an athlete and young man.[2] This is not to say that one could dress well and therefore increase his status as a ballplayer; but it could operate the other way—dressing poorly could hurt the impressions made on others. People were not concerned with whether or not the impression was real—is a kid really rich when he wears $500 outfits? But there is an association that is made. Girls wanted boys who looked good, like they cared about themselves, because it gave the impression that they were more successful or would be in the future.

"I'm Rich, for a Kid"

Poverty in South Philly doesn't mean that the kids don't have anything, but most don't have much. I often took notice of what kids wore because they spent a good amount of time talking about shoes, clothes, and materialism.

Fifteen-year-old Clarence was noteworthy for dressing en vogue and expensively. He was an only child living with his elderly grandmother in a dangerous low-income housing project. His mother had passed away a few years earlier, and he had never known his father. Details of his mother's death were never given, but his friends said she left Clarence some insurance money when she died. Clarence was given allotments from this pot of money, which he used to buy clothes and elevate his social status. He described himself as wealthy in a conversation with Ray and me.

> "He gay, Scott," Ray said, referring to a pair of white non-athletic socks that Clarence was wearing. "He always be wearing them gay socks. Look at them [the socks read 'I ♥ me']. Why you buy them socks?"
>
> "Because they cost three dollars," Clarence replied, as though paying more for socks made them worth the price.
>
> "Three dollars! That's why you gay. I don't spend more than a dollar fifty for socks."

"That's because I'm wealthier than you," Clarence shot back at Ray.

"Wealthy? You ain't wealthy," I interjected. "How are you wealthy, if you're dependent upon people for money?"

"I mean for my age. I'm wealthy to be young. I'm rich for a kid."

Clarence believed that money spent on clothing was a sign of wealth. Ray was critical of Clarence's socks, but his remark was not to be taken literally. Ray did not question Clarence's sexuality, although it was clearly a derogatory and feminizing remark. If meant literally, being called "gay" was worth fighting over. Ray meant that Clarence was wrong for wearing socks that looked like girl socks—they had a heart on them—and that cost so much money. Ray was appealing to group norms. Again, Clarence was not just dressing for himself. He thought about the social worth of items and how they could add to his identity and appearance of being wealthy. Socks may not add much to his image, but spending money did.

There was a hierarchy and perceived social value associated with specific clothing items. Wearing an athletic jersey was more important than socks, although wearing certain brand-name socks such as Air Jordan or NBA logo socks was very popular and status increasing. Likewise, Clarence had a jersey collection that was also proof of his "wealth" and showed that he knew *what* to wear. At one practice, he said that the jersey he was wearing cost him $95. It was a Steve "Franchise" Francis Houston Rocket (basketball team) jersey. On another day, he wore a Brett Favre (an all-star football quarterback) jersey, which he said cost only $40 or $50. But Clarence's pride and joy was a Darius Miles Los Angeles Clippers (basketball team) authentic jersey. He paid $150 for this jersey. It was an item that really meant something to him because of its cost and the popularity of Darius Miles at the time. Darius Miles jerseys were one of the top-three professional basketball jerseys sold that year.

Clarence's jersey collection ran the gamut: replica, swing-man, authentic, and throwback, and retro jerseys. The list is in order of cost, a sliding scale from about fifty dollars upward. Replica jerseys are simply copies and can be copies of all the other types of jerseys. They are cheaply made in terms of type and quality of material and the craftsmanship and stitching. Swingmans differ from the higher-end jerseys primarily in aesthetics. More creativity is used to produce new styles and even color schemes with the goal of drawing attention. Authentic means that it is made to the specifications of a professional jersey and that the manufacturer is an official manufacturer of the jersey. Companies pay handsome fees to have exclusive rights as the official manufacturer of NBA merchandise—and this is passed on to the buyer. For example, if Adidas is the official maker of NBA apparel, then jerseys made by Nike can only be replicas or swingmans, because Adidas is the only maker licensed to make authentic jerseys that players wear in games for a contracted period. Retro jerseys are made for existing teams but in a previous, no longer current, style. Throwback jerseys are "only a throwback if the team no longer exists" (as explained by rap artist Nore on MTV's 2003 hip-hop fashion show). The distinctions are sometimes very subtle and vague, but one is assured of understanding the difference between a replica, swingman, and the top tier by price. This helped Clarence to look rich and "like he had money."

What's Hot

I learned a lot when I went shopping with Jermaine and Ray. They talked about what they wanted, how they were going to get what they wanted, and made references to how they became aware of the items. They asked questions about fashion as part of our bonding. Had I seen the pair of shoes T-Mac wore during the All-Star Game, or did I see Cam's (Cam'ron, a rapper) sweat suit in a music video, or had I seen the new Kobes? They looked in shoe-centered magazines, such as *Hoop* magazine's "Kicks" edition, or basketball and sports magazine pictures and advertisements or on television.

"Yo, I can't wait. I'm getting money September first for school clothes; I'm getting new Air Force Unos," said Ray.

"What?" I asked.

"Air Force Unos . . . Air Force Ones, Scott."

"I'm stomping in my Air Force Ones," Ray and Jermaine recited in unison, laughing [this is the chorus to a rap song by Nelly about the shoe].

"My moms is giving me three hundred for school shopping, but I got to wait until September fifth," added Jermaine.

"Air Force Ones," by St. Louis native and rapper Nelly, was a cultural anthem that highlighted what people were doing who affiliated themselves with hip-hop culture. They stomped (or danced and walked) in their Air Force Ones, a Nike shoe. The Air Force One, which was manufactured, marketed, and sold first in 1981, has had a particularly strong renaissance. Kids began wearing outdated or "retro" shoes at least a year or two prior to Nelly's song. The retro trend really picked up speed in 2003–2004 when other shoe companies like Adidas, Puma, Converse, and Reebok followed suit and re-released or reintroduced old-model shoes. In fact, some of the Air Force Ones sported an embroidered "20th" in commemoration of its twentieth anniversary. Nelly's video for this song did more than show Nikes. The video served also as a fashion show, showing what the rich wear. Nelly, his partners, and some celebrities were wearing rare throwback athletic jerseys and custom-made jerseys with matching baseball hats and Air Force Ones.[3] The song talked about the variety and number of Air Force Ones that Nelly and the other celebrities buy, illustrating their wealth and social position. They could afford to buy multiple pairs of Air Force Ones to match rare and expensive jerseys and hats.

One afternoon Jermaine, Ray, and I went into a very popular sports apparel store. Mitchell & Ness is a Philadelphia-based company, nationally and internationally known for its production and stock of jerseys and other sport merchandise. It specializes in retro and throwback jerseys priced from about $150 to $600, depending upon the rarity and historical significance of the

jersey. We shopped for a while and then left. On our way back to
their homes, Ray talked about what he would buy.

"When the season starts, I'm getting some authentic jahns,
some shorts," Ray said.

"They cost a hundred dollars!" I responded.

"I don't care, I'm getting them jahns to practice in."

"You probably going to get the Sixers ones, so you can mess
them up. 'Cause he don't like the Sixers and he always be fall-
ing on his butt," Jermaine added.

"But when I fall, it'll be *authentic*." (Jermaine said "authentic" with Ray.)

"I want that authentic AI [Allen Iverson] jahn," Jermaine
chimed in. "It's three-fifty [$350], though. I'd probably have
to save up my paychecks for a year. I don't care, though. I like
that old Phillies [baseball team] one too."

"That's not authentic, though," Ray said critically.

"What you talking about? It's a throwback. So you telling
me this is not authentic?" Jermaine asked, pulling on the Sixers warm-up shirt that he had on.

"It's not authentic. It's not the one they wear in the game,"
Ray shot back.

I intervened. "Authentic means that it's the same jersey
that a professional might wear, but it's made to be sold."

"I want game worn. I want their sweat on my sweat," Ray
said, as though dreaming.

"See he gay, Scott," Jermaine said with excitement, happy
to call Ray out.

Ray clarified, "Nah, I just want they magic. Paul Pierce [an
all-star player for the Boston Celtics] magic, like *aaahhh* [pre-
tending to take a shot]."

The allure of Mitchell & Ness is the fantasy turned reality of looking or wearing authentic sports merchandise. Ray and Jermaine
may emulate their favorite player's moves on the playground
or even in high school, but to wear the same or very nearly the
same jersey as their favorite player is closer to living the dream
of being a professional.[4] Of course, this came with a big price

tag, and although they dressed well enough to avoid criticism, they didn't always get what they wanted.

It's Tough Not Looking Poor

I was hanging with Ray and Jermaine at Espy one summer afternoon, teaching them shooting and ball-handling drills. After the workout Ray told me that he was excited because he was going to buy some new sneaks that day. I asked him what he was going to buy, and he said, "I don't know. Maybe the Ray Allens or the new AIs. It depends if they still on sale. If they on sale, I might be able to buy two of them jahns [pairs of shoes]." He added that he was waiting for his grandmother to get home because she was giving him the money and then he was going to the store. He also asked if I could take him to the store since I had a car. Otherwise, he would have to walk or take the bus. I told him I would take him because I wanted to see what he would get.

We headed back to Ray's house, and when we arrived, Jermaine and I stayed outside and waited as Ray went inside to see if his grandmother was home. He was in the house for about ten minutes, and then he opened the door and told me that his grandmother wanted to speak with me. I was confused—what did she want with me? I had met her and chatted with her several times but had never been asked to come in and talk. Our conversations had always been in passing as I picked up Ray and Jermaine to drive them to and from games and practice.

I entered the dark apartment. It was a hot day, and all of the shades and curtains were drawn to keep the room cool. There were things scattered on the floor and coffee table, but this was expected for a small one-bedroom apartment housing three persons, two of whom were high schoolers. Ray's grandmother, dressed in denim shorts and a white tank top, was sitting on a sofa chair, fanning herself. She had sweat beads on her forehead and looked serious. I took a seat on the couch next to Ray, who seemed distant and depressed. He did not look at me, and his face was emotionless and drawn. It was clear that something was wrong.

Ray's grandmother, Erica, began by asking me if I wanted to buy some flowers. She told Ray to grab one of her arrangements. "I make these myself. This one is thirty dollars, that one is forty dollars, and I can make a special one for you if you want different colors." I was really confused and looked at her sideways, with my neck drawn back, raised eyebrows, and a curled lip. She explained to me that she had promised Ray $60 so that he could buy new shoes. Erica wanted to do something nice for Ray because she felt that he had been working hard in school and needed something to keep his spirits up. Her promise to Ray was dependent upon her getting paid for making floral arrangements. This was a side job, since she was on disability and receiving government assistance. Erica had expected to have the money, but other people didn't come through.

Erica had gone to one of the local hospitals a few days earlier to deliver an arrangement to a patient. While there she met two other persons who asked her to make something for their loved ones in the hospital. She gave them a price and said she would bring the arrangements in a few days. She made her arrangements and went to the hospital to collect payment. The first client had forgotten about their interaction but said that she could write a check. But Erica would not accept a check because it could bounce and cashing the check required a separate trip to a bank, standing in line, and so on. The second client complained that the price was too steep and that he could not afford the arrangement, after agreeing to it initially. Erica was upset. She had not only made a promise to Ray; she had also taken the time to buy supplies, make the arrangements, and had incurred expenses. She had paid for the supplies up front, had used gas to drive to the hospital, and had to pay for parking. Erica had done all of this and come home empty-handed to her grandson. I bought a small arrangement, but it was not enough to make up for the total loss, so Ray could not get new sneakers on that day.

Families worked together at not looking poor. Ray and Jermaine sometimes received large sums of money to spend as they wished. The source and ways to get money varied. Money came from their moms and grandparents or other extended family members and old heads. Money was given to them for birthday gifts and playing well, for getting good grades, for back-to-school shopping and because a mother or grandmother got "her check" (usually meaning for disability, unemployment, or child support). There was a mutual benefit. Monica, Erica, and Tamika, when they could, felt good about providing the funds for clothes. Good parents took care of their kids and were better than those parents who had kids that looked poor.[5] Ray and Jermaine also felt better about themselves because they looked good and *not poor*.

Poverty is not simply economics. It is a way of life, an identity, and a stigma affecting individuals' social experiences, sense of self, and interaction. Looking poor is negative reinforcement. Jermaine and Ray were not simply playing basketball; they were becoming basketball players. This identity worked against feeling poor; and success with young women and looking rich were parts of this effort.

18 IMPLOSION

Blade Rodgers League began again in June, and I looked forward to defending our championship. One year older, Jermaine and Bryant would be our stars on the ninth- and tenth-grade team. They would double up and play on the eleventh- and twelfth-grade team with Ray and Keith, who were eleventh graders. This was an award, allowing them to play up, and it gave them more time, more exposure. But things did not go as planned. Chuck liked having players with "dog" in them, but sometimes they didn't just bark, they bit, hurting everyone around them. The team struggled to blend individual goals with team goals. Chuck and I expected more loyalty and deference as a sign of respect and trust. Our guys expected a lot too. They were eager to play and perform, showing others that the chip was not a fluke, and expected us to be less critical and more tolerant of their mistakes.

Chuck essentially gave me the reins for the ninth- and tenth-grade team. He didn't always come to the games, and when he did, he was late, often missing the whole first half. He didn't tell me that he was going to do this, nor did we talk about it. He said later that this was intentional. It was a sign of his trust in me, and it gave me a chance to "pay some dues" as a coach. It was a shock initially, and I would look around the gym for Chuck, waiting for him to come and take over. He joked, "I'd be hiding in a corner, and you'd look up and say, 'Chuck, get down here.' Like, '*Get your ass* down here. Come help me with these niggas.'" I felt like some substitute teachers feel—temporary, half prepared, and only partially effective. The game was very different from the head-coach position, and I could not juggle all the tasks and relationships. There were referees, parents, and the table staff, who kept score, kept track of the number of fouls and time-outs, and managed the game clock. I focused primarily on my players and what they were doing and not doing, using time-outs to try to keep control. I didn't pay attention to whether or not the score was correct or question referees, but my players and their parents did. They would yell to me, "Coach, Coach, the score. They got the wrong score." I'd tell my players to stop worrying about the score and refs. "Don't worry about them. Worry about what you're doing. If we do what we're supposed to, that stuff doesn't matter." Our play was inconsistent, and we won and lost. My control was fragile without Chuck. I had conflict with players, even when the team won.

During one game, Jermaine and Jamal complained about not getting the ball enough and being pulled from the game. We were playing in the "big gym," with a large crowd and an announcer. We were up against a weak team, but the score was close because we were playing poorly. On consecutive plays, Jamal, our biggest and strongest player, shot long shots and missed badly after I yelled for him not to shoot. I took him out of the game because he did not listen and wanted to do his own thing. Then Jermaine did the same. He handled the ball outside, trying to dribble past smaller defenders, rather than posting up. He lost the ball. So I took him out too. Both walked by me and, in frustration, said something about not being able to play freely and hating our team. This was their way of cursing me out. Bryant played well down the stretch, and we won the game with them sitting and pouting on the bench. After having the players shake their opponents' hands, I directed the team to our makeshift locker room, which was a public bathroom. The guys handed in their dirty uniforms, and we had our usual postgame talk, where each player had the chance to talk about the game and what we could do to improve. The normal things were said: "We didn't rebound"; "We didn't play defense"; "We didn't pass the ball"; and so on.

In contrast, Jamal spoke about hating "this," being taken out of the game and being told not to shoot. He was concerned about his playing time and spoke for a while about my coaching.

"This ain't fun," he said. "I'm not coming back. You always take me out for shooting. Fuck this!"

I raised my voice to Jamal after he cursed.

"Good. Give me my jersey and *get the fuck out!*"

He would not go. He changed out of the uniform slowly in rebellion. In anger, responding to his rejecting my authority, I picked up Jamal's athletic bag and tossed it out of our locker room.

"GET OUT!"

Jamal stood tall and looked me up and down, sizing me up, as though he wanted to fight. I walked up to him, showing him I was not afraid, daring him to do something.

I threatened him, "I'm a grown-ass man with a wife and kids. I ain't gonna fight fair."

Jamal knew that I was serious; I rarely yelled, let alone cursed. He stared into my eyes further before gathering the rest of his stuff and leaving. "Fuck this shit, y'all ain't gonna win *shit* without me," he said as the door closed.

Before I could catch my breath, Jermaine started. "I don't understand why I don't get more plays."

With adrenaline still pumping, I started in on Jermaine. "You don't get the ball because you don't grab any rebounds, and you can't move without the ball. There's nobody who can stop you, but you keep thinking you need to handle the ball and drive on everybody, rather than dominating the boards and getting put-backs; you bigger than everybody out there."

Jermaine responded, "Man, I'm tired of this. I'm always wrong! You guys always telling me different shit! You tell me to help out whoever handling the ball, but then when I do, you tell me I shouldn't drive or shoot. This is bullshit."

"First of all, that's not what I said. But you can go too! We don't need *no* players who think that this is all about them. This is a team game. This ain't the playground."

"All right. You don't need me? You don't need me, huh, Scott," he said, nodding his head slowly with one corner of his mouth turned up. He seemed to be plotting, thinking that he was better off without us and that we would surely need him. Then, with his head held high, he said, "This is bullshit. I quit!" And he threw the jersey on the ground in the pile with the other jerseys.

"GO! Get out!" I replied, shaking my head in disgust.

Jermaine gathered his stuff quickly, looking at me every so often, as though he had something else to get off his chest, but he just shook his head. He left with tight lips and his shoulders lifted, carrying his rage as he stormed out.

This whole ordeal reminded me of the confrontation with Aaron years earlier, but Aaron had talked to me after the game, keeping it between the two of us. Jamal and Jermaine were challenging me in front of the team. They felt that I had disrespected them by taking them out of the game, telling them what they had done wrong, and suggesting that the team did not need them. Determining who played and correcting players is part of my job as a coach. Telling them that they were dispensable was necessary to reinforcing the team orientation. They were part of the team, and not the other way around; we were not simply a part of their individual game. They could not talk to me as though I was one of their friends—someone of equal or lower status. I was the authority, knew what I was doing, and could demand respect from or reject a player, kicking them off the team. We were playing by the same rules—respect—but I had power and would not risk having other players speak to me that way because they had seen Jamal and Jermaine do it. Nor was I willing to ignore Jamal's stepping up to me. I would not put it past some young men to "sneak me" and hit me while I was not looking or paying attention. Fighting was a real possibility because so much was at stake. I had to be on guard and defensive. I was wrong for daring Jamal to fight, but if I had responded differently, he easily could have believed that I was afraid of him and would most likely have fought me in an attempt to gain respect from his peers, since he did not defer to my status as the coach. Besides, how would Chuck and others see me? I had to take the possibility of fighting more seriously than Jamal because he could come and go. I was in a more permanent position as the assistant coach, and losing a fight to a young man, regardless of his size, would have been seen by others as a major weakness.

What disturbed me most about Jermaine's behavior was that he and I had a close relationship. I expected him to have respect for me and show it in public. I could have had a conversation about his not getting enough touches, opportunities to score, but not in the wake of dealing with Jamal. Jermaine's statement showed no tact and considerable selfishness, which I had to address because I had just accused Jamal of this. I had to remain consistent in order to continue to be seen as a legitimate authority with the other players. There were rules and boundaries, from which no player was exempt.

Our postgame talk ended quickly; the other players seemed stunned. I went and sat outside on a bench with TD and some other men. Jamal found me and apologized. It was clear that someone had talked to him, probably TD, and told him to make amends. I accepted apathetically. I had to be an adult and bigger than him, but I didn't want to be; little time had passed, and I knew that he would continue to be trouble. (I was right. Jamal quit two games later.)

Later that night Chuck brought Jermaine and me together to clear the air. Jermaine had quit the ninth- and tenth-grade team, and so his status with the eleventh- and twelfth-grade team was up in the air, plus he and I weren't talking. I could affect Jermaine's basketball career. I controlled how much he played on my team and could even hurt his opportunities with the eleventh- and twelfth-grade team and even other teams by telling coaches about his behavior. Chuck asked Jermaine what had happened, and Jermaine spoke of his role confusion. Why didn't he get the ball more, and why did Chuck and I criticize him so often? Chuck remained soft-spoken but firm, to avoid further escalation.

We ask you to do a lot of things. You supposed to be the leader. You've been with us for what? Two years? You know our stuff. You won with us. But you act like you don't know what we talking about. And we telling you right. But for you to act out against this man [Chuck's voice climbed a little] . . . whoo, boy!

I mean, this man been your daddy. He drive you everywhere; he tutor you. What else can you ask from him? What

you did to him is just plain wrong, and he don't have to take
that from none of you, but especially not from you. Come on,
man! After everything he done for you. He love you. Isn't that
obvious? He got a wife and his own kids, but he do all this for
you. He don't have to do this. He don't owe you anything. But
you owe him everything. You wasn't shit before we got you.
Now, you think you a big-time player. You think you *that guy*.
Come on!

Chuck asked me if I had anything to say, and I rambled on a
bit about how Jermaine disrespected me in front of the team and
how wrong that was after what had happened with Jamal, especially because he and I had a relationship outside of the team.
He apologized to me, and we hugged awkwardly and squashed
the incident. He vowed not to do it again and was back on the
team. Jermaine left to join the rest of the guys, and Chuck joked
with me, "You used to be real nice and quiet, but these niggas
will test you. I knew you'd snap one day. It's just a matter of time.
They'll drive you crazy. One kid said that they made you curse.
You should have took a gun and killed every last one of them
bastards!"

Jermaine's mother, Monica, apologized to me after Jermaine
told her about the incident. She told me that, in the future, I
had her permission to slap him or curse him out or whatever I
wanted, because I had earned her and his respect by investing in
him. She confirmed that I was right in feeling disrespected by
Jermaine. I could demand something more from him because of
our relationship. The altercation solidified our relationship, as
it seemed Jermaine took Chuck's words to heart: "he love you . . .
he don't have to do this . . . he don't owe you anything." But we
still had problems.

Jermaine struggled through the rest of the season wanting
to be the star, but he forced things. He would try to dribble the
ball and drive on smaller guys, which was not to his advantage,
and he often lost the ball. Chuck and I would yell at him, and
he grew more and more frustrated. He saw Keith and Ray handle the ball a lot on the older team and assumed that his status
on the younger team meant that he could and should do the

same. But he was a bigger kid. The game needed to come to him, through passing and trusting his teammates. He claimed that our guards didn't always pass him the ball, and he was right. But this was not an error. He was not the absolute star that he had expected to be.

Bryant was a better ball handler and was known for scoring. Also, Sean, a new kid, had shown me that he could score and handle the ball. Most importantly for me, Sean did not give me attitude. He listened with wide eyes and didn't whine or voice complaints. I sometimes called plays for Sean, which both Bryant and Jermaine grew to resent.

Sean played a big role in our making the playoffs. I put the team's fate in Sean's hands at the end of a game, one that we needed to win. We had been in front of the other team for most of the game but turned the ball over several times as the finish drew near. I called consecutive plays for Bryant and Jermaine because they had been complaining, and Bryant only played defense when he was not getting the chance to shoot. Both failed to score. Bryant got his shot blocked; Jermaine lost the ball on another play and was called for an offensive foul on a third occasion. Our opponent had a one point lead with only twelve seconds left. They missed a shot, we rebounded, and I called a time-out to set up a play.

"We gonna run one-four. Sean, you bring the ball up but don't do nothin' until I tell you. When I tell you, you drive and you look for Bryant or Jermaine. If you ain't got nothin', then you take it. Okay?" Sean nodded. "Now, we not in a hurry. Hold the ball until I tell you. We don't want to shoot until like five or seven seconds left. Come on, we still in this. Let me hear it."

They all put their hands in, and Jermaine led, "One, two, three . . . South Philly," and we broke the huddle. Bryant passed the ball to Sean in the backcourt, and I yelled to Sean, "Go by him." Sean pivoted around and dribbled quickly by the defender. He was moving fast when he passed half-court, and Bryant yelled to him, waving his arms for the ball. I nearly ran onto the court.

I was standing and making a pushing motion with my hands in front of me, yelling for Sean to slow down. "SEAN! SEAN! HOLD UP! HOLD UP!" He put on the brakes and stopped just in front of me, bobbing his head and waiting for my call. He looked at me while he dribbled the ball, and I watched the seconds run off the clock, nine-eight-seven. "Wait . . . wait . . . GO!" Sean dribbled to his right and was double-teamed, but spun back to his left and jumped. He shot a floater, a running lofty shot, over a big third defender. The ball hit the front of the rim and rolled over into the net as the buzzer sounded. We won! I pumped my fist and gave Sean a high five.

Bryant and Jermaine weren't as happy about the win; they shook their heads and waved their arms because they had expected to get the ball. I ignored them but was waiting for them to say something about the play. Bryant had almost cost us the game by yelling for Sean to pass him the ball. Luckily, I had caught Sean's attention and slowed him down.

We got into the playoffs and were matched against a team we had beaten soundly during the season. I was confident because I figured we now had three good players, Jermaine, Bryant, and Sean. Chuck often said, "If you got one player, you can compete. Two players and you can win a lot of games. Three players, you damn near unstoppable." But Jermaine's and Bryant's attitudes would haunt the team.

We controlled the playoff game from the tip-off and had a ten-point lead at halftime. We weren't playing great, but we had spurts that kept us ahead. At one point Jermaine made an unbelievable play. There were two defenders back, and one of them ran to a spot in front of the basket to try and prevent an easy basket. I knew what was going to happen. Jermaine got the pass on the right side and dribbled once. He jumped off of his left leg from about six feet out and stretched his whole body toward the basket. He was almost lying flat and looked like Superman, as his right arm slammed the ball through the rim. Jermaine knocked the defender down and landed on two feet in a crouched position. "AAAAHHHHHHH!" he screamed, and shimmied his shoulders up and down. The small crowd was abuzz. The referee whistled the defender for a foul, and Jermaine made the free throw. I felt comfortable going into the last three minutes of the game, even with just an eight-point lead.

Then things turned. Jermaine was called for his typical offensive foul while driving out of control to the basket. He fell on the play because he had tripped, and then jumped up and got in a referee's face.

"WHAT! That was a foul on *HIM*! You SUCK! You're TERRIBLE."

Bryant put his arms around Jermaine and tried to pull him away, but he pushed Bryant's hands off of him.

I yelled, "JERMAINE! JERMAINE!"

The referee moved to the scorer's table.

"Offensive foul on blue [number] twenty-five and technical foul."

Jermaine walked toward the referee, and I went to Jermaine and grabbed him around the waist, walking him by the referee.

"What are you *doing*? We up by eight points and you going wild . . . Sit down. Justin, go in for J." I shook my head.

Jermaine walked to the end of our bench and kicked a chair.

"This is bullshit!" And he started to take off his jersey. I knew he needed to blow some steam, but I warned him, "*Don't take off that jersey* . . . I'm going to need you. Just cool out." He sat at the end of the bench and sulked.

The other team made their technical foul shot and scored from out of bounds. Our lead was cut to five points. Bryant then went out of control. He grabbed a rebound and dribbled coast to coast, the length of the floor. He cut through two defenders and lost the ball. They scored on the other end. It looked like he was fouled on the play, but he was playing wild. Sean took the ball out. He passed the ball to Bryant. He dribbled down, stopped, and took a long shot, missing badly. I called to him, "Bryant. Bryant. We don't need that shot." The ball was batted around before the other team collected it and headed back toward our basket.

Bryant ran back, trailing the dribbler, who stopped to pull up for a shot. He swung wildly at the player's shot and missed the ball completely, hitting the shooter hard across the face. The player landed and quickly turned to Bryant, who was looking at him. "That's what you get," Bryant said to the player. The player lunged at him but was held back by one of the refs. The other ref gave Bryant a technical foul and said to me, "Coach, Coach, take him out. He has to sit down and chill out." I looked at Bryant in disbelief and shook my head.

> "Jermaine, you ready. Go in."
> "I ain't going in. Fuck that, they cheatin'."

The game unraveled quickly. The other team got to shoot three free throws and take the ball out of bounds. They made their free throws and scored on their next three possessions. Jermaine and Bryant sat on the end of the bench, heckling the referees and laughing at the game. We lost by four points, and our season was over. I couldn't believe what had happened.

I spent some time reflecting on the season and figured that I had made some critical coaching mistakes. My inability to manage all of the coaching tasks made me less effective. Chuck embarrassed players, but he also embarrassed referees. When referees made bad calls, he would question their judgment, stop the game and ask for clarification, and hound them verbally. This was "working" the refs, but it also was a way to influence the game. He knows the game so well that sometimes the two or three refs would stop and confer and change their call because Chuck had raised a valid complaint. His activity also protected our players. They knew that he was going to yell at the refs if they were fouled and that he would ask refs to control opposing players. He "went off" on referees, so that the players didn't have to.

In contrast, I was not always in the moment. I spaced out sometimes—thinking about home stuff, research, and hoping for a quick end when we were losing badly. We started games slowly and would be in a hole, behind by eight or ten points, before really getting on track. Yet kids said, "I like playing for you,

Scott. You let us play." And parents applauded me. "I like how you talk to the kids. You don't yell at them like Chuck. Sometimes they just can't hear him because it's too much. Nah'imean. But you listen to them." Of course, parents weren't around for my postgame talks! Chuck warned me that parents and players would like me as long as I was a nice guy, but when I had to say "no," they would turn on me. They were manipulative and could create a wedge between us, if I believed that the kids played better for me. But I didn't. Being nice didn't get me what I wanted from our players; kids back-talked me, and I nearly fought Jamal. Kids played noticeably different when Chuck was present. He entered and started yelling right away, at practice and games, and they listened more, did what we had practiced, and didn't talk back as much. The parents didn't have much to say to Chuck either, yet they spoke freely to me in criticism and praise. I decided that I needed to be firmer and have higher expectations. I didn't believe in yelling at kids, but wondered if it would help. If I yelled early, maybe I would not have to yell later and seem out of control. I could also support and protect my players by getting on refs and juggling more of the tasks.

Jermaine still earned league co-MVP, along with Hanif Martin, because of several dunks over the season. But I couldn't speak to Jermaine for a while because of how the season ended. I felt disrespected by him again. His behavior was selfish. He cost the team a playoff win and also made a fool of himself. People around the league talked about the game and his and Bryant's behavior. More was expected of him, and any scouts that were present would write negative reports or, worse, not mention him at all. Playing and acting in public was something that he controlled. His bad attitude ruined anything that he had done well. I spent less time with him that summer, and Chuck began to voice his dislike for Jermaine. We heard reports about Jermaine's attitude and antics when playing for other teams too. Jermaine was "bigheaded" and thought too highly of himself, believing that he had "arrived" and was a star player.

19 MOVING NORTH

For the next school year, Ray and Jermaine (now seventeen and sixteen years old) left Thompson High School to play at better schools. This would make it possible for them to gain even more exposure. Ray was recruited by Tillman High School, a public school that won the public league chip in the previous season. Importantly, he was entering his senior season and only had one year left to play and earn a college scholarship. He figured and hoped that his transfer and growing reputation as a great scorer would make this possible. A local preseason basketball guide wrote about Tillman High and Ray:

> The Pub [public league] Champion Bears lost nine seniors from a year ago, but are still back in the mix thanks to two talented holdovers and two more very talented transfers. . . . The transfers are high scoring 6-1 Sr. CG [combination guard position] Ray Webster from Thompson and F/C Kelly Smith from Tech. Webster was only second in the league in scoring last season getting 29 a night. He has a deep/sweet stroke and a quick/shifty handle. He's also the most mentally tough kid on the team and a D-1 prospect that will need Prep School.

Ray was recruited to fill a large void at Tillman left by graduating seniors. It would be very difficult for him to score twenty-nine points per game for Tillman, as he had for Thompson. Tillman's team had better players with whom he would have to share the ball. Still, Ray's decision was a good one. He would gain much more publicity because he was playing for a team that the local press followed and would be associated with a winning team and good players. Tillman had won two public league championships in three years and had former players on college scholarships.

Jermaine transferred to North Philadelphia Catholic High School. He did not get the same media attention because his status was lower, yet some was better than none. The same preseason high school guide summarized North Catholic's standing and Jermaine's addition in this way: "The Trojans of North Philadelphia Catholic could be St. Dominic's toughest challenge with their mix of experience and depth. The depth comes in the Trojans' having virtually two or three of everything. . . . Need athletic wings? They [North Catholic] have plenty of those in 6-4 Jr. high-flyer Jermaine Perkins and . . ." Jermaine recalled another preseason write-up this way:

> When I got to North, it stepped up another level 'cause before the season start they got preseason predictions, and it tell you like who transferred or whatever. So, in one of the predictions, it said North got a big-time transfer in Jermaine Perkins. And first I wasn't even thinking of myself like that; I was just thinking I was unknown, a regular person. And everybody started talking [about] "North got Jermaine Perkins. He transferred, and he gonna kill the Catholic league." And that's when I knew I was getting talked about and I was getting pumped. So it started from there.

Ray and Jermaine both received publicity that added to their personal histories and getting known. They could validate their status with printed publications and the testimonials of others. Their reputations were growing, and more people knew of them and talked about them. Ray was characterized as "a scorer, leader, top-level college prospect and mentally tough," and Jermaine as "athletic and a high flyer." There was no mention of Jermaine's college prospects or potential. Still, Jermaine gave a lot of weight to the fact that he was being talked about.

Like Ray's move, Jermaine's choice to attend North was a career decision. He had other choices but thought about the success of other players from South Philly who had attended North and envisioned himself reaching similar heights.

> I had [St.] Augustine that was looking at me and Bishop John and [Our Lady of] Grace and I had St. Dominic's. But I didn't really want to go to St. Dominic's 'cause I didn't want to stay in South Philly, plus, like, a couple of guys on the team, we was friends, but not friends to be on the same team or whatever. Plus, I mean, North had that tradition. They had a chance to win, and they had a lot of South Philly people that went there and did well, so I just wanted to be the next one on the list—Jameer Ross, Omar Johnson, Jermaine Perkins. So I was thinking I could be the next person on the list or whatever.

Jameer Ross and Omar Johnson both played for Chuck in the Rodgers League and went on to play college locally at Milton University. Omar was a leading scorer in the nation before contracting mononucleosis in his senior year. Many believed this kept him from playing in the NBA, but he played professionally overseas. Jameer played at Milton University for two years and was drafted by an NBA team. A trajectory and path had already been paved from South Philly to North and beyond, and Jermaine believed he could follow in other players' footsteps.

Leaving Thompson High

Transferring to Tillman and North were beneficial for reasons beyond basketball. Monica, Jermaine's mom, did not feel that Thompson could provide him with the academic environment he needed to succeed and escape their neighborhood's problems. Further, she worried about the violence at Thompson and sensed that the school did not and could not protect him. I talked on the phone to Jermaine and Monica about his transferring.

"What'd your mom say about North Catholic?" I asked.

"My mom want me to transfer. She say that she tired of all the fighting at Thompson. She says it's dangerous. Hold on, she want to talk to you."

"Hi, Scott. I just want a change for him. I can't stand Thompson," Monica said. "If he stay at Thompson, I might be putting my baby in a coffin."

Jermaine and a number of his friends had been involved in a rather large fight at school. Detrick, a neighbor and teammate of Jermaine's, was the cause of the fight. D Street gang was looking for Detrick because he "disrespected" a girl whose cousin was one of their members. The gang wanted to teach Detrick a lesson. Some of the gang's members attended the school, but others came from outside the school. Jermaine was the first to see the gang gathering. He attempted to cool the gang out because he knew some of its members. He talked to one of them and gave dap, asking why they needed to fight. This was not effective. Detrick showed up, and a gang member began cursing and pushing him. Then others jumped in and began "throwing" on him, punching and knocking him down. Jermaine ran to protect his friend and started fighting. More people, including Ray, jumped in. Security came and broke it up, removing the gang from campus, but the gang promised to be back with guns. Jermaine and Ray were not hurt physically, but they worried about repercussions and future fights. They all served one-day suspensions from school.

Monica, Erica, and a number of other neighborhood parents went to the school to see "what was up." They wanted to know how the principal planned to prevent another fight. Monica did not feel confident about the principal's ability to resolve the situation. The school staff had identified Ray, Jermaine, and their friends as gang members, which, for her, illustrated that they did not understand the situation and were criminalizing all young black men. If not addressed, this approach could land Jermaine and Ray in jail or get them hurt by fighting or killed by guns.

Ray and Jermaine continued to be involved in fights. Personal relationships and associations had histories and consequences. In following a street code, they needed to protect their friends. Further, it was likely that they would be mistaken for being directly involved and that they would be victims by association. Jermaine and Ray found it difficult to avoid fights because they went to school with other kids from their block and took the same buses and trains. Jermaine described the situation as follows:

"And it's just, South Philly is surrounded by hood. Once you get past Chesapeake, it's mostly nice neighborhoods. But from about K [Street] and Georgetown all the way down, it's nothing but gangs and drugs and violence. It go by street, really. You got D Street, they represent they block; H Street represent they block; K Street, J Street, like P Street. We ain't really got like Bloods and Crips. It just go by your street. So it's like people go to war over dumb stuff, like blocks, that don't really belong to them."

"What was school like?" I asked Jermaine.

"The metal detectors, you gotta be scared. People bringing guns in, knives, selling drugs in school, gambling in school. I mean, you had to be scared for your life a lot of times at Thompson. Man, 'cause, I mean, that's when the gangs started coming up. D Street, H Street, they didn't like each other, but they [really] didn't like us 'cause we wasn't from nowhere. We was from Bank Street. So even though they hated each other, they got together to fight us, and we had to catch a bus to the sub[way] to get home. So, it was like, just to make it on the bus you gotta fight; to get home you gotta fight every day. I mean, they'll walk down the hallway [and someone would say], 'Look at them Bank Street niggas, we gonna fight you after school.'

"So, it would start in the school. We'd fight in the school. It was only like ten of us. Fifty people from D Street, about twenty people from H Street 'cause they wanted to get rid of us. They'd work together—it was like an alliance. I mean, one bull [boy] told me and Ray they was plotting on us, and one of they girls or whatever, from down they way [from D Street], used to talk to my homie. So, she called him and she said, 'They in the parking lot plotting to get y'all, one by one. They gonna get Ray and Jermaine because they play basketball.'"

"What did the school do?" I asked.

"Nothing really. They tried to call us a gang, and we wasn't really a gang. Security wasn't doing nothing. The security guards was scared to death. I mean, they had cops at the school. They just started having cops at the school, but when the cops would leave . . . The cops wouldn't let us out the door until everyone would leave, but the cops was so dumb, that they'll [the gangs] hide behind they little blocks or whatever and wait for us to come out.

"But when we off school property, they'd get us, and then we had to make it to the bus, and then sometimes they'll wait at the sub for us. So, there was nothing else to do but fight, unless you got off two blocks down from the sub and walk to the other sub stop that's two blocks away. We just fought. I was the type [of person], I was gonna get home regardless, nobody gonna scare me from getting home, nah'imean."

The recurrence of violence had serious consequences. Jermaine and Ray fought regularly for no apparent gain and began skipping school to avoid the violence. Being targeted made the threat even more real. Jermaine and the other Bankers sought to avoid fights and grew to fear for their lives. The threat of death became too great, and they were outnumbered and outmatched in guns and a willingness to shoot people. Ultimately, a young man from Bank Street was shot and killed. Jermaine and Ray were transferring just in time. I asked Jermaine, "What do you think would have happened had you stayed at Thompson?"

> I'd a died. I think I woulda died. 'Cause my man got killed. His name was Rone; he went to Thompson. They came to the block and shot him. And he lived on Bank Street and Montross, two blocks down from me. They came down there in the car. He was standing outside, and they drove around the block, a bull hopped out, and they shot him.

Rone's brother retaliated, shooting a young man from the rival gang. Others gave up the fight. Ray and Jermaine believed that they had a future in basketball and that fighting and dying over territory or interpersonal disputes was less significant. Basketball had given them an opportunity to leave Thompson and escape the violence.

Going to a New School

At North, Jermaine was moving into a smaller, wealthier, and predominantly white school setting, which took some getting used to. Initially, he faced culture shock as he interacted with his new classmates. He was no longer worried about personal safety, but he had new issues.

> So I went there, and it was like, it was kind of a struggle the first year. I had to try and adapt to a new coach, new school environment I wasn't used to. In the beginning I felt good, but then I started slacking off because it was different. Like it's an all-boys school, and the school I went to before wasn't a lot of Caucasians—it was mostly black—and I had to get used to them and putting up with a lot of they stuff.
>
> Like they joke a lot and I wasn't used to that. Like they would make racial jokes, like they would be playing, but like, one bull was like . . . What he say?
>
> "What looks good hanging from a tree, besides a cherry?"
>
> And we said, "What?" And he said, "A black man." They said he was playing, but I wasn't used to that so I spazzed on him. I was about to hit him. So I got in trouble a lot the first year, and I had to get used to wearing a little shirt and tie, and keeping your shirt tucked in, and demerits, and all that. So it was kind of a struggle.

Jermaine's initial struggles were due to his unfamiliarity with the culture of North. Jermaine left a girlfriend of two years and neighborhood buddies at Thompson, as well. He was used to living, playing, and going to school in predominantly black settings. What he experienced at North was an integration of sorts. His blackness made him different, and he was no longer an insider and part of the majority. As a minority, and one with special status—as an athlete—he had to learn a new set of rules and to respond differently to authority and others' behavior. He came to see behavior, such as the racial joking, as a process of assimilation. He was in a white space. It is unlikely that the white kid would tell the same joke outside of school or where he was not in the majority and in a "safe" space. Jermaine also had to work hard academically because the curriculum was challenging. Following all of the school's rules helped him to become more disciplined at school.

> Academically, I thought it was a great school. 'Cause it pressured me a lot, like it made me step my weight up [work harder], and work in the books. 'Cause like at Thompson, you just, I really didn't have to do nothing. I was happy, [I'd] do the work and just leave [cut school]. But there, it was a different atmosphere, 'cause if you leave, they got people looking for you. Like they got people following you. You couldn't cut school. You cut lunch and they find you and catch you in the lunch room. It matured me more in the classroom, academically, in how to become a man, than I would have if I been at Thompson. Because at Thompson, I'd probably be the same person [that I was], leaving school early, doing this and doing that. So, academic-wise it was a good change: it helped me out a lot; grade-wise I produced a lot better.

Jermaine recognized an important difference between North and Thompson—supervision. He had to go to school, do his work, and play basketball because he was being watched. Although restrictive, close supervision also implied that school was serious and that kids were being looked after. Jermaine adapted and measured personal success in new terms, like productivity. North also helped his self-esteem and made him feel like a star.

> When I came in, for some reason, everyone knew who I was. The teachers knew who I was, so I had all the support. The students were cool, I mean, I thought it was gonna be weird because I hadn't never been around that environment. I mean, it was good; I didn't have any problems with anybody at the

school, nah'imean. I met a lot of friends that was different races.

Whenever I needed something, I got money. Like if I needed money for lunch. And plus my mom wasn't working at the time. So they knew I didn't have it [money]. Momo [Jackson's coach who recruited him to North] and them, they gave me a mentor named Mr. Rose and whatever. He always talked to us [other black players] after the game and [asked], do I need something to eat, do I need money to eat dinner? Do I need money for the rest of the week? Or if I had a tournament, I just call him and he'll give it [money for the trip] to me. I ask for money and he just like, when I go to school, he just give it to me. He was like a little alumni.

And the students, they'll buy me lunch. I mean, I knew a lot of them, I met them during the year, and I talked to them or whatever. And a lot of times, I really didn't have to pay for lunch because I played on the basketball team and I was something like a star. So, lunch people, I mean, they gave you lunch. You got in the line, and they'd pick you out of line to be the first person to eat. And I wasn't used to that. I mean, you got to wait your turn in the public school system, and I came there and I had to adapt. My first day I didn't see no metal detectors, and I didn't know what I was doing!

Jermaine received the "real" star treatment that he had seen on television and in movie depictions of "blue chip" players on scholarship at predominantly white schools. He was known because of his basketball and minority status—most black males at North were recruited to play sports. The positive interaction and admiration by teachers and students felt good and supportive, rather than adversarial and resentful. Jermaine also learned that his basketball play was a form of labor garnering informal wages, tips, and benefits. Little to nothing was said, yet he knew what was expected in return. He was expected to perform on the basketball court, and he received more money for outstanding performances.

Quickly Jermaine got a glimpse of how his basketball career at North might go. North had two big rivals, Our Lady of Grace and St. Dominic's. Our Lady of Grace was in North Philly, and St. Dominic's was in South Philly. St. Dominic's was a big game for Jermaine because he was well acquainted with most of the team, including his archrival, Hanif Martin. Jermaine played a memorable first game against St. Dominic's.

> It was the second game of the season, and we played St. Dominic's at St. Dominic's. So it was a big deal, I mean, me coming back home, me coming back to South Philly and playing a South Philly team. And plus that was against my rival Hanif Martin. So I think that was my burst [a special moment] because I just came there, I scored twenty-two points, and I dunked on William Evans. He was one of the top big men of the city at the time. I think that just burst me; ever since that I just got so much confidence, I just play harder and scoring on everybody. I was in the mode that I think nobody is better than me, I mean, in my class [grade], I was in that zone.

Jermaine was excited to play St. Dominic's; he knew that there would be a large crowd and that status and pride were at stake. He was implicitly in competition with Hanif and other players, in the same grade and position, and of similar or higher reputations. Hanif could have made fun of him again and claim that he was still a "nobody" if North lost to St. Dominic's and he played poorly. But North won this game, and Jermaine had risen to the challenge and cemented his status as "a player to watch" throughout the city, which he carried into other games against known players. Jermaine showed well for the season, averaging a little over fourteen points per game and becoming the team's third leading scorer behind two seniors.

20 LEARNING OTHER STUFF

Increasingly, Ray and Jermaine turned most of their attention to how to become college players. They went to basketball events—such as high school, college, and pro games. They practiced in new ways and continued expanding their networks, looking for small but significant ways to distinguish themselves from others.[1]

I went to a national high school tournament in New Jersey—about an hour's drive from Philadelphia—and ran into Jermaine. He was with three other teammates from North. One of them was white and his father had driven them to the game. They were there to see some of the nation's best high school players at the time: Sebastian Telfair, Josh Smith, Dwight Howard, Rajon Rondo, and Kyle Lowry, who are all now professionals in the NBA. We ran into each other while watching a game between a Philadelphia school and Oakhill Academy (a perennial prep-school powerhouse from Virginia).

Jermaine's and Ray's frequency at the playground increased too. Basketball had become their business, and practicing and working out, especially at the playground, was their job and routine.

> I was playing there every day [at Espy]. *Every day*. Soon as I get out of school, soon as practice was over, I wouldn't even go home. I just go straight to the park. Marcus Sr. & Jr., Ray, Darren, and a lot of different old heads; everybody from all parts of the city come down there and play. Like we would play games or whatever, and then when it died down, all the

old heads, like Marcus and them, they'd take us to the back [court] and we would work out in the back while everybody else was playing. Like shooting drills, dribble drills, like the agility [drills], work on your hops [jumping ability], play in the strength shoes, like basically your ball handling, your shooting. And then he [Marcus] started getting a gym, so we didn't have to work out outside, and we'd have workouts and stuff like that. Anybody was welcomed, but he had his few he'd do extra with because he knew them for so long.

Jermaine seemed to be at Espy all of the time, going whenever he had a break between other activities. The change in "practice" activities marked an even bigger distinction between Ray and Jermaine and recreational players. Over time they gained different skills from different old heads. They began as hopeful high school players, became playground regulars who played with old heads and some of the best players at any age, and then began working out with pro and college players who had returned home.

I looked for Jermaine and Ray one evening and was told by Monica that they were probably at Espy. I drove by and saw them playing on one of the side courts with two older men, whom I didn't know at the time. One of the older men was leading. He would bark orders, ridicule the others, and start and stop the drills/games. They played a shooting game called "knock out." They stood single file at the three-point line and shot, and each player had to make a basket before the person behind them. If they didn't, they were "knocked out" of the game and would have to wait for a new game. They did a shooting drill as well where they would shoot from three spots on the court and have to make ten baskets from each. The last two to finish would have to do twenty-five push-ups.

Jermaine and I talked later, and he told me that he and Ray were working out with Smoosh. Smoosh played pro ball overseas and was home for his off-season. He was one of Chuck's former players and different people said that he was "certified," "51/50," or crazy and wild. He had been kicked out of one college for stealing before becoming an All-Conference player and Student

Athlete of the Year at a second college. Later he was cut from a couple of NBA teams for fighting and intimidating players. Ray and Jermaine worked out with him consistently for a month or two. They were impressed and influenced by him. They loved to say that they were doing "pro workouts" and claimed that they were getting stronger and learning "pro moves."

The playground had remained a constant and necessary part of their development. They believed that it enhanced their over-all training; it was complementary, and the different people in each context (playground, school, Blade Rodgers, and AAU) were useful in overlapping but varying ways. Ray and Jermaine needed different people, knowledge, and opportunities as they advanced,[2] and Philadelphia had plenty of resources.

21

A STAR IS BORN; ANOTHER IS STILL WAITING

Tillman High had a great season, was top seeded, and was predicted to win the public league championship by a newspaper journalist. Ray was the team's leading scorer and captain. They knocked off Keith's high school in the quarterfinals but lost in the semifinals to the eventual champion 67–70. Ray shot poorly, five of seventeen for sixteen points (and seven rebounds and two assists), and the team gave a lackluster performance. The newspaper captured him in the game's featured photograph. He and an opposing player were in a tug-of-war over a loose ball. The caption said that the play was symbolic of Ray's and Tillman's struggles throughout the game. The loss was heartbreaking for Ray, but he gained a lot from the experience. He was much more known because of Tillman's reputation and their success. He averaged 18.5 points per game—down more than ten points per game from his junior year at Thompson when he averaged 29.1 points per game. But while playing for Thompson, he *climbed* from Third Team All-Public honors to First Team All-Public honors at Tillman. He was highly sought after by Big University, the paper reported during the season—an indication of his ascendance; Big U recruited only the city's best players.

Jermaine was not in the headlines, and North was not a top team in their league. He played alongside one of North's all-time leading scorers who garnered a lot of attention. He was sometimes written about for playing a supporting role, making a defensive play or a key basket to help the team. North lost in their second playoff game to Hanif Martin and St. Dominic's by ten points. Jermaine received informational letters from colleges about their team and school, but he did not earn individual All-League honors nor any scholarship offers or personal calls from coaches. He had another year, fortunately, and expected to be the star next season.

Jermaine's and Ray's busyness had become frantic. Ray traveled year-round with different teams, and Jermaine's high school team played in preseason and postseason tournaments outside of Philadelphia, in North Carolina, Washington, D.C., and Hawaii.

Summer arrived, and Jermaine and Ray—as well as Keith, Bryant, Miles, and Justin—returned to our team. They rarely showed up for practice, because they were busy with other basketball teams and considered our practice "kid stuff" compared to their pro workouts and other commitments. We were just another team that they played for. They competed on the eleventh- and twelfth-grade team, and the team's pecking order mirrored the championship team from two years earlier with a slight twist. Keith was still a star, but Ray was no longer secondary; he had grown into a star in his own right. He even surpassed Keith, as indicated by Tillman's defeat of Keith's team in the public league playoffs. Bryant's status slipped—he went from being one of the best players in his grade for two years to not being mentioned at all. His skills had peaked in his sophomore year, and he did not grow much thereafter. Bryant was also getting into more and more trouble off the court, such as failing classes. Jermaine said that Bryant was now "gangsta." He was seen smoking weed and hanging out on the street with drug dealers. Jermaine, Justin, and Miles remained role players.

Ray's improvement was obvious beginning with our first game of the season. Jermaine jumped for the tip-off and tapped the ball to Ray. Ray pivoted and faced the basket. Chuck called a play from the side. "Ray! Move the ball. Open, open!" The guys spread out, opening the middle of the floor and passing the ball to one another. Ray passed the ball to Bryant. Then Ray ran to the other side of the court and set a screen for Keith by standing in the way of Keith's defender. Keith ran around Ray and down the middle of the floor. Bryant passed the ball to Keith, who caught the ball on the run and tried to score. He was fouled and would shoot two free throws. Chuck clapped and called Ray over.

"That's it, baby. Take your time. Take your time. We in no hurry. We take what they give us. Move the ball around, get everybody touches, and pick 'em apart. You get yours on the back end."

Ray nodded. Keith made the first free throw, and Ray left Chuck to be ready for defense. Keith missed the shot, and a big defender snared the rebound. Just as he was passing the ball to a guard, Ray darted and cut in front of the guard and stole the ball. He drove to the basket with no hesitation and laid the ball up on the backboard over the big rebounder and scored. He was fouled and fell down. Jermaine quickly ran over to Ray and put one arm out to pull him up. He slapped Ray on the butt as he picked him up and then rubbed the back of his head. Ray sunk his free throw and we had a quick four-point lead.

The opposing team took the ball out. Their guard got the pass, and Ray tracked him closely. He moved swiftly at angles to stop the guard and bump him with his stomach and hip. Ray swatted at the ball, and the guard pushed back with his non-dribbling hand. "Ooooh, Ref. He pushing off," he said, while laughing. Ray was pressing him, and the guard was clearly bothered.

Ray ran the show. He was a constant threat and controlled the game with his defense and playmaking. This set the tone for the rest of our team. Jermaine squatted and slapped the floor with both hands in front of the player he was guarding. And Keith, Bryant, and Justin all played their guys tighter. We kept them from scoring on three consecutive possessions and took a ten-point lead. In that time Ray stole the ball from the guard, tapping the ball from behind. Keith scooped it up and tossed the ball to Ray, who was streaking down the court, for an easy basket. Keith made a jump shot, and Jermaine made a move around the basket and scored. The opposing team called for a time-out.

"YEAH, BOYYYY," Ray said loudly, sensing that the call was a sign of their coach's frustration. Our guys slapped hands excitedly and encouraged each other as they came to the bench. "Good shit." "Stay in 'em." We huddled and Chuck told them to keep it up. "Don't let 'em breathe. And don't get stupid; it's still early. Keep the pressure on. Let me hear it, gentlemen." Jermaine led, "One, two, three . . . South Philly."

We continued to score easily and led by fifteen points at half-time. The other team started the second half much better and cut into the lead after scoring two uncontested baskets. Their guard got excited and hollered after one basket, "YEAHHH, BOYYYY," mocking what Ray had said earlier. He looked over at our bench and smirked.

"Oh, you think you done something?" Chuck asked. "I'm gonna fix your ass! Ray, Ray. One-four. One-four."

Ray got the ball from Jermaine, who had taken the ball out of bounds after the scored basket. He yelled the play to the rest of the team. "One-four, one-four." Jermaine hustled down the floor and echoed Ray, "One-four, one-four." Ray looked at the guard, who was now guarding him closely. "You too little. You too little." And he turned and dribbled while sliding backward and bumping the guard with his hip and butt, protecting the ball with his body and moving the guard back because he outweighed him. Ray got over half-court and turned sideways.

Chuck gave Ray the green light, "All right, kid. That's your meat, your meat."

Ray faced the basket and dribbled right at the guard quickly and then stopped, but kept his dribble going. The guard jumped to cut Ray off and then nearly lost his balance as he tried to stop.

"YEAH, BOYYYY," Ray chuckled.

Jermaine added, "*Got him.*"

But Chuck interrupted, "Stop playing with the ball and take his little ass to the hole."

Ray patted his chest and nodded. He passed the ball to Jermaine and got it back to start again. He stood tall with the ball in both hands in front of him and then bent forward over the ball, putting his head in the guard's chest. He moved his right foot forward, pushing the guard back, and then he straightened up and darted to his right with three dribbles, stopped, dribbled once more, stepped back, and shot a twelve-footer. All net!

We won the game easily and the next four of five games. Ray had tremendous confidence and was having a lot of fun, which showed on the court. He was blossoming. He was smarter than everyone else on the court and controlled the game. Sometimes his confidence got the best of him and he did too much, playing with defenders, trying to do the spectacular, then losing the ball. Chuck would yell at him, and he would pat his chest and say, "My bad, my bad." And Chuck would ease up. He trusted Ray to regain intensity and manage the game.[1]

We had high expectations for this team, but our season was derailed. Ray and Keith missed games to play in tournaments outside the city. They believed that local leagues, including Blade Rodgers, were less and less necessary. Both had graduated but had uncertain futures. They hoped that playing elsewhere would shore up scholarships for them. Bryant quit the team because of intra-team competition. He had fewer opportunities to score and played less than in previous years. There were a few new players on the team who played his same position and were good. Jermaine did not get the ball a lot either and felt that he was again a role player with little opportunity to show what he could do. I spent a lot of time trying to convince him of his worth to us. He was not a primary scorer but could be a strong defender and our best rebounder if he played as he had during our chip. We lost our last four games and the first game of the playoffs. Keith had disappeared, and though Ray worked hard, he could not beat the best teams alone.

Ray's activity paid off. Big University offered him a scholarship, but there was a contingency; he had to get a minimal score on the SAT to be academically eligible for admittance. Keith only received offers from community colleges. Jermaine, on the other hand, hadn't "made it" and still wasn't considered among the elite players in the city. Fortunately, he was asked to play for the Philly Jazz, which was one of the most regarded AAU teams in Philadelphia. He traveled with them a lot during the latter half of the summer and into fall. This would be his chance.

What happened was Little Marcus used to play for them [the Philly Jazz]. So, Marcus [Sr.] used to always try to bring me up there and ball. And Anthony [the coach] was like, "He tough but he not good enough to play with us yet." So I used to just work hard. And then he [Anthony] saw me play, end of my junior year, and was like, "Oh, we going to a tournament"—he got my number—"we going to a tournament, you trying to come with us? I'm a pick you up; you ain't got to pay for nothing." So I went, "All right." I played with them there, and then he took me to Vegas.

I was just figuring it out [the recruitment process] 'cause I saw everybody [talking to coaches], like I started getting letters and all that. Like I'm new to this, I didn't even know who these [coaches] is. I didn't know no Division-1s, mid-majors, highs. I was just happy to be getting letters then. And they [higher-status players on his team] was like, "Yeah, and I got Duke, North Carolina." And, "Who you got [letters from]?"

And I like, "I got Wagner, Robert Morris [names of colleges], and all them. And they tough [good basketball schools], right?"

And they like, "They lows."

"Lows? I thought Division 1 was just Division 1."

They was like, "Naw." And then Morgan [a teammate] started schooling me to the game. Todd Giles was schooling me to the game. They was like, "There's like different levels to Division 1. And high majors, like Duke, is big-time. Mid-majors they all right, but like low majors, they horrible. You wanna shoot to be a high major."

And they was telling me like what they did to get they publicity, what you do. You only do what you can do. Don't try to do what you can't do and the coaches love it. Like play hard and all that.

In the hotel room and all that and after games, they would tell me what I did wrong, 'cause I was new, I was new to this. So they'd tell me what I did wrong and what I got to work on. Morgan took me under his wing in the AAU season, 'cause he was that big-time bull; everyone knew Morgan Douglas. So, I was happy to be around him.

Anthony's team was the top AAU team in Philadelphia, largely because of his younger brother, Jason Landon, who was a nationally ranked high school player and went on to become a standout college player.[2] Anthony was protective of his team and cautious about allowing players to join, because his team's prestige was based on having the best players. The team was given a shoe contract with an athletic company, and their travel was fully funded. Morgan Douglas and Todd Giles were the next big-time college prospects sought after by top-ranked schools. Not surprisingly, Jermaine benefited a great deal by joining such players. He roomed with them and learned about "the game," gathering insights and knowledge he might never have learned otherwise.[3] Furthermore, by playing on their team, Jermaine also gained exposure by sharing Morgan's and Todd's "shine," or recognition. He played well in some big tournaments at the end of the summer and began drawing attention.

> It was the Player's Ball at Seton Hall, so like all of . . . Ronald [Simmons], Ralph [Lewis], Randy Gibson, like every big-time player in the country had their AAU team there. And we played against Randy Gibson and them, and I just went off [played extremely well]. Yeah, [against] Big East [University]'s Randy Gibson. And I had twenty-four against Randy Gibson and them. It was like, the publicity was there, 'cause I had, for one, Morgan Douglas. He was like one of the top-three [position] guards in the country at the time, top five, top ten. Every big-time school in the country come and see him play. That helped me out 'cause they looking at him, that's gonna give me publicity, so even if I can't get the big ones, I'll get the mid-majors, the lows [low majors].

Jermaine was very hopeful about his chances of getting a scholarship in his senior year. He had learned the *real* game, what it took to get the attention of scouts and recruiters, and had played well against some of the best players in the country. Would this be enough?

22 POLITICS AND "PUB(LICITY)"

I moved from Philadelphia in the summer after Jermaine's junior year and Ray's senior year. I followed their careers via personal reports (on the phone), talks with Chuck and other coaches and friends, and newspaper box scores and articles. Beyond court achievements, they had to be academically eligible and have good character relationships with coaches and other key people. College recruiters and scouts look for players who are coachable. They search for clues to tell if a player will get into trouble (i.e., criminal) once they leave home. They talk to their coaches and family, and use school achievement to give indications and proof of this. They want players who have heart and "get after it" (remember the college coach's words), but who are not too "street." Those who do not meet social, athletic, and academic standards struggle and typically "fall off." Only the most gifted are worth this gamble. Some players have a distinct advantage over others because of personal connections and support from coaches, old heads, and family members.

Ray, now eighteen years old, worried no longer about building his reputation and getting "pub(licity)." Big U offered him a scholarship, but it was contingent upon his passing the SAT. He had failed to get the minimum score required (700)[1] on his first attempt. Big U's coach advised him to get tutoring and prepare for the exam. He attended tutoring sporadically and failed on his second attempt. Big University rescinded their offer. At the end of Blade Rodgers, he was "offered" (a scholarship) from a smaller Division 1, historically black college. Chuck and I were

disappointed in Ray. He was so close to playing for a top program, but he landed on his feet anyway and was a great catch for
a smaller school. Ultimately, getting to college was the blessing.
He was a Proposition 48 student athlete and couldn't play his
freshmen year, according to NCAA eligibility rules. The school
admitted him and he took courses and practiced to be academically and athletically eligible his second year.

Jermaine wasn't at the same point. He had not been *the* star
player anywhere; neither at Thompson High or North, nor on our
Blade Rodgers teams. His past performances were helpful, but he
needed more to garner support, increase his pub and buzz, and
be a star in his senior year.

For me, I needed the exposure to get the networks. So I had to
show [play well]. You got to show the networks, like the scouting services and all, that you can do more than post up. So,
you got to get them on your side first. If they don't like you,
they can destroy you, no matter how good a player [you are].
Like Hoop Group, 5 Star camp, they come to all the main tournaments like Vegas, Big-Time Tournaments, Bob Givens's Tournament, all them. Like, they basically looking for the next big
thing. And they got their opinions on everything, even if the
college coach don't see you, they [the scouts and recruiting]
buy they books and it's telling what you can and can't do. So
I mean they can help you or hurt you. So you definitely need
the networks on your side first.

I mean, you got to be able to play well, but you do got . . .
Well, I say about 75 percent is about your game and 25 percent
is about who you know. No, I'll say it's fifty-fifty. It's where
you play too, but you still got to get pushed [promoted, publi-
cized] too. Like you got to have somebody who gonna stay on
recruiters. Stay on the scouting services, like, "He really could
do this, he could do that"; that's why I say it's about fifty-fifty.
You gotta do your job, but your old head got to do his job trying to get you in college: call the coaches, call the recruiters,
like, "He really doing this, he could do that. You gotta come
see him play."

So, it's just like a fifty-fifty thing. Like you got your select few you know is gonna do something for you. Like some coaches, you can't really just trust [them]. They'll just use you just to win a championship. And you got some you can really trust.

My high school coach [at North] didn't know what he was doing. He was a Caucasian man that just sat there and let us play. If we win, he get a little raise or whatever, but he didn't really know what he was doing, what he was talking about. He just thought he had [good] players, [and] he put players on the floor.

Jermaine learned that being an elite player and getting a scholarship was not simply about playing ability. He received letters from low Division 1 schools, and coaches at higher levels had seen him play, but he did not get offers from them. He was frustrated by this and later figured that he was lacking support from old heads, coaches, and scouts.

Jermaine was not North's star in his senior season, averaging less than fifteen points per game. He had memorable games, but he didn't live up to the high expectations that his coach had for him. His struggles and frustration showed in his behavior. He had temper tantrums and complained, sulked, and talked back to his coaches. He fell out of favor with the whole coaching staff and played fewer minutes per game. He fought Jamal, who played for another Catholic school, and was suspended from a few games. Jermaine's personal experience and lack of powerful networks initially reflected his marginality when compared to other elite players and the advantages that some people had because of their extended "weak ties" and affiliations. Strong ties are associations based on primary group connections, family connections, or kinship. Weak ties are networks of secondary group ties made through friends, friends of friends, and so on. He talked more about ties and networks:[2]

The only way you get known, it's all politics in the city, like you gotta know somebody that knows somebody or you gotta be with the right people. Know the right person basically. You got to play with the right person. It's like, it's a lot of people that's better than a lot of the people that's talked about, but they ain't got the same opportunities or go to the same showcase tournaments because of where they from. Philly is so divided, if we from South Philly, we really not going to go anywhere with someone from North Philly, 'cause they gonna get somebody that's known from their hood. You just got to be liked really from everybody in the city.

Jermaine's interactions with others and the impressions he made were important. The politics he faced impacted his opportunities. He had to impress certain people to garner attention from college coaches and add to his networks. Jermaine needed to get playing time, get along with and be liked by others, and to have people say favorable things on his behalf.

Coaches and old heads have some control over their players because they give playing time, and they talk to recruiters and scouts, offering favorable or poor recommendations. Some coaches use this power and have great influence, although better players generally get more latitude. They can leverage their status, big performances, and exposure to counter bad recommendations. Jermaine talked about the ideal situation and his high school coach.

"Yeah, they [coaches] got power in everything. Even if you do play and a college ask, 'How was he?' He could say, 'He was an a-hole, he complains a lot, he's a baby,' and that could hurt your recruiting. So they got a lot to do with your exposure and what type of schools recruiting you. But it's still your job. You're on the floor, so you got to show your talent. So, it's like they job to politic you, so if you have a bad game they could still say, 'Well, he usually can make that shot off the dribble. Well, he had a bad game today, come and see him again,' and everything like that."

"Did you feel like your coach helped you? Or did he hurt you?" I asked.

"Yeah, he hurt me bad. I had Niagara [University], James Madison [University], William and Mary [College]. I had Penn State. He told them I wasn't that big-time player, I couldn't play in they conference. So he turned them off because he had that word of mouth, and he seen me all year long. So in his eyes, I wasn't that big-time player that should be in their conference. In his eyes, I wasn't that good."

Jermaine was surprised and hurt by his coach's lack of support. His coach was well respected because he was successful. North had won several league championships, had been ranked nationally, and a number of its players had graduated and gone on to play in college. Jermaine didn't get any help from scouts at this point.

John Franklin, scout for the scouting network of the Northeast; Antoine McKnight, they rank all the players in the city. Those are the basic two main ones [scouts] in Philly. Now, my senior year he [John Franklin] never smiled at me, but I always smiled and shook his hand. Antoine McKnight, he just didn't think I was that good. He thought I was a big-time D-2 player. And he never gave me a chance [to show that I could play D-1].

Jermaine felt that he was disadvantaged. His coach had done him dirty, and scouts didn't like him. Ray had Marcus and other old heads behind him, pumping him; and other players had help too. He recalled how Anthony Landon (coach of the Philly Jazz AAU team) campaigned for Jason, Anthony's little brother.

Jason had the pub since ninth grade; like, he had everybody on his side. His brother [Anthony], he politicked him so well, that even his [Jason's] attitude, all the scouts got away from [forgot about] his [bad] attitude because he was a good player. Plus, his brother made him better by talking about him.

Anthony made the whole AAU team [Philly Jazz] 'cause of him. He did that just so he could give his brother publicity. So he [Anthony] was like, "He [Jason] this, he tough and he that," and he was talking to all the scouting services. He [Jason] was politicked his whole [career], ever since high school, so when it came down to it, everyone knew who he was.

With no offers, Jermaine contemplated his options. He visited a junior college in New Mexico and a small low Division 1 college in Pennsylvania. He was offered a scholarship to the Pennsylvania school but did not know whether or not the scholarship was real because the school never sent the official paperwork that needed to be signed. They eventually reneged on their offer. Jermaine graduated from North with a 3.3 grade-point average, but his cumulative high school GPA was just below a 3.0. He got a 670 on the SAT and was academically ineligible to play college ball. Schools stayed away and his future looked grim.

Then he was recruited to attend and play for Philadelphia Covenant School, a local high-profile prep (college preparatory) school.[3] It offered a thirteenth grade, an opportunity to take college prep and SAT prep courses, and retake remedial coursework. The school's team traveled an extraordinary amount, at least twice a month, and was not limited to a winter season. They played all year long, as a school and AAU team. The team included players from different parts of the country who were in Jermaine's position or younger, seeking maximum exposure. Jermaine planned to get even more exposure and do a SAT prep course offered at the school to land a scholarship at a big-time college, mid-major, or high major.

23

GETTING IN (SCHOOL) AND GETTING OUT (OF THE HOOD)

Jermaine played for Philadelphia Covenant beginning in the summer, prior to his entering the school in the fall. He drew attention after only a few games and was offered a scholarship by Northern New York State University (NNYSU), a small mid-major program. Bigger schools had talked to the Philadelphia Covenant coach about "offering" Jermaine, but none had followed through. An NNYSU assistant coach had seen Jermaine play in a Las Vegas summer tournament. He called and spoke with Jermaine's mother, Monica, soon after. She told him that I was an influential person so that he would call me too; she wanted my advice and recommendation. He called and told me that he had gone to Vegas to see another prospect but Jermaine stood out.

"Scott, I've got to tell you. Jermaine really impressed me in Vegas. He had like ten dunks in the game I saw. He's really athletic, a great leaper. But, I've got to ask you, and I don't know because I only saw him dunk. How's his jump shot? Can he handle the ball a little bit?"

I responded, "Jermaine's got a nice jump shot from ten to fifteen feet, and he's much more than just a dunker. He's a good passer, and he can handle the ball a little bit. I mean, he's not a point guard. But he can use the dribble to go by someone and get to the basket. And he's smart with the ball. And more importantly, he's a great kid who's not going to give you any trouble."

"I know that, Scott. I mean, I have to say, sometimes when I talk to these kids . . . I just don't know how they get through school. It's a challenge for them to put a sentence together. But with Jermaine—he was such a breath of fresh air. He had manners and was articulate. He's a great young man, just the type of kid that we would love to have."

We talked for a while, swapping stories about kids, and I continued to push for Jermaine, highlighting his strengths. I didn't need to do this; the coach had called me to build a rapport, with hopes that I would encourage Jermaine to accept their scholarship. But I was proud of Jermaine and really wanted him to get to college so that I could stop worrying about him. The problem was that NNYSU is a very good school, and I knew of its academic reputation but nothing about its basketball program. I told Jermaine and Monica about its academic reputation but didn't know how much to advise them regarding basketball. It was a good thing he had only one offer.

Jermaine was very excited about getting offered. When the head coach and assistant coach made the home visit, Jermaine committed verbally without having first visited the school. I told Jermaine that he had jumped the gun. "How could you say 'yes' before you've seen the school?" I asked. The assistant coach wooed him with a good sales pitch. "I told Jermaine," the coach began, "other schools might say this and that, telling you exciting things to try and date you, but we want to marry you and we're the only ones making a real commitment." Jermaine said that he was just tired of the whole process and since no one else had offered, he might as well go with this school. Jermaine wanted to have an offer so that he could say he was going somewhere, and many of his basketball peers had signed in the spring and were heading off to their first year of college. Jermaine later visited the school and had mixed feelings. He liked his prospective teammates, but they were scared to play pickup ball against him and seemed "small time." The school also felt a lot like North Catholic—too white. We talked and he decided to renege on his commitment. This was risky, but he figured that bigger schools would offer him, in time.

Philadelphia Covenant had a stable of players and played feverishly throughout the year. They beat well-known prep schools and AAU teams with nationally ranked players. By Christmas the *USA Today* ranked the school as one of the top prep schools in the country. Jermaine caught fire and began considering multiple offers from ranked programs in the Midwest and East. In February he was offered a full scholarship by the head coach of Middle University, a top-twenty program in the Midwest. He quickly accepted. A newspaper article reported on the signing.

> "I am very excited to add a versatile player like Jermaine to our program at Middle University," the coach said. "Jermaine will play a very important part in the future of our program."

Jermaine was extremely proud. He had beaten the naysayers—coaches, old heads, and scouts—but he still had to get an acceptable score on the SAT or ACT. He studied, he said, and took both exams two times through the summer. Jermaine did not get the score, failing by a narrow margin. The school pulled back their offer, and he was lost again. The coaches continued to speak with him, though, and other schools entered the hunt, but all said that they would wait for him to get the proper score. A small mid-major school in the Midwest, Red State, however, offered him a scholarship and, like Ray, he would have to sit out a year of basketball to prove himself academically. He accepted.

Jermaine learned to manage his reputation on different teams, in varied settings, and with a vast and amorphous network of persons. His success depended upon five things: his learning and performing up to expectations; gaining exposure to multiple settings and audiences; creating buzz by impressing influential people; managing the politics; and having a support system—family, coaches and old heads, and networks that sustained him and created opportunities for him to play. This was not easy. His support was sometimes tenuous and fragile, largely because he was hotheaded and created trouble for himself.

Jermaine's college opportunity meant that he would be leaving his neighborhood, and poverty, at least temporarily. Most young men from the area never leave, and the relatively few who do often leave for prison. After losing the scholarship offer to Middle University, he wondered if he would ever leave his neighborhood and get to college on an athletic scholarship.

24 BEING USED

Chuck and I talked about Jermaine's good news. He offered congratulations. "Well, Daddy, you did it. You need to get a cigar, champagne and enjoy this. Celebrate. 'Cause what you done is a miracle, and you should be proud. From where that boy came . . . now, he in college! You done something. You treated him like your own son. Didn't nobody know nothin' about him till we got our hands on him."

Chuck's words were special to me because Jermaine has truly become "my guy." Jermaine played for me and Chuck, but he claims me and I claim him—Jermaine refers to me as his godfather, he calls me on Father's Day and other holidays, and he has visited my family three thousand miles from his home. We usually end phone conversations and visits with "Love you." Jermaine talked about our relationship and how it evolved.

> I see you as a father, friend, a big brother. It happened toward the end of the summer [the first summer I coached him], like even though you was doing research,[1] like you was still taking your time with me. I rarely, like, get attached to certain people. But I can feel if something's good, [or] something's not. I told my moms, like, "I just always wanna be around Scott." You [Scott] wasting your time, your money. You didn't have to do none of that. You was taking me out [to eat]. You was somebody to look up to. So from there, you was something special. Like you don't really got that people that come around in your life many times, that do anything for you, when he could be doing for hisself. Like, he got kids but he still come and see

me. But that's time he could be with his kids, so it was like . . .
I mean, it was like every time I was with you I usually had fun,
like you ain't got those old heads, you just chill with, relax
with, talk, like, you talk to them about anything.

No matter what, you [Scott] listened. You got your opinions,
but you always steered me in the right direction no matter
what. When I'm wrong, you tell me I'm wrong. When I'm
right, you tell me I'm right. And you tell me why I'm right or
why I'm wrong, and I needed that. It's like you that support
system, and no matter what, I know you gonna be there, and
you told me that when we first started getting close. You called
me and you wanted to talk or whatever, and that just got to
me. It just seem like it was something special. Like you was
just meant to be there, for you to come into my life.

She [my mom] must have had to feel something different
[about you] too. She be telling coaches that "if you want to
recruit him [Jermaine], you gotta call him [Scott]." 'Cause she
knew you knew more of the basketball game than her and
how I was always spending my time with you. And I call you
almost every day, and it was like that and she knew that. She
don't really trust a lot of people, and like for her to say that,
I knew she trusted you and she trusted I wasn't going to get
into trouble or be in the streets or whatever. [When I was with
you] I was always doing something right or whatever and doing something productive.

It's clear that some of what Chuck said after my blowup
years earlier with Jermaine had stuck. I have been a coach, father figure, and mentor to Jermaine. He learned not to take this
for granted, although not without his mother's lectures and
my drawing boundaries. Jermaine thought deeply about our relationship and considered my opportunity costs—what I could
have been doing instead of coaching and hanging out with him.
He realized that I was not like other men and old heads that he
had met and interacted with. He came to see our relationship as
something special. He believed that I was a part of his support
system, someone who would be there for him, someone he could
confide in, and someone who would also give him constructive

criticism, feedback, and advice. Monica trusted me too. She told me that she was "giving him to me." This meant that she was giving me authority over him and a responsibility; I was expected to treat him as my son and do whatever I could to help him.

Chuck knew exactly how I felt because he has been a coach, father figure, and mentor to many older and younger men. Chuck says that taking a kid on and coaching them is more than just basketball. It's a socialization and life-skills activity for the kids. The kids need Chuck's and my help because of the absence, busyness, fear, and neglect of parents and the structural inequality and racism of society. Many parents who struggle to provide for their families spoil their kids with materialistic gifts and leniency as a way of dealing with living in poverty and the accompanying guilt, shame, and fear of its possible impact on their children. Chuck and I could be critical and correct the kids and push them to act according to higher expectations because we did not have to provide for them; we did not carry the guilt of raising them in poverty. At the same time, we believed in their potential and knew that they could achieve if they had more resources, information, and opportunities.

Chuck and I are bridges to other worlds. We have specialized knowledge, and Chuck has strong influential networks in basketball. At one point during my research, he knew the head and assistant coaches at five of the six Big 5 schools. Some were *his* guys and close friends. Because of his relationships, Chuck is in a great position to help young men.

Chuck took me along to a birthday barbecue in honor of Sean, a former assistant coach at one of Philadelphia's Big 5 schools who is now a head coach outside of Philadelphia. It was an intimate party; family, childhood friends, and several other college coaches were there. Chuck had some personal connection to most of them and was asked to give a few words about Sean before the cake was cut.

"I remember when this lady comes to me and says, 'My son needs help going to college and he's a real good basketball player.' I said, 'Wait. Hold it right there, lady.' 'Cause mothers always think that their kid is the best, the next Michael

Jordan. I say, 'If he so good, how come he ain't got no colleges recruiting him?' Then we was all right."

Sean's mother was smiling and giggling, remembering this conversation with Chuck. And he continued, "That's right, Gloria. You remember. She bring this scrawny little guy to me and introduce him. And that was it. He was MY GUY from then on. I set him up with my man, down at South State University. Then, I talk to him [on the phone] and he tell me he gonna quit, because my man, the head coach at South State, ain't playing him. He call him [the coach] all kinds of bad names that I can't repeat because there's ladies and children in the room. [Sean starts laughing.] That's right, you remember. And I say, 'Just cool out, baby, and get your degree. You be all right.' 'Cause he wasn't going to be no big-time player no way. He was tiny."

Chuck speaks directly to Sean. "Now look at you, baby. What they say, 'You've come a long way, baby.' And it's true. It's a miracle, God has blessed you, and I love you, man."

Chuck was part of Sean's history, and telling stories affirms his usefulness as well as the value of basketball in changing the lives of young black men. Chuck helped Sean get to a college. Much to Sean's disappointment, he was not good enough to play much. Then Chuck encouraged Sean to continue to work on achieving his degree. This might have been sufficient, but Chuck hooked Sean up with another one of his guys, Gabe, who was then an assistant coach at Catholic University. This led to Sean's first coaching job in the college ranks. Sean's story is particularly good for Chuck, because Sean has coached at some of Philadelphia's universities and colleges and has had much success.

Chuck's gratification comes in the form of hearing "good stories" about players going off to college, graduating, or doing something to show that they are taking themselves seriously and trying to better their lives. "It's not about the basketball; it's about getting 'em in school, graduating [from college]. They come to me and tell me they got a job, they got a family, that's better than the life they was gonna have." Chuck views basketball in much the same way that middle-class America perceives education—as a means to upward mobility. And Chuck chooses to be used through basketball. He says, "It's not being used, if you're being used." He hopes to be used by kids, to be effective, referred to, and to be called upon to give more help when needed. He maximizes his own experiences and relationships to former players, coaches, and families for the development of young men.

I share Chuck's mission. I hope and expect to be used as a resource, as an advocate, but not simply for basketball. My common refrain, when talking to Jermaine, is "Just finish school, graduate. Basketball is nice, but it's not the end. Education has to be the end." My concern is with how Jermaine's life (and the lives of others I coach) has been changed through basketball and how this will impact his children's life chances. This is a long-term project.

CONCLUSION

There are numerous factors that are significant in black male athletic achievement in basketball. Natural ability is important, and people vary in their "God-given" skills; some people are quick, while others have uncanny hand-eye coordination or extraordinary strength or leaping ability. Undoubtedly, there is a minimal level of ability that is required to become an elite basketball player. Yet there is no formula; if so, scouts and recruiters would have a much easier job assessing talent and finding the best players. Some major factors are often overlooked. Only highlighting players' "natural" superior ability diminishes the hard work, effort, planning, strategizing, and decision making required to become elite players. It negates their intelligence, learning ability, and their ability to perform well under pressure.

Elite basketball players do not merely play. They are learning continually throughout their careers. They learn from others that it is important for them to play for status and sociability. They learn to play in particular ways and are taught skills and moves. Players are also tested in different competitive environments and learn how they might move beyond neighborhood and school competition. They learn from different people: from peers, older boys, and from men who have often been declared "missing in action," unreliable, and selfish by research and popular media reports. Simply learning to play and practicing does not lead to success either. Basketball is a perceived niche opportunity that is extremely competitive. College and professional coaches have their pick of players, and few players are indispensable. Therefore, *networks*, *opportunities*, and *exposure* are especially important. An elite player learns how to build his reputation using local, regional, and national image promoters in the form of old heads, media representatives, scouts, school and college recruiters, and fans.

There are formal factors in achievement like where players go to school, the teams they have played for, and in which leagues they have played. Jermaine and Ray gained a lot by playing in Blade Rodgers and transferring out of Thompson and into schools that were more competitive and were followed by the news media. Family history may also be important, having a well-known parent who is or was an elite athlete. Kobe Bryant is the son of Joe "Jellybean" Bryant, who played at La Salle University and professionally in the NBA as well as overseas.

There are also informal factors in achievement such as family, support, coach and player relationships, the quality of play at the playground, the old heads in one's neighborhood, local networks, and the networks' influence. Mothers, grandmothers, brothers, aunts, and uncles were some of the most significant people in young men's lives. For Ray and Jermaine, they gave unconditional support and encouraged them to *become something*. They remained hopeful in times of disappointment, such as when Jermaine did not make Thompson's varsity team and was kicked off junior varsity for fighting, and when Ray and Jermaine did not receive public recognition early on. Ultimately, it was hoped that Ray and Jermaine would mature and grow to become men. As a survival strategy, Monica "gave" Jermaine to me to coach in life. Other mothers, grandmothers, and fathers gave their boys to other men or the military. Non-kin father figures—in the form of old heads, coaches, pastors, and moms' boyfriends—were present every day. This was surprising. Urban sociology has considered the plight of black men a central component of contemporary urban poverty. Their joblessness, underemployment, and general absence in families and households are common and unifying themes for theories of urban social disorganization (crime and violence) and social isolation.[1] Single parents have difficulty raising children on their own. Their children are more likely to be victims of crime, neighborhood violence, and the underground economy or to be involved in them. And specifically, single female-headed households have lower incomes because women earn less than men. Non-kin-related men can have a big, positive impact.[2] To be sure, some of these men seek to take advantage. But in the context of basketball, men can be more effective as old heads, picking up the slack left by absent fathers. Although no organization can be perfect, the Blade Rodgers League is a shining example of social organization. Its network of men/old heads enables it to be more than just a basketball league. It is an institution that gives hope through the investment men make in younger men.[3]

An Alternative Identity and Possibility

Being a basketball player is undoubtedly attached to a black masculinity: a masculinity inherently defined relative to and in contrast with ideas about white masculinity and black and white femininities. Black men are considered the best athletes. At the same time, black men have a unique socioeconomic position. They are not considered *real* men, at least by the standards of masculinity set by the wider society. It is said that they don't provide for their families financially, leaving black mothers to be single heads of households and children fatherless.

In this world, dominated by systems of white patriarchy and capitalism, black men seek to define and claim themselves in a world of suspicion, conflict, competition, and limited opportunity. They must combat how others see them and how they've come to see themselves, and gain hope in the midst of intractable hopelessness and immobility. How does this struggle against the broad media-maintained construction of black men as thugs, criminals, pimps (literally, and metaphorically as promiscuous lovers), and irresponsible adults play out at a local level? Young black males do not wholly accept this presumption of criminality, nor do they see themselves as failures. Instead, they see society as skewed and opportunities largely determined by factors beyond their control. They are encouraged to do certain activities and take on identities that belie low social status. Many feel that they have to succeed on their own, solve their own problems. Thus, they imagine how they might succeed via mainstream paths and institutions. Young men in South Philly become basketball players because it is a positive identity, an alternative to being in "the street," and a possible means of escaping poverty.

Jermaine and Ray (and others) were working out an alternative identity: becoming basketball players by learning and constructing a plan for mobility and gaining recognition, getting known, and utilizing local resources.

John Edgar Wideman, Pulitzer Prize–winning author and former collegiate basketball player at the University of Pennsylvania, writes about basketball as the key to "alternative possibilities" for young, poor black men in his autobiographical memoir *Hoop Roots*.

> Growing up, I needed basketball because my family was poor and colored, hemmed in by material circumstances none of us knew how to control, and if I wanted more, a larger, different portion than other poor colored folks in Homewood [Pittsburgh], I had to single myself out. . . . Imagining a different portion is the first step, the door cracking between known and unknown. A door on alternative possibilities. If you want more and you're lucky enough, as I was, to choose or be chosen by some sort of game, you may then begin to forge a game plan. If you believe you're in the game, you may be willing to learn the game's ABCs. Learn what it costs to play. Begin making yourself a player. (2001, 10)

Wideman played basketball to distinguish himself from others, to have alternative possibilities, and to get more out of life. In short, becoming a basketball player is a way to become special, and it is this "specialness" that enables young, poor black men from inner cities to imagine a future different from their peers. He also recognized that one learns and makes themselves into a player. This does not happen overnight; a kid has to "forge a game plan" to learn how to use basketball as a "door on alternative opportunities" and learn what it takes to be good.

Everett C. Hughes writes that *professions* are typically

> entered by long training, ordinarily in a manner prescribed by the profession itself and sanctioned by the state. The training is assumed to be necessary for learning the science and technique essential to practice of the function of the profession. The training, however, carries with it as a by-product, assimilation of the candidate to a set of professional attitudes and controls, a professional conscience and solidarity. (1928, 762)

For players like Jermaine and Ray, basketball became a career and a profession. They organized their lives around basketball activities, playing at the playground with old heads and peers, playing at school with friends and as part of the school team, competing in leagues outside of school/organized basketball, and traveling with teams. Moreover, they learned what it took to become a player socially: how to dress, how to talk, and how to interact with others. All of this was indicative of their assimilation into what it meant to be a basketball player: someone who was trying to be somebody, who wasn't wasting his life, and who was trying to do something for himself and his family. Being a basketball player took one out of his neighborhood and poverty, both physically and mentally. Unfortunately, this can also have deleterious effects on poor communities lacking in resources and accessible role models. Young black men learn to leave their communities, and few give back in significant ways that might create lasting change for younger children (Powell 2008; Smith 2007; Edwards 1997). On an individual level, "putting all your eggs in one basket" offers little wiggle room or backup plans. Most basketball players who dream of NBA stardom and riches fail, and many sink into depression, drug use, and violence—the effects of failing and unfulfilling their alternative possibility. They feel as though they have let down loved ones and have been misused by a system that gives no consolation prizes.

Therefore, many scholars and former athletes claim that black boys' participation in the highest levels of basketball, and sports generally, is pointless—a "dirty trick" that misleads and gives empty promises.[4] Undoubtedly, basketball as a business exploits young black women and men, and we all are complicit in this.[5] However, at a micro level, participation cannot be measured just by the probability of becoming a professional, even if this is a major motivation for young men. Only a *few* young men get a chance to go to college and then fall short of their dream. Instead, short- and long-term, immediate and latent effects must figure into our understanding. Young men are looking for the alternative possibility, a new world that Wideman talks about and has attained.

Chuck pushes for this by rejecting the myth of "making it," explaining during practice sessions his hope for players and their use of basketball:

> I don't see no NBA players in here. One in 25 million make it. And how many teams are there in the NBA? Twelve make it, and there are twenty-nine teams how many is that? Two hundred fifty-six. And you got thirty coming out of the SEC [South East Conference—a top collegiate athletic conference], ten from the ACC [Atlantic Coast Conference—another top conference], ten from the Big 10 [a Midwest Athletic Conference, made up of arguably the ten best athletic schools in the Midwest], five from the Big East [an athletic conference made up of schools along the East Coast], the PAC 10 [the major West Coast athletic conference, the PAC is short for Pacific]. And that don't include those coming out of high school and foreigners! The Turkonlink [an attempt to say the name Türkoğlu—a Lithuanian player for the Orlando Magic] and the Nowitkees [another attempt to pronounce the name of an European player, Dirk Nowitzki, who plays for the Dallas Mavericks] whatever they name is . . . But if you listen and learn I am going to give you everything that I think you can handle. And you can be a good player. Maybe you can get a scholarship, go to college, get a degree and get a good job. 'Cause if you don't, I can tell you where you gonna end up, that's right, I know right where

I'll find you. On the corner, looking out this way [hands put in front of his face crisscrossed]. You know what this is, these fingers are bars. That's jail. Or dead.

As Chuck figures, as well as many young men like Jermaine, basketball is in competition with the street—not education. At its best, it is an identity—a lifestyle and perspective that informs and guides decisions. Chuck stresses that the "good" story is not simply a basketball dream; it is whether or not they "become somebody," according to their own expectations and standards, limited by larger structures—whether or not they nurture a new future for themselves, open another world, or even something less grandiose. It does not have to lead to fame and fortune. Hope is not intrinsic and can't be taken for granted. Kids work at success and gain momentum, gain opportunities, and ultimately gain hope. From hope, alternative possibilities can grow. Basketball may simply maintain communities and sustain relationships by providing a social space and platform for young men to feel redeemed and bond with older men based on shared experiences and moments that can be revisited.

EPILOGUE

Jermaine entered college in January 2007 and completed one semester of course work. He was offered a scholarship, but it only partially covered tuition and fees, books, and room and board. Grants and financial aid, for which he had to qualify, covered the rest; he would have some loans to repay. In addition, he arrived out of shape, due to an ankle injury. As an academically ineligible student, he couldn't practice with the team or go to away games, but he worked out hard to regain form. He lifted weights, did conditioning, and practiced his shooting. However, class was a struggle and he failed two courses (Intro to Religion and Health Sciences); he retook Health Sciences in summer 2007, earning a B grade.

Before Jermaine could play a game, the head coach resigned. Jermaine was unsure about staying, but academically eligible. He made the decision to stay and was one of two players to start every game. At the season's end, he was the team's third leading scorer and second leading rebounder. Jermaine continues to play in Blade Rodgers' college summer league and is entering his second basketball season at Red State.

Ray entered college in August 2004 and completed a full year of course work before playing. It was worth the wait. He became the team's second leading scorer, earned All Conference Second Team honors and Freshman of the Year. He also scored twenty-one points against one of the nation's top teams. This was just in his first year of play. As a second-year player (third year academically), Ray was the team's leading scorer and averaged better than sixteen points per game. He became the team's captain and a conference star (First Team All-Conference). He returned for his junior season (fourth year academically) with high expectations and did not disappoint. Ray led his struggling team to the conference championship and won the TOP (tournament outstanding player) award. The win earned his team a NCAA tournament berth and a nationally televised game. They struggled and lost in the first round, but again Ray had gained exposure. Ray was talked about extensively during the television coverage and was the subject of a special feature in one of the most widely read sports magazines. He still hopes to become a professional player and considers this a realistic possibility. He is on track to graduate in June 2009.

Keith attended a community college in the Midwest before transferring to a four-year college in the South on a basketball scholarship. After only one season, he is transferring again, but to a smaller four-year college. He has played in Blade Rodgers' college league each summer and is on track to graduate in June 2009.

In Bryant's final year at Buddy Strong High School, he was involved with drugs and his life was threatened at a game. In the summer, he rejoined our team and showed up for a couple of games. He said that he really needed help from Chuck and me because playing ball was his only chance to stay out of trouble. Bryant attended Philadelphia Covenant Prep School with Jermaine but dropped out. He then disappeared for about a year before landing at a Southern California community college.

Chuck runs into other former players or hears about them. They are doing different things. Some are away at college, playing ball, or just going to school. Others are working, doing entry-level fast-food jobs and military service. Inevitably, a few have gotten into the street life. One kid has been shot, and another has been in and out of jail.

Chuck and Me

Chuck remains South Philly's coach, and his 2007 Rookie league team won the championship again (we won the sixth-, seventh-, and eighth-grade championship once during my tenure). He says that he will continue to coach as long as he enjoys it and has the passion. It is clear that he can still perform "miracles," "taking turkey shit and making turkey salad." But who will be his predecessor? He has been looking for one of his former players to step up and be consistent in coming to practice. He wants someone to learn under him, and then he will give them the reins. He has done this before, at least for one team, right before I came onto the scene. But this person left and so have others. Some come to learn his system and approach, and then set up their own leagues and teams. Recently, Bobby, Keith's uncle who coached AAU ball with Alvin, has shown great interest and consistency in coaching South Philly. He is an assistant with Buddy Strong High School and brings some of his players to the team. Bobby looks to be the next coach when Chuck is ready to step down, but I don't expect this to happen soon.

Chuck and I stay in weekly contact via scheduled phone calls, where we speak mostly about "our guys," what they're doing, and who he has seen. We talk about other players (current and former) in the league, and basketball and sports generally. We also discuss our families, our daily lives, and how we miss the old days. He is one of my closest and best friends. I usually get back to Philly two or three times a year, especially in the summer. When I do, we talk daily and meet at the league. I'm right back in the groove when South Philly has games. It's as though I've never left.

APPENDIX 1: METHODOLOGY

"That's My Man": The Ethnographer as Friend

Scholars have produced wonderfully rich representations of the life of "common" folks in the city: from street-corner men and bar regulars (working and middle-class blacks); to Chicano and "Spanish," Italian, and black youth in the inner city; and people in poor ghettoes and black middle-class ghettoes. In many accounts, researchers present some part or whole stories of their "getting in"—how they gained rapport and could be trusted. These are really stories of relationships, namely, how they met and befriended a key informant(s). To name a few, there's Anderson's Herman, Horowitz's Gilberto, Duneier's Hakim, Bourgois' Primo, and Whyte's Doc. There are countless other examples. Ethnographers make clear how important their relationships with these persons are to the outcome—an ethnographic document—as they discuss the contours of their relationships with these teachers of local knowledge and sponsors.[1] In fact, it might be said that ethnographies are the relationships that fieldworkers have with people in their research setting.

Students generally learn that objectivity is the ideal and necessary to research and writing. Hammersley and Atkinson (1995) write that informants should not be considered how one chooses a friend. Yet one does not always have it easy in fluid research such as participant observation. The ideal may not even be desirable because of how this restricts data gathering, understanding, and the ability to check findings with subjects. Researchers enter the field knowing that they will need others, but they may not know how much they will be needed and even that their needs may go beyond research. Duneier discusses his personal dilemma with helping sidewalk vendors and homelessness by giving small change (1999, 354–57). In the appendix Duneier asks, should researchers intervene or not, or when should they intervene in the lives of people that they are studying? Researchers need friends and may need to be a friend. Textbooks that talk about qualitative research, and ethnography in particular, identify separation or divesting as a final research phase. Getting *too* involved is cited as an issue of subjectivity, and pulling out can be hard to do. The experience of ethnographers is complicated.

Rarely are the relationships between fieldworker and informant discussed and divulged as "regular" friendships, whereby maintenance rituals occur, trust is established and confirmed, researchers become emotionally vulnerable, and researcher and subject express affinity and commitment to one another, verbally and nonverbally. The "getting in" process is often presented linearly—once a researcher has gained rapport, it is simply maintained and they go about doing their work. However, relationships take work, and there are ups and downs, times of near and far observation, and bumpy relations. This is what largely distinguishes ethnographers from other researchers.

Research is a relationship, whether it be quantitative or qualitative, and we create a history with our research that typically begins before the formal research project. Anderson and Allard (2004) talk about ethnographies being a part of the ethnographer's *own* story, a way of resolving or attempting to work out something inside of the ethnographer. Objectivity is an ideal for some, but it is not only unrealistic at times; it can be undesirable. As a humanistic endeavor, shouldn't our goal be to get personal? More to the point, I learned that ethnography is not merely active; it is real life.[2] I developed relationships, gained a lifelong friend, and have been changed by my research. From the outside in, I learned what it meant to be a friend in this space and how this affected my research.

I was a young, middle-class, educated black man from the West Coast doing research in a South Philadelphia community of poor blacks. This affected how I was able to gain access and trust, and shaped the expectations Chuck and others had of me. I had to manage impressions and the feelings I had, which changed over time. I was not simply a researcher. I had little choice in the matter, if I was to become an observing participant. Chuck's ideas about me and my relationship with him and others were significant (Brooks 2004). I became a friend, a mentor, and a coach, roles that I had to learn. I had joined a club, an organization, a network of people. This network was filled with history and shared experiences. Their status ranged from legends and star basketball players to scrubs (poor players) and knowledgeable spectators who looked up to the stars and legends. They "spoke for" each other and vouched for past basketball ability as a matter of inclusion and defining who belonged to the group.

Getting In

As I mentioned in the book's introduction, I met Chuck through a reference, via snowball sampling. Chuck was the only one, from a list of men that I contacted, who returned my call. Chuck was eager to respond to my call because I left a message stating that I had been referred by Henry Ryan and was interested in learning about Philadelphia basketball. I needed some reference or lead to bridge and get into this basketball network. Chuck told me this straight up, "You called the right name—Henry Ryan. That's my MAN! I'd do anything for Henry; he a great man, a GREAT man! If you all right with him, you all right with me. How my man doing? I ain't seen him in a long while, since he been dealing with his health situation." We talked briefly about Henry, and then Chuck took on a particular role, befitting his local status. He quizzed me on early Philadelphia basketball legends and general black basketball history.

Chuck was also excited about my call because he's a self-proclaimed, and socially validated, "guru" (pronounced ga-roo). This meant that he considered himself knowledgeable and useful—a sage and teacher. "I don't know nobody in the world who know as much basketball as me. I been at every level—high school, college, pro. I ain't telling you from what I seen; I'm telling from what I know, what I lived, what I done. I not only coached—I played for forty years!" His sense of being a guru was based upon experience and success. He showed me news clippings from his high school and professional careers and pictures of teams and players that he coached. What he did most was tell me lots of stories. His social status and position was validated when I met other men involved with the league. "You got the right guy," Blade Rodgers, the president of the league, commented. "Chuck's the guru. He's a legend. And not many could play like this man [Chuck]. He was the Truth. Wilt Chamberlain, Earl 'the Pearl,' he right up there with the best of them to ever come out of Philadelphia."

You're Black, Right?

Before we got too far along—ten to fifteen minutes into our first conversation—Chuck stopped midsentence and asked, "Now, let me ask you one question . . . Are you black?" I said, "Yes." Thereafter, he continued with very little pause, "I can tell you the truth, but if you black, then I can tell you the *real* truth, know what I mean." Race definitely played a large role in my relationships. Race was the starting point, a group connection; I belonged to the same broad community—a black community—and therefore it was believed that we had some level of shared experiences and understanding about the world. It allowed me to observe, listen, and join in some conversations without introduction. My presence was not threatening or odd—the league was filled with other black men who were *strangers*[3]: fathers, coaches, spectators who moved about anonymously and without specific purposes.[4] Still, being black and male did not guarantee acceptance as a member of the group of men who coordinated and ran the league. Membership required more; I had to invest time in the league and be vouched for (Brooks 2004).

While I thought that my relationship with Chuck was solitary—just between him and me—he let me know otherwise early on. I volunteered in the league for a month or so and got to know some of the other five or six older men who helped in running the league. Then Chuck had a proposition for me. "I talked to the guys and they said that you 'all right.' You checked out," he said in a very straightforward manner and with a serious, even tone. "I got something that I think you gonna love. How'd you like to get closer to the kids and really see what's up? How'd you like to coach with me?" I said "yes" with no hesitation. I hadn't expected this but didn't see it as a huge deal. I knew that coaching was a volunteer effort, not a paid job, and something that many people didn't take on, especially if their kids were not involved, because of the time commitment, frustration, and mixed payoff. I was excited because I had been a volunteer coach before—this was my preferred method of community service—and it would be invaluable to my research. How much so I didn't know. At the same time, Chuck's formal offer and reference to "the guys" and "they" seemed strange. Who exactly were "the guys," and how did they have power or influence over me? I understood naturally that I was being watched, in terms of basic socializing and impression management. However, I didn't know that I was being evaluated in such a formal way. This foreshadowed the seriousness of the endeavor I was joining and the significance of bonds between men in this setting.

Summer Break

I joined Chuck and three other men in coaching South Philly's contingent for the league. We had different, but overlapping roles based upon our status. Chuck was obviously the head, followed by Ali, who was Chuck's age and whom Chuck described as a "great guard." Ali had helped Chuck on and off for over twenty years and had coached separately at a local YMCA. DeAndre was one of Chuck's former players who was known for his high school and local college career. His career was cut short by drug addiction and its concomitant effects that led to a rapid downward spiral into obscurity. He worked in a halfway house and was trying to put his life together because he was married and had children. DeAndre had been a consistent assistant coach, but his obligations busied him and his consistency waned. Another man, Murph, whose stepson was a member of this particular team, recruited other young men from the community. He had very little basketball experience. Murph did not play past high school junior varsity. He enjoyed basketball, admired star players, and learned as much as he could because it allowed him to talk to others about basketball and vie for status. He also hoped to help his stepson become a great player and to coach on his own. Chuck, Ali, DeAndre, and Murph were local guys and knew many families and their kids because of this. They had attended high school or played basketball with mothers, fathers, grandmothers and grandfathers, sisters and brothers, aunts and uncles.

I was the outsider, a graduate student from California. I did not have a long relationship with Chuck, was not a Philadelphian, and did not know the kids or their families. So I did not have any significant vested interest in the kids or the other men. However, I did develop this over time as I committed myself to Chuck, the league, and our team.

In my first year, I helped coach the three teams (sixth, seventh, and eighth graders; ninth and tenth graders; and eleventh and twelfth graders) from March through July. Then I went on summer break. School had been out since May, I was anxious to return home to California before classes resumed. I then used the fall as a break from gathering data. The league was not active, and I reviewed my data and wrote, gave a presentation at a conference, and thought of what would be next to do once the league resumed. I thought little of my absence, of the relationship that I had begun with Chuck. I was on my school schedule. Chuck was my informant, and coaching in the league was my research site.

I called Chuck in January to check in and ask about when we would be starting back. Chuck was very short on the phone. He did not sound animated as he had in the past. I thought maybe he just wasn't feeling well and told him that I would catch up with him at the preliminary housing project league that Blade Rodgers operated. He still had not thawed when we met up again.

He did not tell me that he was upset with me. He did not tell me to stay away, yet he was aloof and avoided eye contact. He did not introduce me to others, and he sometimes turned away from me and carried on other conversations. He did not joke or say much to me. I felt alienated and stayed away from him, though I continued to volunteer in the preliminary league. In contrast, my relationship with other men in the league had deepened. They greeted me warmly, calling my name loudly when they saw me: "Scotty!! Beam me up, Scotty." They inquired about what I had been up to, asked me to do things, and included me in their conversations.

I confided in my wife, Kara, and she smartly clued me in. Basketball was not just community service or research for Chuck. It meant much more to him, and therefore the relationships that he developed with others through basketball were not seasonal. Within this context, I had entered a relationship with Chuck and then left, leaving him feeling jilted. I had disappeared for nearly six months, reducing basketball and our relationship to research, an activity to be done between more important things—like school and school breaks. Worse, my disappearance may have signaled that I was selfish and had only volunteered for personal gain. I had "dissed" (disrespected) him. The meaning of basketball involvement was much deeper than research for Chuck. He had invested in me, and we had become partners via coaching, working with young men, sharing part of our lives, and gaining common experiences. He thought I would love the opportunity to coach and get closer to the kids and implicitly wanted to get closer to him.

Getting Back In

Getting back in good graces occurred in little time because our practices began and I saw him a lot during the week. I did not speak to him directly about what had happened. I knew that he was a no-nonsense guy and excuses would be lost on him. I could not just say, "Sorry, I did not know that we were in a relationship. I didn't mean to hurt your feelings or lead you to believe that I was not grateful or uninterested in coaching with you." I had to work my way back in, showing him that I was committed via my attendance and attitude. We practiced five days a week, and I was the most consistent and dependable assistant coach. Practice was held from 5 to 7 p.m., so I would show before 5 p.m. and stay the whole time. DeAndre, Ali, and Murph had erratic attendance, and Chuck would arrive no earlier than 5:30 p.m. and usually kept the boys until 7:30 or 8 p.m. I also called Chuck twice a week just to check in. In one conversation, after his thawing, he asked me what I had been doing from August to January. I told him about my schedule and tried to fill in the time as much as possible, to account for my absence and appear busy and pulled from him. This was my apology, and he seemed to accept it. He said that he wondered what I was up to during the fall and figured that I had been back in school but would reach out to him at some point. It was awkward, a funny dance; my indirect apology and his wanting an apology and needing an explanation without making it explicit that he needed an apology—this would have been an acknowledgment of his hurt. We began to meet again before practices to hang out. We would drive around the city while he told me about points of interest, as they related to basketball and blacks.

My investment increased all around. I began to reach out to our players, tutoring kids before practice and driving kids home when they needed rides. By the end of the sixth-, seventh-, and eighth-grader season in my second year, Chuck and I were pretty much all alone as coaches. Murph and DeAndre had completely gone missing in action and Ali died. During the high school summer session, I got some solo game-coaching experience, when Chuck would come late or miss the game completely. He would come to me after the game or call and ask me how the game had gone. He would also ask others how I had done and tell me what these men had said. Again it was clear that I was being watched, albeit passively and seemingly for positive ends. If they were watching me, then perhaps they were also protecting me. Chuck's lateness became regular, and he would show up and observe from afar until I waved to him or called him over. We would talk about the game, and he would say that I was doing all right without him. I would affirm that I needed him. And we'd laugh about what my body language said: "Come help me and hurry!"

Why You Asking Them?

In my second summer, I began using my association with Chuck to interview other men who coached and were involved, many of whom were on the original list of people to call given to me by Henry Ryan. I also interviewed parents. This was part of my efforts to triangulate information and cast a broad net. Chuck sometimes saw me talking to others and would come over to see what was going on, then would realize what I was doing and walk away. We talked about this directly. I told him that I had to interview other people to make sure that I got as many perspectives as possible. He didn't understand this in a practical manner. "Why you asking them? I'll give you everything you need to know. They don't know as much as me." I agreed with him, and at times folks I interviewed were confused as well. It seemed disrespectful; my actions did not show that I understood his position. He knew the *Truth* and was the source. Others generally gained their knowledge from him or from others taught by him. How did it look for me to have the source, yet go to secondary and tertiary sources? Did it suggest that I did not believe him? Or perhaps I wasn't as close to him as it seemed? Chuck and I worked through this dilemma by talking. I blamed my interviewing on research and my professors who demanded that I talk to others because numbers confirmed ideas. He understood and accepted this. I was up front about whom I was going to interview; I didn't want him to feel as though I was doing something behind his back. Ultimately, he came to offer names of people to interview, and when we talked to some men in passing, he would prompt them to tell me their stories. These people spent time talking about how they learned from, admired, and respected Chuck and some of his cronies.

Interviewing others was more problematic when Chuck disliked the people I interviewed; they might have been longtime adversaries or had done something that Chuck did not like and vice versa. Chuck considered parents the worst part of coaching because they generally had the least amount of knowledge but a high amount of influence on the child's behavior and self-perception with regards to basketball ability. In varying degrees, they were opponents. They asked why we didn't play their sons more and why we insisted that the team play a certain way, which they always felt limited their sons. It was clear that Chuck and I held divergent expectations and evaluations of their sons than they had.

Over time, interviewing other coaches was strained by my gaining a position, not only as Chuck's "guy" but also as an opposing coach. Early on, I could play up my role as an outsider, being "green" as a coach, and talk about the league from an outsider's view. However, after a couple of years, I was fully entrenched, one of South Philly's coaches, and opposing coaches did not speak much to one another. Competition forced social distance—and South Philly was a feared part of the city with a reputation for being the toughest area in the city (South Philadelphians often believe that North Philly is the worst/most violent area).

Part of History—Relationships Forever

Our younger team (sixth, seventh, and eighth graders) had some success in my first two years, but the high school–aged teams were a crapshoot. In fact, in my first year, we had to forfeit the season for the eleventh- and twelfth-grade team because we could not get enough players to show up consistently. The younger kids seemed to listen and do what we asked, not yet jaded by the inflated egos and self-perception that came with playing high school varsity basketball and traveling to tournaments around the country. Things improved greatly and surprisingly for the ninth- and tenth-grade team in my second year. This was the year that Ray, Jermaine, and Keith's team won the chip.

The championship story solidified our team. The core players stayed together for two more years, and Chuck and I bonded to them and vice versa. The story of the playoffs and the championship became a bookmark for my personal relationships and my connection to South Philly basketball. Chuck often referred to the story, our interactions, and how much we went through. The sense of struggle and being an underdog made the story more fantastic, and our trust in one another and working together seemed much more significant. Chuck and I became even closer friends. We had overcome something together with the odds against us. Chuck expressed that I had also become a permanent member of the league because winning the championship was a historical moment. "You a part of history now," he said and told me that I was an unforgettable person in the lives of our boys because championships last forever. "These boys got something special—can't nobody take it away from them. All they life, they can say, 'I was a champion.' And you had a hand in that, a big hand in that. Whatever they do, you can say you 'put your hands on them.'"

Conclusion

My four-year story of "getting in" leads to three main points about fieldwork methods and relationships. (1) You don't know where you'll meet your friends, in life and research. My relationship with Chuck does not seem likely. People are more apt to develop friendships and relationships with others similar to them (i.e., race, class, education, religion, and gender). (2) As a researcher, you may be needed as a friend and you may need a friend. It is obvious that ethnographers will need others to do their research. The types and tones of relationships will vary as some will become close friends and others mere acquaintances; some will be helpful and supportive and others suspicious, perhaps even hostile. The research setting evolves based upon your relationships and negotiation with people. Importantly, you may be needed because of what you bring to the table as a person, an academic, and as a person with privilege and resources. Your subjects' view of you and what you are doing is important to your relationships; it is not simply what you believe that you are doing. (3) Lastly, how you navigate relationships, being a friend or remaining distant/apart, has profound implications for data gathering, understanding, and ultimately the final report. It is not a simple matter of claiming one way is better than another—close and intense participant observation over a passive role. You may have very little control of how close you become; the social setting may be closed out of necessity. Each setting and research has its own unique factors, people, culture, and conditions, and ethnographers have to find their own story each time they begin a new research endeavor.

APPENDIX 2: SETTINGS—POLITICS OF SPACE

As Jermaine and Ray progressed, they grew more aware and concerned about their opportunities. They considered who would be watching, with whom they would be playing, and how much they would play. This chart describes how settings and types of basketball compared.

	Playground[a]	School[b]	Leagues[c]	AAU[d]
Exposure	Low	Low	Medium	Low-High
Competition	Low	Low-Medium	Medium-High	Medium-High
Opportunity	High	Medium-High	Medium-Low	Medium-Low

[a]Playground includes playground leagues.
[b]School includes summer leagues for school teams, with summer leagues being a place of low competition but high opportunity for underclassmen to show their potential.
[c]Leagues include citywide prominent leagues like the Blade Rodgers League.
[d]AAU includes the range of city/regional/national with more local tournaments having less competition and exposure, but offering more opportunities to play.

APPENDIX 3: JERMAINE'S PATH

Freshman Year

- Thompson High School, Junior Varsity: kicked off team for fighting
- Dunked on a known player, Tommy Handy

Spring and Summer

- Blade Rodgers League: championship game Most Valuable Player (MVP); team wins championship; dunked on six-feet-eight-inch known player
- Selected to play for Amateur Athletic Union (AAU) team

Sophomore Year

- Thompson High School, Varsity: second leading scorer

Spring and Summer

- Selected to play on AAU team that travels to Italy
- Blade Rodgers League: First Team All-League; named Mr. Charisma and League Co-MVP (with Hanif Martin); team loses in second round

Junior Year

- North Catholic, Varsity: third leading scorer
- Great defensive play against known player earns praise in newspaper

Spring and Summer

- Blade Rodgers League: Second Team All-League; named Mr. Hustle; team loses in first round
- Selected to play on Philly Jazz (AAU) with city's best players

Senior Year

- North Catholic, Varsity: second leading scorer
- Dunked from foul line on Seniors' Day in front of mother and close friends
- Voted second team All-Catholic League by coaches

Spring and Summer

- Offered scholarship to small low-level Division 1 university in Northeast—declined
- Blade Rodgers League: First Team All-League; named Mr. Charisma; team loses in second round
- Continued playing for Philly Jazz AAU team
- Tries out for, and is given, scholarship to prep school
- In Vegas tourney, notable defensive performance against one of nation's top players at same position and narrowly missed dunk over nation's best player, who is seven feet tall
- Offered scholarship to mid-major university in Northeast—accepted, then reneged

Prep School

- Dunk on nationally ranked player, the son of an NBA Hall of Famer, signed to a high-major university
- Dunk on nationally ranked player who attended a high-major university in California
- Top scorer in league (26 points per game)
- Team MVP and Defensive Player of the Year
- Third Team All-America
- Offered scholarship to attend high-major university in Midwest—accepted but failed to qualify
- Offered scholarship to attend mid-major university in Midwest—accepted and admitted

College

Academics only, Athletic Redshirt
Freshman, 2007–2008

- Started every game of the season
- Team's fourth leading scorer (6.7 points per game)
- Team's third leading rebounder (5.7 points per game)
- Conference's second leading offensive rebounder (3.0 points per game)

NOTES

PREFACE

1. Harry Edwards (1973), black activist and sports sociologist, has criticized blacks for being "co-conspirator[s]" in the exploitation of their own children by a white-dominated sports establishment. Hoberman (1997) agrees that the sports fixation by blacks is damaging. He asserts that blacks have put an enormous stake in athletics because of a social need to have some claim of superiority over whites. It is believed that this fixation on sports and athleticism impedes social mobility because it has translated into an overemphasis on athletics and physical ability at the cost of academic and more traditional occupational pursuits.

2. The debate over whether sports enhance or impede mobility rages on. Some research suggests that sports have had positive and negative impacts upon the educational attainment of blacks (Coakley 1988). However studies of graduation rates suggest that black scholar athletes are better off than black students. They graduate at a higher rate than non-athletes from four-year universities, which might suggest that scholar athletes have increased their possible options for employment over non-college attendees and college dropouts. Edwards (1973) counters that this may overlook what majors athletes are steered into (i.e., jock majors or majors that have little to no practical value outside of an undergraduate education) and athletes' actual preparedness to enter the real world after being used up by athletics. Other studies conclude that educational aspirations may be enhanced by one's involvement in organized sports. Skills, abilities, and talents may be developed through athletic training, and local or national occupational opportunities may be expanded due to an athlete's visibility and popularity. Thus, many urban and poor blacks have viewed athletics as a gatekeeper to options and opportunities that have otherwise been closed to people of their social class and race.

3. For an extremely helpful step-by-step guide to conducting this type of research, see Spradley (1980).

4. Matza (1969) provides some foundational thoughts on how to do fieldwork and comes to represent the social world they are studying from an insider's perspective; also see Van Maanen (1988) for understanding different types of ethnographic goals and writing. See Glaser and Strauss (1967) for an

explanation of how theory is developed inductively from data, also called "grounded theory."

5. I abided by the standard of writing thick description. "Thick" description, as opposed to "thin" description, is recording human behavior in context such that its meaning is conveyed (Geertz 1973).

6. See Hammersley and Atkinson (1995) and Denzin and Lincoln (1994). Multi-site qualitative research is useful and relevant to understand the connections between social spaces and meanings. Meanings are not simply created in a vacuum; they are influenced by outside factors (such as outside discussions, actors, and spaces). Multi-site research provides greater reliability and validity. Moreover, it enables a researcher to understand the role of specific spaces in meanings, how these meanings are different in other spaces, as well as the different roles that actors play.

7. The voices of players and other involved parties are of central importance to this type of work as my goal is to show their perspective, meanings, and thoughts about life.

INTRODUCTION

1. Names of people, leagues, and places have been changed to preserve anonymity.

2. This information was validated by newspaper clippings, letters, pictures, and awards.

CHAPTER ONE

1. Naturally, I wonder how Jermaine's life might have been changed by the presence of his father. This is a central finding of this research—some men fill in where other men have been absent. Scholars have looked into the role of fathers (see Furstenberg and Harris 1993), and particularly black fathers (see McAdoo 1988). Furstenberg and Harris find that fathers and father figures in the home have a significant impact on children's outcomes (dropout, teen pregnancy). Father figures present an interesting factor, and Anderson's (1999) analysis of old heads suggests that father figures outside of the home can be significant in children's lives.

2. Anderson (1999) also speaks about the corner as a space where young men involved in drug dealing gather, where shootings generally occur because of territorial competition, and where "decent" kids who want to appear tough mix and blend in with those who really are "street." Bourgois (1995) also documents activities and the corner scene via the "game room" in his ethnography detailing the selling of crack in a New York Puerto Rican barrio.

3. Anderson's chapter "The Black Male in Public" in *Streetwise* (1990) illuminates the social dilemma of young black men: they carry a stigma and are presumed to be suspicious, criminal, and deviant, and their presence provokes fear, caution, and reaction. To avoid discriminatory treatment, a black man "must work hard to make others trust his common decency" (163).

4. This is not a personal viewpoint. Basketball as a savior is the view held by parents, kids, and involved community members. May (2008) comes to a similar finding. It is important to note that saving lives through basketball

is largely temporary, since few young men become college and professional players or enter some other basketball-related career. Smith (2007, 10) adds that young black men from inner cities are not deciding between sports and education or professional athlete and doctor or lawyer. Instead, they are choosing athletics over dead-end, low-wage jobs.

CHAPTER TWO

1. Connell (1987) explains masculinity as a collective practice and socialization where young men learn to be men through their interactions with other men and in contrast and often opposition to what women do believe. Kenyon and McPherson (1973) have written the textbook standard on sports socialization and cover multiple theoretical perspectives.

2. Fine's (1987) study of Little League baseball offers a comparison of how baseball was a predominantly male space, central to how young white men in the suburbs play and engage in teenage masculinity rituals that are encouraged and monitored by men. Messner (1988, 1990) found that black men, particularly poor black men, consider athletic ability and participation more central to masculinity than white men.

3. Patillo-McCoy (1999) writes about how young black men idolize and wear Jordan brand merchandise in Chicago as a way of connecting themselves to Michael Jordan's iconic black masculinity. May (2008) discusses this more generally, similar to what I found, in the collapsing of basketball and black masculinity. Basketball is considered a birthright by many young black men.

4. The game Ray watched was important at the time it was played, approximately seven years earlier. It was a college game that featured Iverson and Ray Allen on opposing teams. Both are all-star professional players.

5. Michael Jordan was not raised in the inner city but was born in Brooklyn, New York. Still, his birthplace has been played up (i.e., on T-shirts, in movies) to reinforce the image that the best basketball players come from the inner city.

6. All names of persons, places, and other points of identification have been changed for anonymity.

7. It is obvious when watching girls' and women's basketball that black women have a love affair with basketball as well. But there is very little scholarly literature in this area. Research on black girls and women instead has been in family, poverty (welfare), or gender literature that speaks mostly to the sexism, racism, and poverty that they face. Ladner (1971) has written a classic ethnography on black womanhood, how black women in the inner city make sense of their world and possibilities and define self-worth. On a side note, there is a necessary and growing interest in the area of criminology. Black girls and women represent the fastest-growing segment of the incarcerated. One sterling example is the work of Jones (2004). Her work is the counterpart to Anderson's *Code of the Street* (1999). She has written about black girls in Philadelphia who abide by the "code of the street" as well and how some manage reputations as fighters to both avoid and win fights.

8. Drexel University has played in the Big 5 since 1987 but is not an official member to date.

9. This information about Philadelphia basketball was gathered anecdotally and verified through some books about Philadelphia's basketball history. See Hunt (1996), Lyons (2002), and Philadelphia Daily News (2003).

10. Rooney notes that from 1961–1980 young black men from the inner city were courted rigorously and paid to play for colleges, often far away from their home—in distance and culturally.

> New York City and environs, Philadelphia, Washington, D.C., Detroit, Pittsburgh, Chicago, and Los Angeles are the hunting grounds of most serious recruiters. In these seven cities, the talent seekers could have observed over one-quarter of the major college players recruited since 1961. Some of the best players are veterans of the rigorous competition associated with high schools of multi-thousand enrollments, as well as of years of ghetto playground experience, and the fact that they perform in the shadow of numerous city universities, coaches, asphalt hustlers, and scouts greatly enhances the probability of their being recruited. (1980, 133)

Playgrounds in the blackest and poorest neighborhoods were considered the best places to find black talent, and two classic books by sports journalists document this trend intimately via participant observation in New York: Pete Axthelm's *A City Game* (1970) and Rick Telander's *Heaven Is a Playground* (1976). This rush to the inner city by colleges created a local industry of sorts. Basketball became an economy where white colleges and universities feverishly sought after young black men from the inner city for their perceived athletic superiority and mental and physical toughness (Brooks and McKail 2008).

CHAPTER THREE

1. Hall (1948, 1949) and Dalton (1951) wrote classic studies on getting a job. Hall wrote about doctors having private practices and institutional affiliations that supported the most professional and socially connected people. Dalton considered different factors in the success of doctors and found that informal factors like ethnicity and class were significant and important to job advancement. Becker (1951) later highlighted how individual motivation influenced orientation and behavior. Jazz musicians who wanted consistent work had to know a particular music repertoire, show up for work on time, and play to the audience's expectations and the expectations of whoever pays the band.

2. This reiterates Charles Horton Cooley's essay (1902) on what individuals get from genetics versus what they absorb from their social environment.

3. This information was taken from the league's website.

CHAPTER FOUR

1. Petey's comment is instructive in understanding girl-boy interaction as well. He says that Jermaine's performance on the court impacted the attention he received from girls. In this way, girls seek boys who have high status in masculine activities.

2. Jermaine's move was doing masculinity—an action that exhibited physical dominance over someone (Messner 2002).

CHAPTER FIVE

1. Anderson (1990, 1999) has a definition of "old head" that refers to local neighborhood figures and "fathers" who act as pillars of the community and symbols of decency, civility, stability, and law-abidingness. Young (2007) extends this "decent" notion of the old head by considering redeemed old heads who have troubled pasts and are still capable of going "bad" if pushed. Still, Young's old heads are redeemable in their sense of community and social purpose and their desire to be viewed positively by others.

2. The percentage of drug dealers as old heads to ballplayers cannot be known; this is a very informal relationship and is not always seen. Of course, the old head–young bull relationship exists in many urban contexts (and beyond as a mentoring relationship), including in the underground economy. It is important to note that drug dealers can have a "softer" and community-minded side (Patillo 1998).

3. In an earlier work (Brooks 2004), I discuss borrowed identity and the status that comes with being vouched for by one with credibility. Networks create opportunities, but individuals must work to stay in and benefit from the opportunities.

CHAPTER SIX

1. Playgrounds vary in rules and norms, as well as physical dimensions. See Jimerson (1996) for a contrast to Espy's stratified play. Jimerson studied pickup basketball in Chicago and found that players cooperate and organize play toward maximizing equality and "flow" (playing time).

2. Expectation states theory (EST) describes status organizing processes. People stratify themselves in small group contexts, creating expectations for behavior and power and ordering. See Berger et al. (1977); Zelditch et al. (1980). EST has been criticized for being too parsimonious and failing to account for the multiple identities and statuses that people carry into interactions with others. Moreover, EST has focused on initial status evaluations and not dynamic and ongoing status negotiation.

CHAPTER SEVEN

1. Lane (2007) examines the cross-section of basketball, hip-hop, and drug culture in these overlapping worlds where young black inner-city males are both cultural producers and exploited.

2. Athletic play, in general, is considered gendered work—where gender norms are taught and strictly adhered to. There is a price to pay for deviance, as known by the experiences of gay and lesbian athletes who "come out." For examples of gender work and social control practices in sports, see Messner (1999, 2002) and May (2008).

3. "Gunner" (shooter), "black hole" (the ball is passed to them but never comes out), and "uzi" (machine gun) are derogatory characterizations of players who monopolize the ball. They shoot nearly every time the ball is in their hands. They dribble, pound the ball into the pavement so it boomerangs back to their hands, and lean one way and the other trying to fake out

the person guarding them in order to jack up a shot. Those who question a "black hole's" status, or do not like them, consider them selfish and indifferent to teammates, unless the other person can somehow enable them to shoot. Gunners and black holes, like Jackson from the previous chapter, rarely pass to anyone else unless it is someone they know well or consider to be better and of higher status.

4. Goffman (1963) speaks to the role of teammates in helping individuals to present a self and their ability to also cause "trouble" in rejecting their presentation of self. Behavior by teammates that disrupts another's performance is inappropriate.

5. See Goffman (1959) for a description of self-protective practices such as "saving face," whereby individuals act to resolve conflicts between expectations and their behavior.

6. Nate's use of "bitch" is a homophobic and feminizing comment that supports Connell's (1987) theorizing that male practice and behavior is inherently about not behaving as a woman. See Lemelle and Battle (2004) about black male attitudes about gay men; and see Messner (1990, 1999, 2002) and May (2008) for other examples of feminizing and homophobic talk in sport used to reinforce masculine boundaries.

CHAPTER EIGHT

1. In this way, Chuck and his network of former and current players is a lot like Anderson's (1978) "extended primary group." Chuck has an affinity for all of his players, relative to the wider society of young men, but "my guys" represents Chuck's stratification of players and ultimately how he treats them differently.

2. Anderson (1990) talks about old heads keeping "accounts" on the young men whom they help.

3. Messner (2002) writes that violence is at the core of male athletics and that boys and men construct and maintain a hegemonic masculinity through a "triad of violence" committed against girls/women, other boys/men, and themselves. Chuck's actions fit easily into a form of everyday hegemonic masculinity that includes race and class. He sees violence, albeit juvenile practices, as a natural part of being black and male—it is something that poor black men understand. Undoubtedly some kids quit playing for us because they didn't understand and feared Chuck's wrath. This put me in a difficult position, as I did not espouse violence and I found myself in a quandary or two with young men who "sized me up" as though they wanted to fight (see chapter 18).

4. Research discussing coaching styles and masculinity is growing rapidly. Fine (1987) provides an early look into the Little League clubhouse culture and the leadership of fathers/coaches. Grasmuck (2005) offers an update on baseball, which includes mothers/women coaching young men; and May (2008) talks about the coach as a role model and father figure for young black men on a rural Georgia high school basketball team. Coaches generally reinforce traditional masculinity—be tough, don't give up, don't cry—but they also act as support in certain contexts. Chuck was called a "youth advocate" by one of his former players, as a way to describe Chuck's influence outside of basketball.

5. Initially, this was extremely uncomfortable for me to take in. However, I came to understand that context was important and that boys adapted and gained a sincere appreciation for Chuck and his methods. His over-the-top antics were memorable, predictable, and part of a team culture that developed. It also showed his passion, love, and commitment to building relationships beyond basketball. Most came to see him as a crazy and dedicated old head and coach.

CHAPTER NINE

1. Their skill sets, natural abilities, and height/size enabled them to do a number of things, but also placed them at a disadvantage in particular situations because they could not dribble well enough to handle the ball against tough defense, or they could not shoot well enough to be shooting or scoring guard, or they were not tall enough and big enough to be really successful against other taller and bigger and stronger players who naturally play that position (e.g., Allen Iverson as a shooting guard at five feet eleven inches creates a defensive problem for his team if he is playing with a teammate who is his height/size or smaller because it means that this tandem is undersized and overmatched).

CHAPTER TEN

1. See Becker (1966) for a discussion on the musician's struggle to appease his audience because he wants to feel as though he is "reaching" them and that they are getting enjoyment, leading to his giving in to their demands. Not being "hated" by the audience is desired because it helps job security and adds to the musician's self-identity and presentation as a good musician.

2. Coaches are required to register and be certified with the NCAA (National Collegiate Athletic Association) so that the league maintains its accreditation. This registration costs $45 and the coach must pass a test.

3. The names of persons and companies have all been changed to maintain their and the league's anonymity.

4. And 1 is a basketball shoe and apparel company, based in a Philadelphia suburb. It created a traveling playground basketball team that stops in cities to take on all comers. The video series is an ingenious marketing tool that implicitly pushes the merchandise while documenting the team's travels and experiences, while paying the athletes poorly.

CHAPTER ELEVEN

1. No player was cut during my tenure, although Chuck cut players before my time. One reason is that fewer and fewer players tried out.

2. This argument illustrated that Aaron and I judged his performance and whether or not he should play on very different standards; I considered teamwork and efficiency, while he was confused that I did not play him, since he could do things that most others on the team could not as individuals. This lends support to Becker's analysis of the musician and square (1966).

3. Again, see Becker (1966) for a description of how musicians see themselves as having special gifts that are not fully appreciated by "squares."

CHAPTER FOURTEEN

1. Goffman (1967, 58) describes deference as a show of appreciation and sentiment that must be given—an individual cannot give it to herself. Respect, in this context, works similarly. Jermaine and Ray needed others to acknowledge their accomplishments for validity. Status is confirmed externally, by what others say, do, and feel (Brooks 2004).

CHAPTER FIFTEEN

1. This lyric was from hip-hop artist Nas's "Made You Look" on *God's Son* (2002) album.

2. Space is determined by how people use space. In *Urban Fortunes* (1987), Logan and Molotch speak of this as use-value. Becker's "Jazz Places" (2004) speaks of the "expected uses" of space; the shared expectations held by participants in a space and time and the social arrangements, including financial, which underlay the social activity in a space.

CHAPTER SIXTEEN

1. See Danley (2007) for a mainstream article on the marriage of collegiate athletes and sneaker companies.

2. AAU has its own stratification and range. Tournaments are hosted by a bevy of sponsors and held throughout the year, around the country. There are local (city) tournaments and regional and national tournaments. For the biggest tournaments, with the largest number of college coaches and scouts, teams have to qualify by playing (not necessarily winning) in lesser tournaments. Teams with reputations and known players are guaranteed to play in the most competitive divisions, against other known talent, and in gyms that accommodate more spectators. They are the featured show and draw attention from coaches, players, and outside spectators.

CHAPTER SEVENTEEN

1. May (2008) writes about the hoop dreams of high school boys in rural Georgia. The pursuit of basketball fame is perpetuated by race (racial advantage in athletics), meritocracy and the American dream, and masculinity. Young boys are able to prove that they are viable men through their performances and status. Basketball is used as a means to get women and secure resources.

2. Anderson (1990, 1999) presents a framework for understanding gender dynamics here.

3. Largely, demand for retro jerseys has continued to increase since this video; jerseys that were once rare are no longer so rare due to increasing supplies to match demand.

4. Jermaine's and Ray's consumption of athletic gear is tied to the larger issue of relative deprivation.

5. This connection between caring, pride, and children's dress has been written about elsewhere. Anderson (1999) describes how young mothers dress their children as a means to gain status, equivalent to "not looking poor." Hannerz (1969) writes about "ghetto" style in the ethnographic classic *Soulside*, and Patillo-McCoy (1999) provides a needed update and shows how some Chicago gangs incorporated Michael Jordan brand apparel into their

gang uniform and how young people kept up-to-date with fashion trends as a source of pride.

CHAPTER TWENTY

1. Ray's and Jermaine's increasing status and recognition, as well as their dressing and playing the part of known players, shows how young players become engulfed in the role of star athlete. Adler and Adler (1990) document how this happens at the collegiate level.

2. Gibson (2003) studied how workers emulated multiple people over their career because aspirations, skills, and knowledge change over time.

CHAPTER TWENTY-ONE

1. Burke and Reitzes (1981) highlight the link between identity and performance. Ray was not simply playing—he was performing—and living up to his status and the expectations he and others held for him. Even in group contexts, individual actions and performance are affected by role identity.

2. He has since become a professional player, drafted recently in the first round.

3. Research on mentoring confirms the importance of others for job satisfaction, job learning, and career mobility (Speizer 1981). People have different needs and use a range of persons, including peers (Kram and Isabella 1985). Moreover, people select role models differently and in nuanced ways. As people mature in their careers, they seek different persons to emulate and they may piece role models together, paying attention to the work ethic of one person, the communication and networking skills of another, and so on (Gibson 2003).

CHAPTER TWENTY-TWO

1. This was the minimum level score at the time, but it has since changed.

2. Granovetter's classic work (1973) introduced the concept of "weak ties" and describes how people use contacts to effectively gain employment and information beyond their primary group.

3. His low GPA plus his failure to earn a "relative" passing score on the SAT and ACT did not meet NCAA Clearinghouse standards, which calculate a "core" GPA based upon considering the courses a young woman or man has taken in high school, their earned grades, and achievement test score (either SAT or ACT).

CHAPTER TWENTY-FOUR

1. This statement shows that I made it clear to folks that I was doing research, which did not preclude me from creating enduring relationships and becoming a member of Jermaine's social world.

CONCLUSION

1. Since the 1980s, the field of urban sociology has been framed by the work of William Julius Wilson. Wilson's landmark book, *The Truly Disadvantaged* (1987), outlines the large structural economic factors—a shifting economy from goods producing to service providing and industrial migration to

the suburbs—that have intensified contemporary urban poverty and created the underclass. These factors have led to economic dislocation and social isolation of the underclass due to joblessness, black middle-class migration, and an increasing absence of black men in households.

2. Anderson's work (1990, 1999) has done much to bring this to light. In *The Code of the Street* (1999), Anderson shows boyfriends who adopt their girlfriend's kids and play daddy to them. In *Streetwise* (1990) he defines old heads: "A man of stable means who believed in hard work, family life, and the church. He was an aggressive agent of the wider society whose acknowledged role was to teach, support, encourage, and in effect socialize young men to meet their responsibilities regarding work, family, the law, and common decency. Often the old head acted as surrogate father to those who needed attention, care, and moral support" (70).

3. Hartmann (2003) and Hartmann and Wheelock (2002) have studied the effectiveness of sports participation in crime and violence intervention, particularly "midnight basketball" programs. The obvious and significant differences between midnight basketball programs and Blade Rodgers are the career orientation and focus on developing character—becoming a basketball player as an alternative identity.

4. May (2008) is very insightful and reflexive in his theorizing about basketball's "dirty trick." After spending seven years coaching high school basketball, boys and girls, he reasoned that his culpability in perpetuating hoop dreams was lessened by a more immediate issue—basketball saved, at least temporarily, the lives of some young men. See Axthelm (1970), Telander (1976), and Frey (1994) for classic docu-journalistic accounts of the "dirty trick."

5. Michael McKail and I (2008) have written about the exploitation of young black men in particular. Young black men from inner cities are ideal for cash sports because they do not have the social, political, or economic capital to demand better conditions and fair wages. Rhoden (2006), Smith (2007), and Powell (2008) provide cogent and damaging analyses of sports and how sports effectively maintain the racial order. These works follow the macro-structural tradition of research on race and sport. *Black Men Can't Shoot* does something different in presenting the career of young athletes—it does not question whether or not playing basketball is politically, economically, or socially empowering; instead it presents the perspective of people engaged in the activity as a means of making sense of how they see the world and how they see their obstacles and possibilities in the midst of macro-structural inequality.

APPENDIX 1

1. Adler and Adler (1987) describe the different roles that a researcher might take in field research, ranging from peripheral membership (passive observer) to active membership (participant observer/observing participant) to complete membership (full immersion with and without researcher disclosure).

2. Becker (2007) adds a thoughtful statement on the researcher's role in settings. In some cases, like mine, he was very similar to the folks he studied (he was a musician trying to stay busy). I was a black man volunteering to

coach. Being a grad student didn't give me authority or power in a basketball world where seniority and known ability (past and present) determined a person's status.

3. "Stranger" is used by Simmel (1971) as an ideal type that describes how groups, like Jews, have historically lived as minorities in many different cities, towns, and countries and maintained their own distinct culture. They have been among, but separate from other people because of their lack of investment in the native cultures. They maintain and adhere to their own religious and professional/business practices.

4. Duneier (1999) writes about "getting in" in a cross-racial context and how larger racial dynamics/concerns remain. Although he was treated as an insider, he heard (via tape recorder) the skepticism and distrust that some sidewalk vendors held about him. (1) He was white and a Jew, and beliefs about white privilege, selfishness, and Jewish aggressiveness informed their views about him. (2) He was not being honest in helping the black men; he wanted to know something for his own interests. Yet, Duneier points out, they also did not believe that he was an undercover cop or government agent—meaning that he was largely considered benign.

REFERENCES

Adler, Patricia A., and Peter Adler. 1987. *Membership Roles in Field Research.* Thousand Oaks, CA: Sage.

———. 1990. *Backboards and Blackboards: College Athletics and Role Engulfment.* New York: Columbia University Press.

Anderson, Elijah. 1978. *A Place on the Corner.* Chicago: University of Chicago Press.

———. 1990. *Streetwise: Race, Class, and Change in an Urban Community.* Chicago: University of Chicago Press.

———. 1999. *The Code of the Street: Decency, Violence, and the Moral Life of the Inner City.* New York: Norton.

Anderson, Elijah. 2001. "Urban Ethnography." In *International Encyclopedia of the Social and Behavioral Sciences,* ed. Neil J. Smelser and Paul B. Bates, 16004–8. Oxford: Elsevier.

Axthelm, Pete. 1970. *The City Game: Basketball from the Garden to the Playgrounds.* Lincoln: University of Nebraska Press.

Becker, Howard. 1951. "The Professional Dance Musician and His Audience." *American Journal or Sociology* 57(2):136–44.

———. 1966. *Outsiders: Studies in the Sociology of Deviance.* New York: Simon & Schuster.

———. 2004. "Jazz Places." In *Music Scenes: Local, Translocal, and Virtual,* ed. Andy Bennett and Richard A. Peterson, 17–27. Nashville: Vanderbilt University Press.

———. 2007. "How We Deal with the People We Study: 'The Last Seminar' Revisited." In *Crime, Social Control and Human Rights: From Moral Panics to Denial—Essays in Honour of Stanley Cohen,* ed. Christine Chinkin, David Downes, Conor Gearty, and Paul Rock, 26–36. Cullompton, UK: Willan.

Berger, Joseph, M. Hamit Fisek, Robert Z. Norman, and Morris Zelditch Jr. 1977. *Status Characteristics and Social Interaction: An Expectation States Approach.* New York: Elsevier Scientific.

Bourgois, Philippe. 1995. *In Search of Respect: Selling Crack in El Barrio.* New York: Cambridge University Press.

Brooks, Scott N. 2004. "Putting the Blessings on Him: Vouching and Basketball Status Work." *ANNALS* 595(1):80–90.

———. 2008. "Fighting like a Ballplayer: Basketball as a Strategy Against Social Disorganization." In *Against the Wall: Poor, Young, Black, and Male*, ed. Elijah Anderson, 147–64. Philadelphia: University of Pennsylvania Press.

Brooks, Scott N., and Michael McKail. 2008. "The Preferred Worker: A Structural Explanation for Black Male Dominance in Basketball." *Critical Sociology* 34(3):369–87.

Burke, Peter J., and Donald C. Reitzes. 1981. "The Link between Identity and Role Performance." *Social Psychology Quarterly* 44:83–92.

Chambliss, Daniel. 1989. "The Mundanity of Excellence: An Ethnographic Report on Stratification and Olympic Swimmers." *Sociological Theory* 7(1):70–86.

Coakley, Jay. 1988. *Sport and Society*. St. Louis: Mosby.

Connell, Robert W. 1987. *Gender and Power*. Stanford, CA: Stanford University Press.

Cooley, Charles Horton. 1902. *Human Nature and the Social Order*. New York: Scribner's.

Dalton, Melville. 1951. "Informal Factors in Career Achievement." *American Journal of Sociology* 56(5):407–15.

Danley, Stephen. 2007. "Trying to Corner the Market on the Best Players." *New York Times*, July 11, 2007.http://www.nytimes.com/2007/07/11/sports/basketball/11camp.html?ref=ncaabasketball (accessed July 13, 2007).

Denzin, Norman K., and Yvonne Lincoln. 1994. *Handbook of Qualitative Research*. Thousand Oaks, CA: Sage.

Duneier, Mitchell. 1999. *Sidewalk*. New York: Farrar, Straus and Giroux.

Edwards, Harry. 1973. *The Sociology of Sport*. Homewood, IL: Dorsey Press.

———. 1997. "Law, Race, and Change in Sport and Society." *South Texas Law Review* 38:1007–27.

Fine, Gary Alan. 1987. *With the Boys: Little League Baseball and Preadolescent Culture*. Chicago: University of Chicago Press.

Frey, Darcy. 1994. *The Last Shot: City Streets, Basketball Dreams*. New York: Simon & Schuster.

Furstenberg, Frank, and Kathy Mulan Harris. 1993. "When and Why Fathers Matter." In *Young and Unwed Fathers*, ed. by Robert I. Lerman and Theodora J. Ooms. Philadelphia: Temple University Press.

Geertz, Clifford. 1973. *Interpretations of Culture: Selected Essays*. New York: Basic Books.

Gibson, Donald E. 2003. "Developing the Professional Self-Concept: Role Model Construals in Early, Middle, and Late Career Stages." *Organization Science* 14(5):591–610.

Glaser, Barney, and Anselm Strauss. 1967. *Discovery of Grounded Theory: Strategies of Qualitative Research*. Chicago: Aldine.

Goffman, Erving. 1959. *Presentation of Self in Everyday Life*. New York: Anchor Books.

———. 1963. *Behavior in Public Places*. New York: Free Press.

———. 1967. *Interaction Ritual: Essays on Face-to-Face Behavior*. New York: Anchor Books.

Granovetter, Mark S. 1973. "The Strength of Weak Ties." *American Journal of Sociology* 78 (May):1360–80.

Grasmuck, Sherri. 2005. *Protecting Home: Class, Race, and Masculinity in Boys' Baseball.* New Brunswick, NJ: Rutgers University Press.

Hall, Oswald. 1948. "The Stages of a Medical Career." *American Journal of Sociology* 53 (5):327–36.

———. 1949. "Types of Medical Careers." *American Journal of Sociology* 55 (3): 243–53.

Hammersley, Martin, and Paul Atkinson. 1995. *Ethnography.* New York: Routledge.

Hannerz, Ulf. 1969. *Soulside: Inquiries into the Ghetto Culture and Community.* New York: Columbia University Press.

Hartmann, Douglas. 2003. "Theorizing Sport as Social Intervention: A View from the Grassroots." *Quest* 55:118–40.

Hartmann, Douglas, and Darren Wheelock. 2002. "Sport as Prevention? Minneapolis' Experiment with Late-Night Basketball." *CURA* [Center for Urban and Regional Affairs] *Reporter* 32(3): 13–17.

Hoberman, John. 1997. *Darwin's Athletes: How Sport Has Damaged Black America and Preserved the Myth of Race.* New York: Houghton-Mifflin.

Horowitz, Ruth. 1983. *Honor and the American Dream.* New Brunswick, NJ: Rutgers University Press.

Hughes, Everett C. 1928. "Personality Types and the Division of Labor," *American Journal of Sociology* 33(5):754–68.

Hunt, Donald. 1996. *The Philadelphia Big 5: Great Moments in Philadelphia's Storied Basketball History.* Champaign, IL: Sagamore.

Jimerson, Jason. 1996. "Good Times and Good Games: How Pickup Basketball Players Use Wealth Maximization Norms." *Journal of Contemporary Ethnography* 25:353–71.

Jones, Nikki. 2004. "'It's Not Where You Live, It's How You Live': How Young Women Negotiate Conflict and Violence in the Inner City." *ANNALS* 595(1):49–62.

Kenyon, Gerald S., and Barry D. McPherson. 1973. "Becoming Involved in Physical Activity and Sport: A Process of Socialization." In *Physical Activity—Human Growth and Development,* ed. G. Lawrence Rarick. New York: Academic Press.

Kram, Kathy E., and Lynn A. Isabella. 1985. "Mentoring Alternatives: The Role of Peer Relationships in Career Development." *Academy of Management Journal* 28(1):110–32.

Ladner, Joyce. 1971. *Tomorrow's Tomorrow: The Black Woman.* New York: Doubleday.

Lane, Jeffrey. 2007. *Under the Boards: The Cultural Revolution in Basketball.* Lincoln: University of Nebraska Press.

Lemelle, Anthony, Jr., and Juan Battle. 2004. "Black Masculinity Matters in Attitudes toward Gay Males." *Journal of Homosexuality* 47(1):39–51.

Liebow, Elliot. 1967. *Tally's Corner.* Boston: Little, Brown.

Logan, John R., and Harvey Molotch. 1987. *Urban Fortunes: The Political Economy of Place.* Berkeley: University of California Press.

Lyons, Robert S. 2002. *Palestra Pandemonium: The History of the Big 5.* Philadelphia: Temple University Press.

Matza, David. 1969. *Becoming Deviant.* Englewood Cliffs, NJ: Prentice-Hall.

May, Reuben A. Buford. 2008. *Living through the Hoop: High School Basketball, Race, and the American Dream.* New York: New York University Press.

McAdoo, John Lewis. 1988. "The Role of Black Fathers in the Socialization of Black Children." In *Black Families*, ed. by Harriette Pipes McAdoo. Newbury Park, CA: Sage.

Messner, Michael. 1988. "Masculinities and Athletic Careers." *Gender & Society* 3:71–88.

———. 1990. "Boyhood Organized Sports and the Construction of Masculinity." *Journal of Contemporary Ethnography* 18(4):416–44.

———. 1999. "Becoming 100 Percent Straight." In *Inside Sports*, ed. J. Coakley and P. Donnelly. New York: Routledge.

———. 2002. *Taking the Field: Women, Men, and Sports*. Minneapolis: University of Minnesota Press.

Pattillo, Mary E. 1998. "Sweet Mothers and Gangbangers: Managing Crime in a Black Middle Class Neighborhood." *Social Forces* 76(3):747–74.

Patillo-McCoy. Mary. 1999. *Black Picket Fences: Privilege and Peril among the Black Middle Class*. Chicago: University of Chicago Press.

Philadelphia Daily News. 2003. *Philly Hoops: The Magic of Philadelphia Basketball*. Philadelphia: Camino Books.

Powell, Shaun. 2008. *Souled Out? How Blacks Are Winning and Losing in Sports*. Champaign, IL: Human Kinetics.

Rhoden, William C. 2006. *Forty Million Dollar Slaves: The Rise, Fall, and Redemption of the Black Athlete*. New York: Crown.

Simmel, Georg, and Donald N. Levine. 1971. *On Individuality and Social Forms: Selected Writings*. Chicago: University of Chicago Press.

Smith, Earl. 2007. *Race, Sport, and the American Dream*. Durham, NC: Carolina Academic Press.

Speizer, Jeanne J. 1981. "Role Models, Mentors, and Sponsors: The Elusive Concepts." *Signs* 6(4):692–712.

Spradley, James P. 1980. *Participant Observation*. New York: Holt, Rinehart and Winston.

Telander, Rick. 1976. *Heaven Is a Playground*. Lincoln: University of Nebraska Press.

Van Maanen, John. 1988. *Tales of the Field: On Writing Ethnography*. Chicago: University of Chicago Press.

Whyte, William Foote. 1943. *Street Corner Society: The Social Structure of an Italian Slum*. Chicago: University of Chicago Press.

Wideman, John Edgar. 2001. *Hoop Roots*. New York: First Mariner.

Wilson, William Julius. 1987. *The Truly Disadvantaged*. Chicago: University of Chicago Press.

Young, Alford. 2007. "The Redeemed Old Head: Articulating a Sense of Public Self and Social Purpose." *Symbolic Interaction* 30(3):347–74.

Zelditch, Morris Jr., Patrick Lauderdale, and Stephen Stublarec. 1980. "How Are Inconsistencies between Status and Ability Resolved?" *Social Forces* 58(4):1025–43.

INDEX

The names of all persons and places that were a part of the research have been changed.